THE EXPERTS SAY YOU CAN'T AFFORD TO IGNORE DR. BATRA'S STARTLING ADVICE.

"The forecasting record of this widely respected . . . economist has won glowing praise from many pragmatic investment masters."
—Tom Peters, *Chicago Tribune*

"His predictions in the early 1980's of low inflation, falling oil prices, and a wave of mergers—mocked for years—have proved close to the mark."
—Thomas C. Hayes, *The New York Times*

"So far Dr. Batra is close to five for five. Pray he doesn't go six for six."
—*People*

"Clear, straightforward . . . Dr. Batra raises issues any sensible person should stop and reconsider."
—*Dallas Times Herald*

"Enlightening and thought-provoking . . . Batra has a stunning record of being right. . . . Everyone from the general reader to the stockbroker will find something here to chew on."
—*Daily Press,* Newport News, Virginia

DR. RAVI BATRA, author of the number-one best seller *THE GREAT DEPRESSION OF 1990,* is widely acclaimed as one of the world's top trade theorists. Appointed to full professorship at the age of thirty, he teaches at Southern Methodist University and is ranked third in a group of forty-six "superstars" selected from all American and Canadian university economists by the prestigious journal *Economic Inquiry.* He *rents* a home in Dallas. "I believe in practicing what I preach." says Dr. Batra. "All the advice I give you, I have followed myself or will follow at the appropriate time."

BOOKS BY RAVI BATRA

The Great Depression of 1990
Studies in the Pure Theory of International Trade
Theory of International Trade Under Uncertainty
Capitalism and Communism: A New Study of History
Muslim Civilization and the Crisis in Iran

Surviving the Great Depression of 1990

PROTECT YOUR ASSETS AND INVESTMENTS— AND COME OUT ON TOP

Dr. Ravi Batra

A DELL BOOK

Published by
Dell Publishing
a division of
Bantam Doubleday Dell Publishing Group, Inc.
666 Fifth Avenue
New York, New York 10103

ISBN: 0-440-20461-5

Reprinted by arrangement with Simon and Schuster

Printed in the United States of America
Published simultaneously in Canada

November 1989

10 9 8 7 6 5 4 3 2 1

OPM

To my wife, Sunita

CONTENTS

PREFACE

In *The Great Depression of 1990*, I set out to convince a skeptical public, media establishment, and government that the world was headed toward a major economic disaster by the end of the 1980s, and that it would dwarf all previous depressions unless some bold reforms were undertaken in time. Because my purpose was to wake up a complacent planet and its governments, the book was 80 percent theory, data, and charts—aimed at proving a depression was on its way—and only 20 percent advice to individuals about how to prepare for, and ultimately survive, that depression. I soon realized that the advice section was inadequate. Wherever I went, I was bombarded by questions from both the public and the press. It seemed that I no longer had to convince the country of the coming depression. The Wall Street crashes of October 19, 1987, and January 8, 1988, implicitly anticipated in my book, had occurred despite loud claims by economic experts that such eruptions were nearly impossible in an economy cushioned by myriad New Deal reforms.

But false theory is one thing, reality is something else. That is why this book is about financial survival. It tackles a wide range of concerns and answers the hundreds of questions raised by viewers and listeners when I appeared on television and radio talk shows and spoke before groups nationwide. *Surviving the Great Depression of 1990* offers you practical advice to prepare yourself financially for what could turn out to be the worst social and economic turmoil of the twentieth century. The crash of 1929 and the Great Depression that followed hit the globe like lightning, and everyone was caught unaware, unprepared. Society's agony was much greater than it would have been if economists, whose job it is to warn us of looming troubles, had had the vision to foresee the coming disaster. But no one had predicted the Great Depression of the 1930s, even though numerous financial excesses occurred during the 1920s. Even among those who could see the handwriting on the wall, no one dared to challenge the conventional wisdom.

If you are like me, you are worried about your future. I believe the nation is about to face its toughest challenge since the Second World War. Right now is the time to prepare yourself for any eventuality. You should hope for the best, but prepare for the worst. Believe me, if current economic trends persist, the worst will indeed occur. This time, however, I hope you won't be caught by surprise by the impending cataclysm, which, according to my calculations, will begin in 1990. I see rough waters ahead, and you and I and our families will have to navigate through them. My purpose is to help you do so with the least financial discomfort.

I don't profess to be infallible, and I must offer you conservative advice, so that if I am wrong you will not be hurt. But if I am right you will have saved yourself from a major calamity. I also believe in practicing what I preach. All the advice I give you I have followed myself or will follow at the appropriate time.

My advice is not limited to your personal financial survival. I also hope to raise your economic and political awareness. Some say it's too late to stop the coming depression. I say it's never too late to try to be part of the noble cause of curing the world economy. Perhaps you and I can't prevent the depression, but our collective and strenuous efforts could at least shorten its duration and soften its blows. As *Time* magazine put it: "Everywhere, from bookstores to boardrooms, from trading floors to ivory towers, speculations about the financial future fill the air. . . . All the talk of recession and depression, while unsettling, is probably healthy. Since the biggest crashes occur as a result of surprises, nervous discussion may produce some vitally needed preventive measures."[1]

Here's what you can expect from the chapters that follow. The book has been divided into four parts. Part I explores the causes of the economic problems we face, predicts what's coming in the near future, and describes how the painful scenario will probably unfold.

Part II deals with whether you are likely to face an inflationary or deflationary depression, what kinds of businesses and jobs are likely to survive better than others, what types of banks and thrifts are safer than others, and what help you might expect from Social Security programs.

Part III is concerned with comprehensive strategies and tactics for financial survival in the years ahead, with emphasis on both what you can do now to prepare for a depression and what you can do when it actually hits.

Part IV deals with preventive measures: what we as a nation and we as part of a global community of nations can do to plan for the coming years. You will learn what policies the world ought to adopt to blunt or shorten the coming crisis, and what we as individuals can do to persaude government to enact the needed legislation.

[1] *Time*, October 5, 1987, p. 46.

All need not be gloom and doom in the years ahead. There is hope. We are strong and resilient people. And with proper preparation and informed action, that hope will grow brighter.

PART I

Economic Upheaval

CHAPTER 1

Racing Toward a Depression

IT'S 1786 IN FRANCE. Louis XVI is the reigning king, and Marie Antoinette his queen. The French masses often go hungry, while the royal family and the aristocracy continue to be wildly extravagant. A commoner barely earns a livre a day, but in one year the queen spends 272,000 livres on her wardrobe—an amount equal to at least 60 million francs today (approximately $11 million)—which is more than twice her allotted budget. Such are the costs of royal display in the midst of hunger.

The queen faces a cruel dilemma—a nasty deficit. Her spending is more than twice her revenue. Her finance minister has been secretly borrowing millions from the affluent to support her profligacy over the past several years. By 1786, however, the secret is out. The queen's deficit is the highest ever, and the minister, unable to borrow more, seeks the parliament's approval to meet it. All of France now knows what the royal family, its 2,111 servants, and the 4,000 members of its household are costing the nation. No longer will things be the same for the queen. Henceforth Marie Antoinette will be known as Madame Déficit.[1]

In 1986, exactly two centuries later, the U.S. government had the largest deficit in the history of the nation. The government borrowed $221 billion, surpassing in a single year all that it had to borrow over seven years to finance the do-or-die defense effort of the Second World War. So huge was the deficit that the government borrowed billions not only from wealthy Americans but also from wealthy Japanese, Germans, Englishmen, Canadians, Arabs, Dutchmen, Taiwanese, and Koreans. In President Reagan's first term alone, the United States accumulated a debt exceeding the combined debt of all other thirty-nine presidents. As the chief architect of this unprecedented shortfall, Reagan should go down in history as Monsieur Déficit.

History reveals that the government's extravagance under Madame Déficit in the 1780s led to an economic blight in France by the end of the decade and eventually to the fires of the French Revolution in 1789 and the Reign of Terror in the 1790s. It is not unreasonable to suppose, as I argued in my earlier book, *The Great Depression of 1990*, that governmental extravagance and economic mismanagement under Monsieur Déficit in the 1980s will cause similar economic devastation by the end of the decade and possibly a social upheaval in the 1990s.

What are we to do now? In the history of every nation comes a time when society is caught in a gridlock of vested interests, when confusion abounds and economic anarchy reigns because curing social ills requires bitter medicine. Those placed comfortably in the system paint a rosy picture of the present and the future, but a vast majority of people, who can barely make ends meet, view their prospects with apprehension. Our nation in the late 1980s is

[1] See André Castelot, *Queen of France* (New York: Harper & Row, 1957), p. 220.

caught in the throes of just such times. Indeed, it is now a global problem and every nation in the world is caught up in the dilemma.

America is fast becoming a nation of two classes, with the haves growing richer, the have-nots growing poorer, and the middle class slowly sinking into oblivion. The minimum wage in America is $3.35 an hour, and an unskilled worker working the normal 40 hours a week and 2,080 hours a year would earn $6,968. This is what hundreds and thousands of Americans make per year and have been making for the past eight years, even though prices have risen by 40 percent, because the minimum wage has remained constant. These people live below the official poverty line, which, for a family of four, begins with $11,000. In order to escape the burden of poverty, a minimum-wage earner has to toil 3,284 hours per year or 63 hours a week. He can't afford the luxury of falling sick or even a week's vacation.

Do you know what the *maximum* wage was in 1986? $125 million—17,940 times the minimum wage and 11,363 times the poverty figure. *Financial World* reported that of the hundred highest salaries on Wall Street in 1986, the top pay was $125 million and the lowest $3 million.[2]

Chances are that you earn more than the minimum wage. The average American annually makes about $29,000, which is only 1/4,310th of the maximum salary in 1986. In addition, you have to pay a 7.5 percent Social Security tax, a 6 to 8 percent sales tax, a 15 percent income tax, another 10 to 15 cents per gallon in gasoline tax—and you wonder why hardly anything is left for savings after you have barely met your needs.

Those of you in the middle class make up to $60,000 per year, but after you have paid your taxes, financed your children's education, and serviced your credit card debts,

[2] *Financial World*, July 14, 1987.

you don't have much change to spare for your savings. This is where 95 percent of Americans find themselves— a vast majority. If you have investments, they may have been badly battered by the stock market "meltdown" on October 19, 1987. But far greater dangers lie ahead. You are ill-prepared for the calamity toward which the nation is now racing under the economic mismanagement of Monsieur Déficit.

The Illusion of Prosperity

We have already become a nation of the haves and have-nots. For the haves, this is perhaps the best time in our history, but for the have-nots the situation is worse than it was even under President Jimmy Carter, who lost to Reagan in the 1980 election. As the 1980s opened, there were high interest rates and a high rate of unemployment, along with a double-digit rate of inflation. All these rates had sharply declined by 1987, whereas the stock market was at its all-time high. Surely these are signs of great prosperity. But the prosperity of the 1980s is more apparent than real. It's a borrowed prosperity masking economic troubles that could be disastrous in the near future.

For the first time in this century, America is a net debtor to the rest of the world. Some nations owe us money, but we owe others much more. In fact, we are now the largest debtor to the world, a situation that has occurred amazingly fast. At $500 billion, our foreign debt is more than the foreign debts of Mexico, Brazil, and Argentina combined. We have accomplished this dubious distinction only since 1985, because until then we were a net creditor. America has achieved in three years what it took Mexico, Brazil, and Argentina forty postwar years to achieve. Furthermore, our foreign debt is rising at the rate of $150 billion a year. If that rate continues, by 1991 it will cross the $1 trillion mark. What happens when other nations stop lending us money?

Domestically, the federal government is $2.5 trillion in debt and continues to borrow up to $200 billion per year. In addition, consumers and corporations are $8 trillion in debt. Moreover, the rate of savings, at less than 4 percent, is now the lowest in our history. Without savings, how can the nation invest in its future and continue to grow?

At this time, there should actually be cause for celebration because the United States is now in the sixth year of recovery from the steep recession of 1980–82. Its rate of unemployment is now below 6 percent. Yet, ironically, it has already acquired certain characteristics of the struggling nations of the Third World: an abysmal savings rate, chronic deficits in the balance of payments, exploding budget deficits and domestic debt, increasing homelessness, a slowdown in the growth of productivity, and, above all, greater disparities in income and wealth. These debilitating features of underdeveloped countries are now beginning to afflict the U.S. economy.

Reaganomics

How could all this happen to a nation that in terms of gross national product (GNP) is still the richest on earth? How could it happen in just a matter of six years between 1981 and 1987? The answer, in a word, is Reaganomics, the economic philosophy that created the Great Depression of the 1930s and will now create the Great Depression of the 1990s.

Let's pause for a moment and consider the economic ideology popular until the 1930s. This creed is known as classical economics, which is, in essence, the same as Reaganomics. Classical economics advocates a system of laissez-faire, in which the government has a minimum role in the well-being of both the economy and society. In this view, government intervention creates more problems than it solves. According to the classical theory, markets behave with such flexibility that, under capitalism, long-term unemployment or a depression is logically impossible. Yes, "impossible" was the word commonly used by the classical economists, who were blind to the reality of the three major depressions that had already convulsed society prior to the Great Depression.

In terms of practical policy, the classical ideology recommends low government spending, low tax rates, a balanced government budget, deregulation, and the absence of state intervention in the economy. It believes in free trade and in abolishing the minimum wage, which, it contends, is one form of state intervention that can create unemployment. It also advocates trickle-down economics, wherein the government doles out money to the wealthy in the form of tax cuts, investment credits, or subsidies to create jobs in the economy. Presumably, the prosperity that this creates will then trickle down from the rich to the poor.

During the 1920s the classical theory was still the craze among economists. Under its mesmerizing influence they continued to be blind to economic realities and failed to foresee that the orgy of greed then engulfing financial markets could soon unleash devastation on a mass scale. As the 1920s opened, the federal government found itself stuck with a large budget surplus. Taxes had been sharply raised in 1916 to finance the defense effort of the First World War. As the war ended in 1918 and defense spending sharply fell, the government faced the dilemma of a surplus. The congressmen of those days adored classical ideology as much as the economists did. The budget surplus was an eyesore to them. Unlike today's politicians, they itched to cut taxes, rather than raise social spending, in order to balance the budget. Little did they realize that such actions usually aggravate wealth disparity, which had risen sharply by the end of the war, making many individuals who profited from defense contracts multimillionaires overnight.

A serious recession occurred in 1920, along with double-digit inflation and interest rates. In 1921, the government proceeded to lower taxes dramatically for big business and high-income groups. It also relaxed the enforcement of many regulations restraining corporate behavior, leading to de facto deregulation. All this, coupled with the government's probusiness and antilabor attitude, created a fertile soil for corporate mergers and takeovers. Merger mania developed as a result, leading to a surge in industrial concentration and a decline in competition.

Whenever wealth disparity rises, speculation rises with it, because the rich are able and willing to gamble with their money on risky ventures that bring a high return in a healthy economy. Therefore, a rise in wealth disparity always leads to a quick rise in stock market speculation. When deregulation and merger mania also accompany a jump in the unequal distribution of wealth, the stock market rise turns into a speculative bubble, which is defined as an extraordinary surge in the market, unmatched by a corresponding rise in GNP or corporate earnings.

The combination of rising wealth disparity, deregulation, and merger mania is rare. That's why speculative bubbles are also rare. But in 1922 all the ingredients for this rarity were present. The sharp fall in taxes favoring the wealthy and big business had already set in motion the process of rising wealth disparity. Deregulation psychology had also taken hold, and the government's failure to enforce antitrust laws had given rise to a wave of mergers. No wonder then that there began a stock market rise in 1922 which, with occasional retreats and pauses, went on until 1929.

In 1922, barely 1 percent of Americans owned 31.6 percent of the nation's wealth. They also owned more than 50 percent of total stock. First, this wealth disparity, along with the economic recovery from the recession, initiated a quick jump in the stock market. This further raised the disparity in wealth, which, in turn, led to another rise in the market. This is precisely how a speculative bubble begins and then feeds itself. At a late stage of the game, the general public, lured by quick and easy profits, joins in and the bubble keeps expanding for several years. However, all bubbles burst in the end, to start a depression. That's why we find in history that all great depressions have been preceded by great speculative manias triggered by high wealth disparity. In short, classical economics in the 1920s produced sharp tax cuts, deregulation, and a huge merger wave. These three, in turn, generated a stock market bubble that burst in 1929 to create the Great Depression of the 1930s.

What is the difference between classical theory and Reaganomics? Very little. Reaganomics is the old wine of classical economics in a new bottle, but with a distorted twist—distorted because while Reaganomics seeks to trim the size of the government, it is, at best, indifferent to the classical prescription of a balanced budget. In accord with the classical theory, tax cuts for the affluent, deregulation, and failure to enforce antitrust laws have been President Reagan's policies in the 1980s. The only difference is that the Republican presidents of the 1920s reduced taxes to eliminate a consistent budget surplus, whereas Reagan, another Republican, trimmed tax rates in an attempt to stimulate the economy and thus eliminate the budget deficit he inherited from Jimmy Carter. Otherwise, Reaganomics and classical economics are time-differentiated versions of one and the same theory: trickle-down economics. In both cases, the government doled out money to the affluent so that from them prosperity would trickle down to the poor and middle class.

To further aggravate the situation, the Reagan administration cut taxes sharply for the affluent and simultaneously raised defense spending. Never in the history of any nation have taxes been lowered and defense spending raised at the same time. If you want protection from your enemy, then you have to pay for it. It's as simple as that. But America abandoned this simple truth in 1981, raised defense spending while sharply trimming taxes, and soon found itself with even greater debts and deficits.

It must now be clear that the classical economics of the 1920s caused the depression of the 1930s, even though at the time the federal government had low debt and a persistent budget surplus, whereas America enjoyed a consistent trade surplus in international commerce and was a banker to the rest of the world. All these were positive aspects for our economy. Yet classical economics led the country into a depression. Today, the situation, in terms of those positive aspects, is just the opposite of that of the 1920s. In all those matters, we are now in the negative. In addition to huge twin deficits—budget and trade—the United States also has huge twin debts—domestic and foreign. There is only one conclusion we can draw: Reaganomics will lead us into the worst depression in history. And a financial disaster will occur even though the economic profession, as in the 1920s and always, clamors loudly that another depression is logically impossible.

It is not only possible, it may be inevitable. And many people have come to sense that something is terribly wrong out there, that the policymakers and their high-paid advisers either are acting in their own economic or political interest or are simply captives of conventional economic theory which has proved itself wrong time and time again. A wise man, having discovered that he has made a wrong turn, reverses his course and goes back to the point where the mistake occurred. History, we have learned to our sorrow, repeats itself. Economic history is no exception, and unless we attempt to change its course, we are headed down a doomsday path from which there seems to be no easy escape.

CHAPTER 2

The Unfolding Scenario

FOR THOSE WITH MEMORIES of the 1930s, the word "depression" has a grim and frightening reality. If they had gambled in the stock market, their investments were now worthless. Formerly secure jobs in booming businesses and industries were wiped out, and millions were unemployed. Breadlines and soup kitchens were familiar sights in the urban landscape. Farms and homes were lost to foreclosure, and the savings of a lifetime vanished when banks failed. Is it possible that a mere sixty years later, in a society and an economy that seem more prosperous than ever before, such a disaster could occur again?

In my previous book, *The Great Depression of 1990*, I described the three-decade cycles that have dominated the world's economy for centuries. A further careful study confirms that some important variables in the U.S. economy have moved along an exact cycle of three decades. Specifically, except during the turbulent period following the Civil War in the 1860s, the rate of inflation has reached its peak every third decade over the past two and a half centuries. Simultaneously, the rate of money growth has also crested every third decade over the same time period. Another variable with an identical pattern is the degree of government regulation of the economy. In other words, inflation is a monetary and a regulatory phenomenon, because all three variables have historically peaked in the same decade.

Regarding contractions in the economy, the same three-decade pattern still holds, but with a modification. A steep recession has occurred every decade since the 1780s. A great depression, which is far worse than a recession, occurred every third or sixth decade—that is, if the third decade experienced only a minor contraction, then the sixth decade witnessed an all-time economic disaster. In other words, the country has been able to avoid a third-decade depression but never a sixth-decade depression. Since the last time a major depression struck was in the 1930s, and since the 1960s escaped one, the 1990s will suffer the worst economic crisis in history. [1]

The analysis of these cycles can help pinpoint the approximate year the depression will begin. For the twentieth century, the six-decade cycle of business activity appears to be more pronounced than the three-decade cycle. Of course, if the three-decade cycle holds, then the six-decade cycle will automatically hold, but not conversely.

Economic Cycles

In order to see how the next few years will unfold, let us first examine the similarities between the 1920s and the 1980s. I will also look at important dissimilarities and draw appropriate conclusions. For the two decades under con-

[1] See Ravi Batra, *The Great Depression of 1990* (New York: Simon and Schuster, 1987).

sideration, the six-decade cycle turns out to be as exact as it possibly can be. These similarities must be more than a mere coincidence, for they involve eight of the maximum ten years within a decade.

Table 1 presents a dramatic account of the sixty-year cycle. I made a similar comparison in *The Great Depression of 1990*. I am reproducing it here and updating it through 1987.

Table 1
The Six-Decade Cycle: The 1920s vs. the 1980s

Comparisons of the decade leading up to the Great Depression of the 1930s with the decade of the 1980s.

1920s	1980s
1920	**1980**
A year of high inflation, high unemployment, and high interest rates. A very rare combination.	The same rare combination occurs again.
GM has its first loss.	GM did not lose money even during the Great Depression, but *does* lose money in 1980.
1921	**1981**
A huge tax cut favoring the rich occurs.	The major economic news is the probusiness, pro-affluent tax cut —regarded as the biggest in history.
Tight-money policies go into effect to control inflation.	The same tight-money policies occur in 1921.
Unemployment rises sharply.	Unemployment rises sharply.
1922	**1982**
A sharp fall in inflation	A sharp fall in inflation.
A sharp fall in interest rates.	A sharp fall in interest rates.
A sharp rise in the stock market.	A similar rise in the stock market

1923

Banks offer interest on checking accounts for the first time in history.

A very sharp decline in unemployment.

The stock market continues to rise.

1924

Inflation is low, interest rates are stable, and the stock market continues to rise.

1925

Unemployment falls again.

The stock market rises again, and inflation is unchanged.

A sharp rise in bank failures occurs.

1926

The stock market breaks another record.

Unemployment declines sharply.

The Revenue Act of 1926 sharply reduces tax rates for the poor and the wealthy, while raising them for corporations.

Another jump in bank failures.

The rate of inflation falls.

At the end of the year, energy prices fall sharply.

1927

The stock market reaches new highs.

1983

Banks offer interest on checking accounts for the first time since the 1930s.

A decline in unemployment considered the largest in three decades.

The stock market continues to rise.

1984

Inflation is low, interest rates are stable, and the stock market continues to rise.

1985

Unemployment falls again.

The stock market rises again, and inflation is unchanged.

A sharp rise in bank failures occurs—120 banks fail in 1985.

1986

The stock market breaks another record.

Unemployment declines a little.

The Tax-Reform Act of 1986 will cause the sharpest fall in tax rates for individuals, while raising taxes for businessmen.

Another jump in bank failures, as in 1926. (FDIC reports 130 banks failed in 1986.)

The rate of inflation falls.

Energy prices fall sharply throughout the year.

1987

The stock market reaches new highs.

1927	*1987*
Banks begin to underwrite stocks.	Congress passes a law permitting banks to underwrite stocks again from March 1988.
Stock prices drop sharply in October 1927.	The stock market drop on October 19, 1987, is the largest in seventy-three years.
The economy operates near full employment.	The economy operates near full employment.
The Fed follows an easy-money policy to prevent a recession.	The Feds follow an easy-money policy to prevent a recession.

In 1920, we had high inflation, high unemployment, and high interest rates. Economists generally regard this as a rare combination—in fact, as rare as a great depression. Yet the same rarity occurred sixty years later in 1980. When unemployment increases, aggregate spending declines, so that businessmen are unable to post big increases in price. Therefore, high unemployment usually goes with low inflation, which in turn generates lower interest rates. In other words, high unemployment, high inflation, and high rates of interest rarely occur at the same time.

Let us now consider the behavior of a specific industry. Automobile manufacturing is an important sector of the American economy. General Motors is the dominant firm in this industry, and, in fact, it has been said that what is good for GM is also good for America. In 1920, the auto giant had its first loss, and it did not lose money again until 1980. Incredibly, the company earned profits every single year between 1921 and 1979—even during the calamitous years of the Great Depression. But as soon as sixty years had passed, it lost money again.

The major economic news of 1981 was a tax cut favoring wealthy individuals and corporations. The last time such an event occurred was in the 1920s, starting with

1921. In both years a Republican president encountered stiff opposition from the Democratic Party to this legislation.

In both 1921 and 1981, there was a sharp rise in unemployment created by tight-money policies of the Federal Reserve Board, which controls the central bank of the United States and regulates credit in the economy. In 1982, however, there was a steep decline in interest rates, along with a sharp rise in the stock market. The same occurred in 1922. In addition, inflation slowed down in both years.

The main economic event of 1983 was that banks began to pay interest on checking accounts. The same thing also occurred toward the end of 1923. However, the significance of this practice has yet to be realized. I will examine it in detail in Chapter 18.

In both 1923 and 1983, the stock market continued to rise in the wake of sharp declines in unemployment.

In both 1924 and 1984, inflation remained low and the stock market continued to climb, while interest rates remained unchanged. Similarly, in both 1925 and 1985, unemployment fell and the stock market soared.

Energy prices plunged in both 1926 and 1986, and so did the rate of inflation, while the stock market scaled new highs. Similarly, in both years Congress trimmed taxes for individuals and raised them for corporations. In each instance the legislation had rare support from both parties, and won plaudits from the press. In both 1926 and 1986, there was a jump in bank failures.

The stock market reached new highs in both 1927 and 1987, while bank failures remained worrisome. There was also a stock market crash in October 1927, though not of the same scale as the one that occurred in October 1987. (On this I shall have more to say in Chapter 9.) Banks first began to underwrite stocks in 1927, a practice that Congress banned during its learning years of the 1930s; but in

September 1987 a new law was passed permitting banks to resume the underwriting activity from March 1988. In both 1927 and 1987, the economy operated near full employment, while inflation and interest rates remained well in control. In both years, the Fed abruptly changed its course and followed an easy-money policy to prevent a stock market debacle and a recession.

Thus there are great similarities between each year of the 1920s and the 1980s. Normally, the six-decade cycle is not so exact, but for the decades under consideration, it appears to be as exact as it can be.

There are, of course, some differences between the two decades. But this is only to be expected over time. The surprising part is in all the similarities we have discovered. As noted in the previous chapter, America in the 1980s has faced twin deficits—budget and trade—whereas in the 1920s it enjoyed twin surpluses. Similarly, it has suffered twin debts in the 1980s—domestic and foreign—whereas in the 1920s it was a creditor nation to other countries and had a negligible domestic debt. But these differences are not healthy economic signs; they only make matters worse. In fact, they tend to reinforce the frightening message of the cycles, namely that the sixth-decade depression is worse than the previous depression.

If the differences between the decades of the 1920s and the 1980s contradicted the message of the similarities, you might still have a sense of relief. You could then at least hope that maybe there will be no crisis this time. But I personally don't see any silver lining in the maze of significant but gloomy differences between the 1920s and the 1980s. They only confirm the forecast of the looming cataclysm.

If you want further confirmation of the sixty-year cycle, then compare the 1910s and the 1970s. In both decades, inflation, money growth, and regulation were high, and energy and farm sectors were very prosperous. In addition, the stock market was stagnant in both decades.

Economic Forecasting

In order to forecast future economic trends accurately we need to combine the message of cycles with an understanding of how our economy works and has evolved over time. Today there are two schools of thought as far as foreseeing the future is concerned. One school focuses on the cycles and disregards fundamental market forces dealing with demand and supply, whereas the other school ignores the cycles and concentrates on the analysis of fundamental market forces, using econometrics and computer models. The conflict between these two schools has given forecasting a bad name. Economists of both sides have become notorious for consistently making wrong forecasts. But the public, the victim of faulty predictions, has been very patient and forgives economists as regularly as it does weathermen.

The proper approach to forecasting is one which observes the similarities displayed by cycles over two periods and adjusts their message in accordance with current thinking and trends. Cycles alone may yield faulty predictions and econometric methods alone may totally miss emerging trends. Computer models, however, can be accurate, provided their message does not contradict the message of cycles.

Let me illustrate this point with the help of the following forecasts that I published between 1980 and 1983:

1. There will be seven years of prosperity from 1983 through 1989.
2. Inflation will gradually decline and then stabilize in the 1980s.
3. Interest rates will decline and then stabilize in the 1980s.
4. Bond prices will first rise and then stabilize in the 1980s.
5. Concentration of wealth will rise every year until 1989.
6. Merger mania will occur in the 1980s.

7. Oil and farm prices will decline in the 1980s.

8. The stock market will break records every year from 1983 through 1989.

9. European countries such as Britain and France will suffer from high unemployment in 1986.

10. At the end of 1989 or the beginning of 1990, the stock market will crash for the final time, leading to another global depression.

None of these forecasts has been wrong so far. None contradicts the message of my cycles, which suggested to me that many, but not all, trends of the 1980s would be similar to the trends in the 1920s. I made these forecasts very carefully. First of all, they do not deal with any specific numbers, although later I did make more specific predictions in response to questions from my students, readers, and reporters. For instance, I did say that inflation would hover around a 4 percent annual rate in the 1980s, and the Dow Jones Industrial Index would reach a high of 2000 by the end of 1986 (it reached 1955), and so on. But these forecasts were based more on a gut feeling than on a rigorous analysis of history and of the thinking of economic policymakers.

Secondly, while the above forecasts were based on a sixty-year cycle of business activity, they didn't just blindly replicate the 1980s for the 1920s. The annual inflation rate for several years during the 1920s was either zero or close to 1 percent. However, I predicted not a zero inflation rate for the 1980s, but a rate that would be significantly below the double-digit level prevailing at the end of the 1970s. This is because the current economic policy is more interventionist than it was during the 1920s. Until the 1930s the Federal Reserve System kept the supply of money under a much tighter leash than it does today. For these reasons I adjusted the message of the inflationary cycle for the 1980s from a zero rate of inflation to a low but positive inflation rate.

Thirdly, I first made predictions about variables for which I could discover regular cycles, and then those predictions led to many others. For instance, whenever inflation falls, interest rates fall with it, and bond and stock prices go up. Similarly, whenever wealth disparity rises in an atmosphere of deregulation, merger mania occurs. Finally, falling inflation, coupled with soaring wealth disparity and mergers, turns a rising market into a speculative bubble, which eventually bursts in a series of crashes to start a depression.

In view of the sixty-year cycle and current economic trends, we can look ahead and predict that in many respects 1988 and 1989 will be like 1928 and 1929. Table 2 gives you a bird's eye view of what the late 1920s were like and how the late 1980s are likely to evolve.

Table 2
The Six-Decade Cycle: 1928–29 vs. 1988–89
(events of 1928–29 with forecasts for 1988–89)

1928–29	*1988–89*
1928	*1988*
1. Stock prices rise sharply.	1. Stock prices drift at a high level.
2. Bank failures fall but remain high.	2. Bank failures remain high.
3. Energy prices fall.	3. Energy prices fall relative to other prices.
4. Interest rates rise slightly.	4. Interest rates rise slightly.
5. Unemployment is very low.	5. Unemployment remains low.
6. The inflation rate is unchanged.	6. The inflation rate is unchanged.
1929	*1989*
1. Stock prices rise sharply until September and then crash in October.	1. Stock prices drift wildly; crash by the end of the year or in the first quarter of 1990.
2. Bank failures rise sharply.	2. Bank failures rise sharply.

1929	*1989*
3. Interest rates rise sharply.	3. Interest rates rise sharply.
4. Unemployment is low in the first half, rises in the second half.	4. Unemployment remains low for most of the year.
5. The inflation rate is unchanged.	5. The inflation rate rises.

In 1928 the stock market kept rising, bank failures remained high but inflation and interest rates were more or less stable, while the economy operated near full employment. In most respects, you should expect the same for 1988, with inflation and interest rates hovering around their 1987 levels. However, the outlook for the stock market, because of wide publicity about the coming crash and because of the twin American debts and deficits, is extremely uncertain. All one can foresee is that the final crash will not come until after the presidential election in November 1988, as the government usually ensures a prosperous economy during an election year.

In 1929 inflation and interest rates rose significantly, and the stock market surged until the month of October, when it finally crashed. This time, you should look for a very volatile stock market in 1989, with the final crash occurring by the end of the year or the first quarter of 1990. Keep in mind, of course, that my forecasts could be off by three to six months.

My earlier forecast that the stock market would break records every year from 1983 through 1989 will now come true for Japan, which in the late 1980s is where America was in the late 1920s, with high trade surpluses and overseas investments.

What Will Trigger the Crash?

People often ask me what will trigger the crash. In other words, what will puncture the stock market bubble for the final time?

When the bubble has expanded to its utmost limits, even a pinprick can burst it open. Any number of things could go wrong in the near future. A rise in farm prices, in inflation, in interest rates, in budget deficits, in inventories, in trade deficits, or in other single statistics could topple the economic house of cards. While any one of these events could push the economy over the brink, they are not likely to bring about the crash. The most likely culprit will be a fall of the dollar.

The dollar is now the Achilles heel of the capitalist world, just as the British pound was during the 1960s, except the stakes are now far bigger than before. Throughout this century the pound and the dollar have served as international currencies which were generally accepted in the exchange of goods and services. For several years in the 1960s, however, Britain suffered large deficits in its balance of payments. The world at that time was on a fixed exchange standard—that is, exchange rates among various currencies were regulated. You could, for instance, buy a certain number of yen for a dollar, without worrying about the two currencies' market fluctuations. Each country was ready to back its currency through the participation of its central bank in the foreign exchange market.

When Britain experienced huge deficits in its balance of payments, the world was awash in pounds, which the country was obligated to buy back with its holdings of dollars or gold. Britain also had another choice—devaluation or depreciation of its currency. This, at the time, was considered a humiliating choice, amounting to an admission of a weak economy and declining international prestige.

In order to support the pound, Britain frequently borrowed money from other industrial countries and from the International Monetary Fund. Other central banks also periodically intervened in the foreign exchange market, buying pounds with their own currencies. All these measures propped up the pound by artificially creating extra demand for the English currency. For a few years these measures were successful. But the root cause of the problem, a chronic deficit in Britain's balance of payments, continued, supplying an ever-increasing number of pounds to the world. How long can you treat the symptoms of a malady without striking at its true cause? A time came when the pound was supportable no more. The international supply of the pound sharply exceeded the demand, including that created by central banks. Its value had to fall, and it did. In 1967, Britain had to eat humble pie—to devalue its currency sharply and accept a major decline in its standard of living. It tried to thrive on foreign borrowing forever, but could not, and ultimately the British people suffered greatly for the mismanagement by their government.

In the 1980s the dollar faces the same fate as the pound did in the 1960s. The only difference is that the world is now on a flexible exchange standard, in which the international value of currencies fluctuates daily on the basis of their global demand and supply. According to conventional economic theory, there can be no balance-of-payments imbalance in such a system. But this is another conventional idea which, in recent years, has miserably failed to hold in reality. Since 1982 the U.S. balance of payments has been in a chronic deficit, supplying a mounting pile of dollars to the world.

Much of the U.S. deficit is with Japan, West Germany, Canada, Taiwan, and South Korea. According to economic theory, an American trade deficit should cause a fall of the dollar until the deficit disappears, because the depreciating dollar makes foreign goods expensive to

Americans and American goods cheaper to foreign consumers. As a result, exports should rise and imports should fall until the deficit vanishes. This is traditional economic theory, but the reality of the relationship of the dollar to the deficit has been something else.

In 1982, the dollar began to appreciate against major foreign currencies, such as the yen, the pound, and the mark, generating in the process high foreign trade surpluses and American trade deficits. That part of the conventional theory did work. With the appreciating dollar, American goods became more expensive abroad and high-quality foreign goods became cheaper in America, leading eventually to large U.S. trade deficits. But then the dollar came under pressure and began to decline steadily in the second quarter of 1985, and it has been declining ever since. As soon as the dollar began to depreciate, forecasts of the demise of the trade deficit within eighteen months came pouring in from established economists. As usual, these forecasts also proved wrong. Not only did the trade deficit fail to decline, it kept rising and reached new highs in 1986 and 1987. By spring 1988, the deficit was stuck at $150 billion a year, while the dollar continued to fall. This is another puzzle conventional wisdom has failed to solve. (We will examine this question later in Part IV.)

I said earlier that the dollar is now the Achilles heel of the capitalist world. This is because central banks in seven countries, known as the Group of Seven, have been buying dollars to arrest its decline.[2] Rightly or wrongly, stability or an orderly drop of the dollar, rather than a free fall, is now considered essential for continued prosperity of financial markets all over the world. There is, of course, a connection among the government budget deficit, America's trade deficit, the value of the dollar, and prospering stock markets.

[2] The Group of Seven includes the United States, Canada, West Germany, Japan, Britain, France, and Italy.

The U.S. rate of savings, among the lowest in the world, is too small to finance the federal budget deficit. Funds must come from abroad to purchase bonds issued by the U.S. Treasury. In order to attract foreign funds into federal bonds, the dollar has to remain stable. Of course, the foreign countries, awash with piles of dollars, are also anxious to pour their funds into America. But a quick fall of the dollar tends to scare them away, as no foreign national likes to be paid back in a depreciating currency.

Suppose a Japanese investor buys a U.S. Treasury bond yielding 10 percent interest a year. If the dollar also depreciates 10 percent in that year, then his entire return is wiped out; if it depreciates more, he actually loses money by investing in America. Therefore, in order to keep foreign investors interested in federal securities, the Fed cannot permit a quick fall of the dollar.

Nor is a speedy fall of the dollar in the self-interest of America's trading partners, as they have to raise their prices, endangering the sale of their products in the United States. Therefore, central banks from the Group of Seven, each for its own reason, have been intervening heavily in the foreign exchange market to stabilize the dollar or at least slow down its decline. However, historical experience with the pound reveals that this is eventually a lost cause. Never has a nation been able to stabilize its currency for long in the wake of continued deficits in its balance of payments. America could be an exception, but it will be the first exception in the world's history.

A time will come when the dollar is supportable no more; when the orderly drop gives way to a free fall. This will most likely occur in 1989 when the U.S. foreign debt, growing at the rate of $150 billion a year, nears the psychologically important $1 trillion mark. Although the dollar has been unsupportable for a long time, the central banks have been keeping it alive through artificial respiration, buying billions of dollars with their own currencies. But sometime in 1989 the artificial respirator will collapse under its own weight. After all, when central banks purchase dollars, they create new headaches for themselves. They have to expand their own money supply, inviting inflation in the process. In other words, there are limits to foreign central banks' accumulation of dollars.

Once the foreign central banks have reached their limits, the Fed has two choices. It can stand idle and let the dollar fall, in which case it could scare away foreign investors from U.S. financial markets; or it can tighten the money supply, in effect raising interest rates to make dollar-denominated investments more attractive than before. A rise in interest rates will trigger a recession and a crash in the still-overheated U.S. stock market, eventually leading to a depression. If interest rates are not raised, then the free fall of the dollar will cause panic waves in Japan, as the Japanese perceive that their export industries could go bankrupt.

An overheated stock market is an extremely sensitive plant, and even a little breeze can bring it down. Speculative fever has afflicted stock markets all over the world in the 1980s, but the Tokyo Stock Exchange has been the most feverish. The Nikkei Index has risen much faster than the Dow Jones Industrial Average index. Therefore, the Japanese market is much more vulnerable to adverse news than the U.S. market. A free fall of the dollar will unleash a wave of pessimism in Japan long before its export industries actually go under. For the stock market to crash all you need is a perception that the party is soon going to be over, not an actual end to the party. Thus just a perception in Japan that its export industries are soon going to be badly hurt by the free fall of the dollar will bring its markets crashing down.

As euphoria gives way to gloom, there will be a great sell-off of stocks in Tokyo. If this crash is minor, funds will move from Japan to other parts of the world, especially to New York, and other stock markets could actually gain. However, a free fall of the dollar is likely to produce a stunning crash in the Tokyo market, so that Japanese investors will be forced to liquidate their not inconsiderable assets abroad, ushering in a stock market crash all over the world. They will also have to unload their holdings of U.S. government bonds; at the very least, they will be unable to buy more. This itself will lead to a rise in U.S. interest rates, further crimping the American stock markets.

The world economic system is now sitting on a knife edge, and the dollar is its most vulnerable point. Whenever the inevitable crunch comes under the mounting pressure of foreign debt and the continued trade deficit, the Fed will either have to raise interest rates sharply or let the dollar slide freely to its market-determined level. Those who have seen the Mexican peso fall in the 1980s from 4 cents per peso to its current level of ¹⁄₂₅th of a cent per peso know what the free market can do to a weak currency. Those who remember the fate of the pound in the 1960s also know that persistent trade deficits combined with central bank intervention in the foreign exchange market eventually lead to a bottomless decline of the deficit nation's currency.

What will the Fed do when faced with the cruel choice between rising interest rates and the sharp depreciation of the dollar? Will it choose one over the other? My guess is that the Fed will strike a compromise and do a bit of both. It will raise interest rates and let the dollar fall somewhat. It did that in September 1987, and will do so in 1989. Eventually, this balancing action will fail, because such actions are treating the symptoms of a malady, but not its cause, which, as you will learn in Part IV, is extreme concentration of wealth.

The question in 1980, when the newspapers first printed my forecast of the coming depression, was: Is another depression possible? Today, the question is: How is it not possible? The knife-edge choice that the Fed faces should convince you that it will now take a miracle to stop the depression. All we can do is to pray that it doesn't happen, and undertake bold reforms to shorten it and soften its sledgehammer blow.

Wild Swings in the Stock Market

Not surprisingly, the financial markets have been reacting instantly to monthly trade figures. The markets understand the world better than conventional economists, who hold that trade deficits are logically impossible in a world of free markets. Fluctuating trade figures have produced wild swings in stock markets in recent years. At the end of 1986, the Dow was at around 1900, and it reached its 1987 peak on August 25 at 2722, a rise of 43 percent in eight months. Then, in just one week in October (from the 12th to the 16th), the Dow dropped by 235 points or 9.5 percent, and the following Monday, it tumbled 508 points or 22.6 percent, all the way to 1738. In both percentage and absolute terms, this was the largest single drop since 1929. But then in the next two days the market turned around and rose 286 points, erasing more than half of the record one-day fall. October 19, 1987, is now called Black Monday, corresponding to Black Tuesday of October 29, 1929, when the Dow fell 11.7 percent.

The Tokyo market in 1987 jumped by as much as 53 percent by the month of September, but in the process experienced periodic drops of as much as 4 percent per day. On October 20, 1987, following Black Monday in America, the Tokyo market fell as much as 15 percent. The crash also had its echoes in other parts of the world; there were huge stock market losses in London, Toronto, Hong Kong, Australia, Italy, France, and other countries.

Two laws of motion govern anything that moves speedily. First, what goes up without an underlying foundation must one day come down to its starting point. Second, anything that moves fast has a large variance. In other words, sharply high growth also invites sharply high fluctuations. Thus, wild swings are only to be expected in a stock market bubble, which, by definition, means an extraordinary rise in stock prices unmatched by a corresponding rise in GNP or corporate earnings. The same thing happened in the bubble of the 1920s, when the financial markets witnessed sharp ups and downs. In fact, even in a seven-year-long bull market, there were many minicrashes, before the final crash in October 1929.

Like storm winds before the arrival of a hurricane, wild swings in the stock market actually foreshadow the severity of the looming disaster. The October Massacre was just a mild foretaste of the swiftness and intensity of the calamity about to engulf our planet. In *The Great Depression of 1990*, I predicted that the coming depression would be the worst in history. That means that the minicrashes preceding the final stock market crash of 1989 or 1990 will also be worse than the corresponding minicrashes of the late 1920s. Table 3 presents the biggest single-day drops in the Dow Jones Industrial Average, and Black Monday's drop is the second-highest in U.S. history.

Why have the stock markets been more volatile in the 1980s than in the 1920s even though now they are under the theoretical control of the SEC (Securities and Exchange Commission), established in 1934? One reason is computerized programmed trading, and another is portfolio insurance. Both have the effect of causing sharper ups and downs, and both are used by large institutional investors.

Unlike traditional investors, program traders don't care about a stock's potential earnings and growth. They buy when a stock has risen above a critical point determined by the index-futures market and sell when it has dropped below another critical level. The idea is to cut one's losses when the market is falling and to get in on the action when the market is rising. Consequently, both upswings and downswings are sharper than otherwise. Portfolio insur-

Table 3
The Dow Jones Industrial Average's Biggest Single-Day Percentage Drops

Date	Close	Point Drop	Percentage Drop
December 12, 1914	54	17	24.4
October 19, 1987	1738	508	22.6
October 28, 1929	261	38	12.8
November 6, 1929	230	31	11.7
October 29, 1929	232	26	9.9
December 18, 1899	58	6	8.7
August 12, 1932	63	6	8.4
March 14, 1907	76	7	8.3
July 21, 1933	89	8	7.8
October 18, 1937	126	11	7.8
February 1, 1912	89	7	7.2
October 5, 1932	66	7	7.2
September 24, 1931	108	8	7.1
July 20, 1933	96	7	7.1
July 30, 1914	71	5	6.9

Source: *Investor's Daily,* October 20, 1987, p. 36.

ers, by contrast, buy and sell stocks to protect their holdings, exerting the same influence in the market as program traders.

These trading innovations provide an excellent example of how the safeguards that the government has introduced over the years to insulate the economy from the 1920s-style excesses are totally obsolete today. New reforms have to be introduced—and right away. Program trading is now, of course, suspended if the Dow drops 50 points in one day. This, however, did nothing to stop a precipitous 100-point drop in April 1988, and will do nothing to stop the coming depression.

CHAPTER 3

A Planet in Trouble

THE STOCK MARKET CRASH of October 1987 had its echoes throughout the world. A day after the collapse of the New York stock exchange, share prices plunged from Tokyo and Hong Kong in the east to London and Paris in the west, from Toronto in the north to Sydney in the south. Thus emerged startling evidence of a development that experts have frequently discussed in recent years— the national economies have become highly interdependent. Of course, what happens in America, the world's largest economy, reverberates around the globe; but what happens in Japan, Germany, and the Third World also sends ripples across the oceans. Like it or not, our planet has evolved virtually into a one-world economy.

The Worldwide Stock Market Bubble

The speculative bubble of the 1980s is not just an American phenomenon, it is a global phenomenon. In fact, the U.S. stock surge pales before that in Japan, Sweden, Mexico, West Germany, and France, among other nations.

Since mid-1982 to their peak reached in August 1987, U.S. stocks jumped by a hefty 250 percent; but that hardly compares to the climb of 600 percent in Japan, 400 percent in Sweden, and as much as 900 percent in Mexico. These were the gains to Americans investing in dollars—which, however, have recently depreciated dramatically relative to most other currencies.

If you purchase foreign shares in dollars, you get an extra bonus when you sell if the foreign currency has appreciated. In terms of local currencies, therefore, most foreign stock gains have been a bit smaller than those reported above; yet they are enough to overwhelm the U.S. gains. What is intriguing and worrisome, however, is that similar developments occurred during the 1920s, when stocks in the major trading nations of Western Europe and the United States soared without commensurate gains in their economies.

Chart 1 displays the stock market performance of ten countries between January 1926 and January 1935, and shows that Europe, Canada, and America experienced a stock boom between 1926 and 1929 and then a crash between 1929 and 1933. Japan, for which figures are available only after 1929, largely bucked the depression of the 1930s mainly because, like the Soviet Union, it had a planned economy at the time and its government raised spending dramatically. As a result, Japanese stocks, unaffected by developments elsewhere, gained in the early 1930s, unlike those in America, Canada, and Europe.

Reasons for the global speculative binge are the same as in the United States—lower nominal interest rates, pro-business government policies, and, above all, soaring wealth disparity all over the world. Because of rising wealth inequality, stock rises have extended beyond developed economies to even some poverty-stricken Third World countries, such as Mexico, India, Malaysia, and Brazil, among others.

In the intertwined world today, the main players in the

Chart 1
Share Prices in Selected Markets; 1926–35

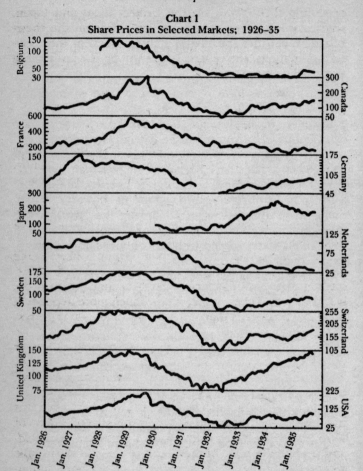

Sources: Charles Kindleberger, *The World In Depression* (Berkeley: University of California Press, 1986); League of Nations, *Statistical Yearbook*, various issues.

economic chess game are the United States and Japan, whereas most other economies are pawns on the chessboard. When the speculative bubbles burst in these two leading nations, the repercussions will be felt around the world—one more time.

Japan

The Japanese economy before and during the 1930s was not tightly linked to the rest of the world. Consequently, the Great Depression left little imprint on Japan which, as I have said, essentially had a planned economy at that time. Britain was then the world's largest exporter, despite an overvalued currency, because of its control over captive markets in its colonies. The United States had a huge domestic economy, but it was the world's main banker. In the 1980s, the roles of different nations have changed. America is now the world's largest importer and Japan is the world's chief banker. Japan is now much more dependent on global prosperity than it was in the 1930s—as is the rest of the world.

The Japanese produced an economic miracle after their country was devastated during the Second World War. Theirs is a Cinderella story worthy of emulation by other nations. The Japanese economy is highly resilient; it adjusts to new shocks much better than any other, a fact that has been proved time and again. Despite the oil shocks of 1973 and 1979, when OPEC raised oil prices manyfold, and despite the huge appreciation of the yen during the second half of the 1980s, Japan's economic engine continues to move faster than that of any other country. Serious problems, however, have already developed under the surface, which, along with the ills in America, would be sufficient to bring about a great depression in the near future.

Like the United States, Japan has a huge budget deficit

and government debt. According to OECD reports, the Japanese debt-to-GNP ratio in 1987 was at 69 percent compared to about 52 percent in the United States. Of course, with a huge savings rate, the debt and deficits are easier to finance in Japan than almost anywhere else. But the fact that the country has needed massive infusions of government spending to keep growing suggests that pressures are developing within the system. Apparently, the wealth disparity has also soared in Japan, so that to counter the debilitating economic consequences of growing wealth inequality, the government has to resort increasingly to deficit spending.

According to *Forbes* magazine, some of the wealthiest people live in Japan, where wealth inequality has surged during the 1980s. Consequently, the country today has perhaps the most speculative economy of all nations. Not only the stock market but also real estate has soared. From 1980 to 1985, commercial real estate in Tokyo appreciated at a 13 percent rate per year; in 1986, however, it climbed by 22 percent, and in 1987 by a whopping 76 percent. Land has risen even faster, jumping by 93 percent in the first six months of 1987. Andrew Tanzer writes in *Forbes,* "Throughout the world investors are fixated on the U.S. budget deficit. If investors thought things through, they would be equally concerned by the high cost of Japanese real estate."[1]

The problem has spilled over to the banks, which are usually involved in any speculative binge. Japanese banks vie with each other in making loans to property owners. The collateral is, of course, the inflating stock price, as property owners, having tasted the forbidden apple of easy money, want to make a quick killing in the stock market. Japan is also the second-largest lender to the Third World, just behind the United States. Thus the Japanese

[1] Andrew Tanzer, "These Prices Are Really Insane," *Forbes,* December 14, 1987, p.76.

banks are also vulnerable to a default by developing countries. On top of all this, these banks constitute a fourth of the country's total stock. Their share prices reflect the speculative environment in the country, selling for sixty-four times their earnings in 1987. An important development occurred on April 1, 1988, as interest from savings came under the purview of taxation. This, in the absence of a capital gains tax, means that a lot of money could move from savings accounts into stocks. Consequently the stock market in Japan could continue to rise in 1988 and the first part of 1989.

Unless something is done to cool down the speculative fever in Japan, real estate and stock prices are bound to crash sooner or later. The continued appreciation of the yen eventually will prove too much even for the Japanese economy, which has so far adjusted well to the falling dollar. But new adjustments will be increasingly difficult to achieve, and bloated internal markets will have to surrender to the rising chorus of contradictions in the global economy.

Japan also faces increasing competition from its neighbors, the so-called NICs (newly industrialized countries)—South Korea, Singapore, Taiwan, and Hong Kong. That increases the vulnerability of the Japanese speculative economy. It is worth noting here that while America might suffer from inflation at the beginning of the depression, there is no possibility of inflation in Japan and, for that matter, in any country with hefty trade surpluses—Germany, Canada, the NICs.

Western Europe

The sixty-year cycle of business activity that I discussed in Chapter 2 also applies to the economies of Western Europe. In terms of several key variables, such as wealth inequality, inflation, unemployment, stock prices, interest rates, farm and energy prices, business mergers, etc., Britain, France, Austria, and, to an extent, Germany in the 1980s are reminiscent of Europe in the 1920s. The United States, of course, has strictly followed the six-decade cycle, but so has Western Europe. The depression of the 1990s will, therefore, afflict Europe as well. But the suffering of Europe, like that of Japan, will fall short of that of the United States. Britain, France, and Germany will indeed suffer high unemployment and loss of incomes, but they will not be hit the worst by the depression. Real pain will occur in America, because the country has lived beyond its means for so long.

Germany now has the strongest economy in Europe and is the largest exporter in the world. Germany does not export as much to America as Japan does, but the German reliance on world prosperity is greater. During the 1930s Germany recovered from the crisis faster than other advanced economies. Whether this will happen in the 1990s, however, is questionable, because the more dependent a country is on world trade and investment, the more vulnerable it is to the coming depression.

Germany sharply lowered its interest rates following the stock market crash in 1987. It is also scheduled to cut taxes by $23 billion in 1990. Some economists suggest that this tax cut should be moved up to 1988. All these are, however, Band-Aid solutions likely to postpone the day of reckoning to the end of 1989 but no more.

Britain and France were among the top three economies in the 1920s. They are not in the same position in the 1980s. In fact, both have suffered from stubborn unemployment since the mid-1970s. Many British banks are also saddled with Third World loans. Both Britain and France have recently followed a policy of privatization, whereby previously nationalized companies are sold, wholly or partly, to private concerns. This has increased productivity and spurred growth, with stock markets responding in kind in both countries.

In terms of percentage decline, neither Britain nor France suffered much in the 1930s. Between 1929 and 1933, while industrial production fell by 36 percent in America, it fell by only 12 percent in Britain and 15 percent in France. The same could occur again in the 1990s, with the two European economies hurting less than that of the United States.

In Italy, Sweden, the Netherlands, and Switzerland, as elsewhere, the stock markets have been roaring in the 1980s. From mid-1982 to the peak reached in 1987, Italian stocks, in dollar terms, jumped by 450 percent, Swedish stocks by 400 percent, Dutch stocks by 340 percent, and Swiss stocks by about 400 percent. Europe has indeed grown rich on paper. Much of this prosperity has been borrowed from the future. It is interesting that Italy, the country with the largest stock gains in Europe, also has the highest debt-to-GNP ratio. According to OECD reports, the Italian ratio in 1987 was 107 percent, compared to 53 percent in England, 38 percent in France, and 43 percent in Germany. Europe, like America and Japan, is floating on government debt.

Canada

America is the biggest purchaser of Canada's exports. That is why Canadian prosperity is almost totally linked with the health of the U.S. economy. During the 1920s, depressed energy costs affected Canada. When the stock market boomed in America, the effect was communicated to Canada. Because of the linkage through trade and investment, key economic variables in Canada rise and fall with those of its giant neighbor.

During the 1980s, the Canadian economy has also moved in the shadow of the U.S. economy. Interestingly enough, even the debt burden in the two neighbors has risen in parallel, with the Canadian government's debt-to-

GNP ratio being 70 percent at the end of 1987. However, there is one crucial difference.

Despite huge government debt and annual deficits, Canada has enjoyed a growing trade surplus with America in the 1980s. This has occurred even though Canadian inflation has exceeded the U.S. rate. Because of higher inflation, shares of natural resources in Canada have performed better than industrials; but overall the Toronto stock market has paralleled its New York counterpart. Developments in the near future in Canada are also likely to parallel those in the United States. For Canada, however, the pain will come mainly from a sharp fall in the world price of oil.

Australia

Australia is also a trade-dependent country. The total of its exports and imports constitute over a third of its GNP; the corresponding figure for the United States is about 25 percent. Australia is mainly a natural-resource-based economy. Consequently, worldwide disinflation during the 1980s has really hurt the country, as Australian export prices fell, but its import prices kept rising. In 1983 Australia had a trade deficit of $5.9 billion, and the deficit continued to rise in the next three years. Consequently, the Australian dollar depreciated substantially first in early 1985 and then in mid-1986. However, the deficit has not budged.

One reason for Australia's worsening trade position has been higher inflation than in other countries. Consumer prices rose by 9.7 percent in 1983, and by 1986 they were still rising at a rate of 9.3 percent. Unemployment has also been stubbornly high, stuck between 8 and 10 percent. In spite of a relatively stagnant economy, Australia has not escaped the clutches of global stock speculation, eclipsing America and Canada in the process.

Like other countries, Australia has had its share of rising budget deficits and debt. The country did announce some austerity measures in the fiscal year 1987–88 to trim the annual shortfall, but it is not clear whether they will make a perceptible dent in the total indebtedness. In the 1990s, Australian export prices will fall relative to import prices.

The Third World

The countries that I have explored so far have at least one thing in common. They are all advanced economies with high living standards. They are also highly industrialized, although some more than others, and most of them export a mix of agricultural goods, manufactured goods, business services, and raw materials.

However, there also exists another group of countries, which are very poor and which export mainly raw materials and import manufactured goods. They suffer from high foreign debts, low savings rates, chronic trade deficits, and abysmal per capita incomes. Even though they are not so trade-dependent, their economic health is critically linked to world prosperity because they receive foreign grants and aid that can make the difference between starvation and survival for a large number of their citizens. Such countries are included in the so-called Third World.

Some of the Third World nations do have a growing industrial sector. India and Brazil are two such countries. They have dual economies, with one sector that is highly developed and industrialized, and another that specializes in low-technology agriculture. But industrialized or not, all Third World countries have extremely high wealth disparities and an unimaginably low per capita income.

The Third World countries will be the hardest-hit group in the depression of the 1990s. As relative deflation sets in, export prices of this group will plummet relative to import prices. With the aid-granting countries themselves in turmoil, foreign aid will simply vanish, imposing a double jeopardy on the Third World.

In the developed world, the depression will first strike brokerage houses, then the durable goods industries, then commodities, and finally the service sector. In the Third World, with a large divergence between rural and urban areas, cities will be hit the hardest. Many urban centers depend on exports, which will plunge, and will be the first to feel the crunch. Rural areas, which mostly supply raw materials to the cities, will also be hurt, but not so badly. Some villages, with self-sufficient economies, could entirely escape depredations of the depression. In other words, cities will take a direct hit, but rural centers only an indirect hit.

The Third World was burdened by foreign debts in the 1920s as well, but it didn't default until the 1930s. Likewise, in this sixty-year cycle, again the Third World has been crushed by onerous foreign debt during the 1980s without an overt default. It's an open secret that very few developing countries will be able to honor their debts abroad. Most of them will not pay even a penny back on their loans. They will have to default openly in the 1990s. Why prolong their misery and increase chances of the coming depression? I suggest their debts should be written off in exchange for their adopting free market policies and competitive practices at home.

Many developing countries are hampered by local monopolies and high wealth inequality. If they promise to reduce disparities, trim bureaucratic controls, and adopt competitive free enterprise, they should be given a chance to become efficient economies. Their debts should be written off, and they should be allowed to start all over again. As they grow fast, they could help us stave off the coming crisis, or at least shorten its deadly duration. As for the lending banks, their accounting practices should be changed so that they could do business as usual. They don't expect to be paid anyway. The current system of de facto default is not helping anybody. It is, if anything, rushing us toward an unprecedented disaster.

Oil-Exporting Nations

As in the 1920s, there has been a sharp decline in energy prices in the 1980s. There will be an equally dramatic fall in the price of oil in the 1990s. As the world demand for oil plunges because of the global downturn, the price could settle at $8 per barrel, well below today's $17 range. Consequently, oil-exporting nations could be among the biggest victims of the coming crisis. They should immediately diversify their exports, reduce imports through national belt tightening, and lessen their reliance on oil.

Communist Countries

The East bloc will also be hit by the coming crisis, although not to the same extent as the rest of the world. Russia and China, being exporters of oil, will be hurt by a fall in its price. Poland, East Germany, and Hungary, among other communist nations, owe a lot of money to Western and Japanese banks and need to rely on exports to service their debts. With world trade plummeting, all communist nations will suffer increased unemployment and a drop in their living standards. Yet, because of their restrained international contacts, their suffering will not be as agonizing as that in non-communist nations.

PART II

Strategies for Business, Jobs, and Social Security in the 1990s

CHAPTER 4

The Challenge for Business

ECONOMIC ANALYSIS and the six-decade cycle of business activity are very helpful in foreseeing the future. As we have seen, numerous economic events of the 1920s have repeated themselves exactly sixty years later in the 1980s, and are expected to do so in the remainder of the decade.

Will the 1990s be an exact replica of the 1930s? I am not sure. But I am sure that the overall direction of the two decades will be the same. I am also sure the depression of the 1990s will be worse than that of the 1930s, but I don't know if each year of the 1930s will repeat itself exactly sixty years later in the 1990s.

I am not certain that I can repeat my predictive accuracy of the 1980s, where not just the trends but also the timing I forecast turned out to be accurate. With all my predictions, if I may say so, I was either right on the dot or was off by only a few days or by no more than a quarter, even though these events had been forecast years in advance. I could be as accurate again for the coming decade, because I am going to use the same methods as before. Then again, I could be off by as much as a year. If you are looking for general trends in the 1990s to guide your present behavior, I won't disappoint you. But if you are looking for the exact year in which any event will occur, then I want you to be cautious and use your own judgment.

For one thing, I don't expect the next depression to be as long as the one in the 1930s, which lasted ten years. The coming cataclysm would historically be the worst in intensity, but it would last only six or seven years, because the American public, much more conscious of its rights today than before, won't stand for another decade of devastation. However, market imbalances caused by extreme wealth disparity take a long time to unravel. No depression in history has been shorter than seven years, and I think the next one would also be that long. This itself suggests that the 1990s will not be an exact replica of the 1930s. Nonetheless, in view of the six-decade cycle and the prevalence of extreme wealth concentration in the 1980s, the coming decade would be ravaged by a great depression.

Let's have another look at Table 3 in Chapter 2 and see what happened in 1929. The stock market surged until September and began declining in October, at first like a trickle, and then like an avalanche. On October 29, Black Tuesday, the bottom dropped out of the market for the second day in a row, producing a horror that was repeated eight days later on November 6. From then on the market trend was downward, as usual in an up-and-down wave, and the trough occurred sometime in 1933. I predict that if the necessary reforms are not undertaken, the same thing will happen to the stock market by the first quarter of 1990.

The Stock Market and the Economy

What is the connection between the stock market and the economy? Normally the market is a barometer of a nation's well-being. As a nation grows, so do its industries and their earnings, which eventually should be reflected in higher dividends, higher stock prices, or both. Conversely, when growth declines, some industries suffer losses, leading to lower dividends and plummeting share prices. Such, then, is the normal relationship between the stock market and the economy.

However, the stock market is much more volatile than the economy even under the best of circumstances, because only an inordinately small minority of people usually participate in the market. In the United States, 50 percent of the total stock is owned by just 1 percent of families, and the other half is in the hands of pension funds, small businessmen, and professionals. Rarely is more than 10 percent of the population involved in the market, except toward the end of a stock market bubble, in which the realization of quick and easy profits by the few over a sustained period eventually lures even those normally averse to buying shares.

There is much greater public participation in the bond market than in the stock market, and that's why bonds are much more stable than stocks. The volatility of the stock market eventually derives from the volatile minds of those who own the largest share of stocks or manage mutual funds. Such people tend to be ultra-acquisitive and materialistic, using virtually all their time and propensities for amassing money. They are always trying to anticipate the direction of the market, the economy, the government attitude toward business, and so on. They and their advisers are the market makers and breakers.

Under normal conditions, as the market grows, the richest 1 percent of the population gain the most, and when the market falls, the richest people are also the biggest losers. However, in a stock market bubble, the wealthiest, as usual, are the biggest gainers, but when the bubble bursts not only they but everyone else tragically suffer from the explosion. For the affluent the bursting means only a loss of a few amenities, whereas for others, who lose their jobs or have to accept subsistence wages, it imperils survival. This is because the economy does not prosper in proportion to the market bubble, but it does suffer tragically in the aftermath of the bust. In the rising stage, the richest wallow in waste and luxury, but in the declining stage the bitter fruit of their greed and folly poisons everyone.

This is exactly what happened in 1929. After the market finally crashed, many speculators, especially the latecomers, were wiped out. They had bought stocks at highly inflated prices, quite often on credit, and their lifetime savings vanished in a hurry. They cut their spending to the minimum. Many firms which had formerly raised funds in the stock market also sharply trimmed their investments. And the rout was on. Production fell sharply, leading to quick layoffs. Those unemployed trimmed their own spending, defaulting on mortgages and auto loans. Banks began to fail in large numbers, wiping out their depositors, who, in turn, had to trim their own expenses, leading to a further fall in demand and hence to more layoffs. One after another, basic pillars of the economy fell like dominoes. By 1933 the unemployment rate reached a high of 25 percent of the labor force, with millions employed only part-time.

The drop was swift and decisive. The Index of Industrial Output declined from 110 in October to 105 in November and to 100 in December—a 9 percent drop in just three months. Commodity prices and imports fell even faster. Pessimism in the stock market quickly brought down the commodity markets and eventually the entire economy.

Something similar could develop in the 1990s. After the final crash of the stock market, for instance, in 1989 or 1990, many investors will be wiped out. Those firms that thrive on the prosperity of Wall Street will have to fire many employees immediately. Others, in the race for liquidity and solvency, will have to cut back sharply, producing a dominolike fall in demand and employment. As households default on mortgages and consumer and credit card loans, many banks and thrifts will fail. The government will come to their rescue, and within a year or less its insurance funds, the Federal Deposit Insurance Corporation (FDIC) and the Federal Savings and Loan Insurance Corporation (FSLIC), will be insolvent, requiring assistance from the Fed. But the Fed will not be able to meet all their needs because of fears of money inflation.

In the meanwhile, the government's revenue will fall sharply. Taxes from capital gains will become negative because of heavy losses in the stock market; taxes from corporate profits will also go down, as many companies suffer a fall in earnings. This will be one legacy of the Tax Reform Act of 1986, which has dramatically transferred the tax burden from wealthy individuals to corporations. With the fall in output will come a fall in the excise tax revenue, which is linked to production. With falling incomes and employment, revenue from Social Security and income taxes will also drop off. And while tax receipts fall, government spending for welfare and the unemployed will rise dramatically. The federal budget deficit will soar, tremendously stretching the bond market. According to some estimates, a 1 percent rise in unemployment currently raises the deficit by $40 billion.

The stock market crash in America will be either preceded or immediately followed by similar crashes all over the world. Foreign lending to the United States will then cease altogether, or else foreign investors will demand premium return, further straining the bond market.

The Fed will be caught in a cruel dilemma. It will then be sailing in uncharted waters, with no guiding precedents. Accommodating the gargantuan appetite of the government deficit and of failing banks, with foreign investment choked off, would require the Fed to print great quantities of new money, enough to threaten the return of crippling inflation along with sky-high interest rates, which in the end would bring about a depression anyway. On the other hand, keeping the money supply under reasonable control, with limitless government borrowing and banking needs, would also sharply raise interest rates and cause thousands of bank failures.

The Fed will then have to choose between two evils—an inflationary or a deflationary depression. My guess is that the government, with the memory of the double-digit inflation alive from the 1970s, will opt for a middle course, but only after it is clear that the depression is unstoppable. It will declare an emergency and, in the process, limit the amount of your bank withdrawals, sharply reduce its own spending, and declare a partial moratorium on interest payments to Americans and eventually perhaps to foreign nationals, thereby giving a breather to the Fed. The Fed will indeed raise money growth, but within bounds regarded as "safe."

Sharp cutbacks in government spending and the supportive foreign lending will, of course, instantly lower aggregate demand, leading to a private-sector depression. But since the Fed will this time come to the rescue of banks to the best of its ability, there will be no inordinate fall in money supply and hence prices. Prices are likely to be more or less stable in the 1990s, with a moderately downward trend. But keep your eyes wide open. There is a 30 percent chance of an inflationary depression, especially in 1990. Later deflationary forces could overwhelm the forces of inflation, leading to moderate deflation after 1991.

International trade, which is normally fueled by foreign lending, will drastically fall. With so much uncertainty generated by a series of events such as stock market crashes, the economic emergency in America, etc., foreign investments in the United States will come to a halt. In the meantime, the Third World countries will be defaulting left and right, as American imports nose-dive. They, too, will be unable to borrow any more. For all these reasons, international commerce will plummet, and a barter system of international exchange will coexist with the current system.

Banks in the 1990s will not fail in such huge numbers as in the 1930s, because this time the Fed won't abandon them. Nevertheless, the 1990s depression will be the worst in history. The reason lies in international interdependence, which is much greater today than ever before.

Foreign trade accounted for less than 13 percent of U.S. GNP in the 1920s; today, the figure exceeds 20 percent. America had a consistent trade surplus in the 1920s, and was also the world's largest economy. It continues to be the largest economic player in the global scene, and even though it has been a deficit nation during the 1980s, the world is now even more dependent on American prosperity than ever before, because in the 1980s the United States has sucked in several hundred billion dollars' worth of imports from other countries, over and above its exports to them. By 1990 the cumulative U.S. trade deficit for the decade will exceed $1 trillion.

The prosperity of Germany, Japan, the Third World, and even communist nations is now linked crucially to American prosperity. That's where the seeds of turmoil lie. If America were a surplus nation, it could continue to lend money abroad, keeping other countries afloat. It did that for three decades following the Second World War. But now the world's largest economy is also the world's largest debtor. It is simply impossible for other countries to keep America prosperous for long. The American appetite is gargantuan. A debtor can thrive on the fortunes of a lender, but a lender cannot forever prosper when a borrower has an insatiable appetite.

Something will have to give. And that will be international commerce, which is fueled by foreign lending. Thanks to multinational corporations and computers, our planet has become a single economy linked by a chain of satellites, giant banks, instant communication, international trade and investment, and above all the stock markets. What happens in America ripples across the globe; what happens to Japan, the Middle East, or Germany echoes in other nations.

During the 1920s, the United States was the world's largest banker; it maintained its large export trade through extensive foreign loans and direct investments in other countries. As a result, Europe was able to maintain a trade deficit and finance its payment of war debt to the United States. But in the late 1920s, the United States trimmed its foreign lending, leading to a sharp fall in world trade by 1930.

In the 1980s, Japan has replaced America as the world's largest banker. The Japanese have not only bought U.S. government bonds in huge numbers, they have also made direct investments in many U.S. industries. Japan has also invested heavily in Europe and the Third World. The real value of the Japanese trade surplus has been much larger than that of the U.S. counterpart in the 1920s. As a consequence, international lending today is far greater than ever before.

Even though America is now the world's largest debtor, it continues to be the largest lender to less developed countries (LDCs), especially in Latin America. Sooner or later international lending is bound to decline, because one-way lending cannot occur indefinitely. And I think it will be sooner rather than later.

Because of wild swings in the U.S. stock market, Black Monday, and the October Massacre, the world economic milieu has become very uncertain, a situation unfavorable to international investment.

When the dollar begins to fall freely, Japanese lending abroad will sharply decline, and so will international commerce. The drop will be faster this time than in the 1930s, because of increased global interdependence. American banks will not fail in as large numbers as in the previous depression, but world trade will come to a screeching halt, causing a much larger disruption of national economies than before.

True, the Fed remembers its follies of the past and won't shirk its responsibility to member banks this time. Yet the coming depression will generate higher unemployment than in the 1930s, because of a deeper depression in international commerce.

Worst-Hit Industries

With foreign trade expected to take a big beating, businesses engaged in exports and imports will be among those suffering the most. But they won't be the first to fail. The first to suffer will be industries providing financial services. Brokers, financial planners, investment bankers, takeover specialists, and the like could be laid off as soon as there is trouble on Wall Street. These have been among the most lucrative positions in the 1980s, and they will be the first to go.

Durable goods industries will come next. Homes, machine tools, autos, furniture, appliances, computers, airplanes—all are big-ticket items for which demand falls sharply in a downturn. Linked to these are the fortunes of companies producing raw materials or intermediate goods, such as iron, steel, copper, aluminum, lumber, chemicals, and plastics, among others, and their demand will also tumble. Defense and defense-related industries will suffer at the same time, since the government will have to cut back its spending drastically.

Farm subsidies will sharply drop, creating havoc for the already depressed farm sector. Farm prices will nose-dive, and so will food prices, generating double trouble for farmers.

Next in line to fall will be services offered by retailers, airlines, hotels, truckers, attorneys, accountants, day-care centers, nurseries, restaurants, banks, entertainers, newspapers, publishers, and beauticians, among others. Yet the service industry will be better off than the durable goods industries, manufacturing, and farming.

Least-Affected Industries

Most, if not all, industries suffer in a great depression, but some less than others. A depression is a cataclysmic event during which the living standard generally declines. Industries suffering the most in the 1990s will undergo massive layoffs as well as wage reductions, but those suffering the least will face only reduced income. Physicians, nurses, and hospital staff will have plenty of work available, as sickness and psychic illness spread in society because of uncertainty and unemployment. But patients won't be able to afford the high fees of doctors and hospitals; Medicare payments by the government will also decline. Therefore, while the health care industry in general will have no shortage of work, its real income could fall slightly. Dentistry, however, will be an exception to this rule, as dental care can be postponed. Dentists won't be as lucky as doctors and nurses.

Education is another industry that won't be hurt as much as manufacturing, farming, and some services. In fact, some segments of this industry could benefit from the economic turmoil. As jobs become scarce, the demand for higher education could rise. Employers will be able to pick and choose from the pool of available skills. People will have to compete hard for scarce positions, thereby increasing the need for technical skills, graduate study, and equivalent degrees.

At this point, I want to give you a word of caution. Even if you are now employed in one of the industries least likely to suffer, there is no reason for unbounded optimism. You should prepare for the worst, which could be loss of your job or a sharp cut in your salary, because even in relatively safe industries, there will be cases of individual hardships. If, for example, you live in a city dependent on manufacturing, which will be hit hard in the depression, that city's revenue will drastically fall. If you are a teacher in that city, you could be laid off or face a large pay cut, even though the education industry in general remains healthy. In making prepartions for the coming crisis, you have to weigh a number of factors: which region of the country you live in, whether it is the East Coast, the West Coast, the North, the South, and so on; what the most important industry is in your state and city; whether you live in a metropolitan city, a small town, or a suburb.

Benefiting Industries

There are a few industries that could actually benefit from the depression. As the demand for durable goods dramatically declines, businesses geared to their repair would flourish. All aspects of repair services could prosper.

Since crime soars amid poverty, the security and crime prevention industries would also flourish. So would businesses dealing with various aspects of bankruptcies, such as resale stores, pawnshops, auctioneering firms, and legal services, among others. And because of the need for inexpensive transportation, industries producing bicycles, mopeds, and minicars could also benefit.

Industry-Wide Analysis

You have seen which sectors of the economy are likely to fare better than others in the coming depression—information that should be especially useful to small businessmen and corporate executives in their planning. Let's now see how various industries behaved in the 1930s. The idea is to use the past as a guide to the future. True, the economy has changed dramatically since then, yet the industrial ramifications are still the same. The 1930s can indeed serve as a guide to the future behavior of most industries.

The Great Depression began in the last quarter of 1929 and steadily deepened until 1933. After that, business slowly improved until it had another setback in 1937. Finally, the U.S. economy was rescued by the Second World War, beginning in 1939.

Table 4 presents data about the state of the economy in 1929 and 1933 to give you an idea of how far and fast things can go wrong. Over these four years, national output (or real GNP) plunged by 30 percent, consumer prices by 24 percent, nominal or actual GNP by 46 percent, earnings by 26 percent, money supply by 31 percent, and foreign trade by 66 percent. At the same time, unemployment rose to 25.2 percent. Actually the purchasing power of those employed full-time did not fall by much, because the drop in incomes was almost matched by the drop in prices.

**Table 4
Key Statistics, 1929 and 1933,
When the Depression Was at Its Worst**

	1929	1933	Percentage Drop
Real GNP[1] or output[2]	203.6	141.6	30
Unemployment rate (percent)	3.2	25.2	−22
Consumer Price Index (1967 = 100)	51.3	38.8	24
Money supply[2]	46.6	32.2	31
Foreign trade[2] (exports and imports)	12.9	4.4	66
Average individual money earnings (dollars)	1,405	1,045	26

Source: *Historical Statistics of the United States.*
[1] GNP adjusted for price changes.
[2] In billions of dollars.

These figures represent national averages and provide yardsticks with which you can compare the performance of individual industries. The worst-hit sectors in a depression are obviously those in which output, prices, and value of production fell more than the corresponding national decline. The opposite holds for the least-hit industries. The rare cases where the output or prices rose are obviously the industries that benefited from the depression.

Table 5 displays the behavior of the construction industry in the early 1930s. This was clearly the worst-hit sector, with fall in output ranging from 78 percent to 80 percent, far higher than the decline in national output of 30 percent. However, prices of existing houses dropped only at the rate of the overall consumer price index, whereas in a large city like Washington, D.C., the median house lost only 20 percent of its value.

Table 5
Value of New Construction, 1929 and 1933

	1929	1933	Percentage Drop
Residential[1]	23,157	4,570	80
Nonresidential[1]	8,144	1,725	78
Public utilities[1]	4,194	847	79
Price index for one-family house (1957–59 = 100)	100	75.5	24
Median asking price for existing houses in Washington, D.C. (dollars)	7,246	5,759	20

Source: *Historical Statistics of the United States.*
[1] *In millions of dollars.*

Table 6 examines the behavior of the durable goods sector during the Great Depression. This sector also fared worse than the national average, with overall output loss of 37 percent. Some of its constituent industries, such as primary metals, transportation equipment, and lumber products, were hit even harder. However, most of the nondurable goods industries described in Table 7 did better than the national average. These could be called the least-hit industries. Except for rubber products, all other nondurable goods industries suffered a decline below the national output decline of 30 percent.

Table 6
Durable Goods Industries, 1929 and 1933
(Index of Industrial Output, 1947 = 100)

	1929	1933	Percentage Drop
All durable goods	56	35	37
Primary metals	65	27	58
Transportation equipment	66	22	66
Stone, clay, and glass products	89	42	53
Lumber and furniture	91	42	54

Source: *Historical Statistics of the United States.*

Table 7
Nondurable Goods Industries, 1929 and 1933
(Index of Industrial Output, 1947 = 100)

	1929	1933	Percentage Drop
All products	67	57	15
Rubber products	57	39	31
Leather products	79	68	14
Paper products	52	44	15
Printing and publishing	72	52	27
Chemicals	35	29	17
Petroleum and coal products	54	42	22
Food	46	37	19
Tobacco	55	48	13

Source: *Historical Statistics of the United States.*

Another way to understand how the last depresssion affected various industries is to analyze the data on personal consumption expenditures presented in Table 8. It is clear that between 1929 and 1933 the percentage of consumer expenditure rose substantially for housing and declined sharply for clothing, accessories, and jewelry. It also fell significantly for transportation and recreation, whereas for other types of products it was more or less unchanged. This suggests that luxury items such as jewelry and recreation suffered badly, whereas house rents declined less than the fall in individual incomes. The travel industry also did poorly relative to others.

Table 8
Personal Consumption Expenditures, 1929 and 1933
(percent distribution)

	1929	1933
Food, beverages, and tobacco	27.5	27.9
Clothing, accessories, and jewelry	14.5	11.9
Personal care	1.4	1.4
Housing	14.9	17.3
Household operations	13.9	14.1
Medical care	3.8	4.3
Personal business	5.4	6.2
Transportation	9.9	8.7
Recreation	5.6	4.8
Other	3.1	3.4

Source: *Historical Statistics of the United States.*

Tables 5 to 8 also give you an overall picture of how some industries fared during the worst years of the Great Depression. If you are a businessman or an employee in any of these industries, you can see which table applies to you, and make preparations for the future accordingly.

In the vast industrial landscape of America, there are hundreds and thousands of industries, businesses, vocations, and jobs. Within each industry, there are different types of products; within each vocation, there are different types of jobs. I have presented a detailed account of how this multitude of products performed during the early 1930s in the appendix to this chapter. Go through this appendix carefully and see which category is relevant to you.

Here I will give you a summary analysis of these data and an outline of the performance of some other industries not mentioned before. Remember that our criterion is how the output, sales, or production value in any sector compared with the corresponding national averages in 1929 and 1933. Thus if output fell more than 30 percent or sales fell more than 46 percent, then that industry did poorly relative to the rest of the nation, and conversely.

On this criterion, some least-hit sectors in the Great Depression not mentioned before were the postal industry, newspapers, most services, communications, general merchandise, department stores, variety stores, drugstores, secondhand stores, life insurance companies, health care, and education. Industries that did especially poorly were radio, musical instruments, luggage, automobiles, furniture stores, tire stores, farm equipment dealers, florists, many wholesalers, banking, and advertising.

In a few rare cases such as bicycles, health care, and repair services, business actually soared. The number of secondhand stores also rose sharply, although their sales fell. Insofar as the past is a guide to the future, it is reasonable for you to expect that industries suffering the least in the last crisis will also suffer the least in the coming depression. This information can be of great help to you and to city and state planners in making contingency plans for the future.

Advice to Businessmen

In Table 9, I have listed small businesses or industries in which economic activity actually increased during the Great Depression. These are also likely to do well during the coming depression. If you are about to start a new venture or to buy an already running business, then take a good look at Table 9. If your current business made this list, you don't have much to worry about. You will find plenty of work in the future, although your earnings could still fall. But you will be much better off relative to others who may have to suffer huge losses or even declare bankruptcy.

Table 9
The Safest Businesses or Industries During the Worst Years of the Great Depression, 1929–33

Repair shops
Educational services
Health-care services
Bicycle shops
Bus transportation
Gasoline service stations
Secondhand Stores
Legal services
Drug or proprietary stores

Remember that a service business is easier to start than one producing goods. Excellence may be all that you need in a service company, whereas in manufacturing you have far more headaches. But any new company must stress honesty and quality. You have to develop a positive image which, in turn, will create the customer loyalty that becomes crucial to survival during hard times. Offer your customers as good a service as possible.

According to James Cook, an entrepreneur and author,

"It takes at least five years to master a business."[1] Take these words seriously if you are ready to start a new business now, because in five years you will be in the thick of the 1990s. Given the choice, I would prefer taking or keeping a job to starting a new venture. I would wait until I can examine business conditions in the next decade before sinking my savings into a long-term project. But if you must get into your own business now, then you should begin or acquire one related to industries listed in Table 9.

Chase Revel, a successful businessman and author, has listed 168 new businesses that anyone can start with a small investment.[2] Although most of his ideas won't work in the 1990s, he does describe a handful that are recession- or depression-proof. These are:

- Home health care
- Day-care center for the elderly
- Consignment used furniture
- Secondhand toy store

Of these, the first two are in the health-care area, which will continue to expand because of the aging American population. They also have a great potential, because of escalating costs in hospitals. The other depression-proof businesses listed by Revel are in the area of secondhand stores, which also did well in the previous depression. To these may be added consignment used appliances, computers, and a whole host of goods that are in general use. The basic idea in these businesses is that a store accepts used products on consignment and pays its supplier only

[1] James Cook, *The Start-up Entrepreneur* (New York: Harper & Row, 1986).

[2] Chase Revel, *168 More Businesses Anyone Can Start* (New York: Bantam, 1984).

after their sale, deducting up to 40 percent of the retail price as its commission. There is no inventory expense of any kind.

Should you sell your present profitable business if it is not listed in Table 9 or if it is among those industries usually hard hit by a depression? This is a very hard decision, one that only you can make. It may be tempting to sell now, take a job when the economy is close to full employment, and then buy a business later at a much cheaper price. For this scenario to work, however, many things must go right for you. You must first disrupt your life now even though things are going well, find a buyer ready to pay you a good price for your business, then get a good job paying you reasonably close to what you are now making, and finally discover another business in the 1990s that is just right for you.

If your business is currently just breaking even or losing money and you are waiting for happy times to come, then I suggest you either sell your business or close it down, and get a job. Long-term prospects for the economy are gloomy, and there is no point in waiting until the 1990s come and overwhelm you. But if your business is now doing well and you want to prepare for the future, there are less onerous options available to you than selling. These are business planning and diversification. Both are essential even in good times, but are indispensable under crisis conditions.

Business Planning

As many as seven out of ten industries and businesses could survive the depression. Whether or not yours is one of them could depend upon your preparations now. You should first make a detailed plan of how to react when sales sharply decline. Your business plan should aim at reducing costs even at this time, when the economy is still prosperous and growing, and in the future when you have to cut back your operations. In times of prosperity, companies have a tendency to be lax in service, quality, and productivity. As Cook points out, "At the top you tend to use more outside consultants, become more generous with office supplies, buy the big computer, become wasteful with postage, pass out fat wage hikes, become sloppy on cost control, print extras that you ultimately waste, over-advertise, and indulge in scores of other minor wasteful procedures."[3]

Some expenses are directly related to the scale of your current operations, and cannot be trimmed when business is booming. Currently, you may not be able to do any pruning there, but still you should develop a contingency plan of cost-cutting in the near future. If possible, don't fatten your payroll; instead of new hiring, use temporary help, unless you lack the kind of employees you might need in the future.

The key to surviving a financial crisis is being able to cut your overhead and operating expenses rapidly. You may have to let some people go or cut their salaries. Unless the labor market dictates otherwise, you should reduce costs by cutting salaries and working hours rather than laying off some employees. This way you will do your part in easing the burden of depression on some people, because those unemployed would have a very hard time finding another job.

In economic contractions, in order to trim expenses companies usually fire some workers without cutting the salaries of remaining employees. This is not healthy for a stable society, because then the entire burden of the downturn falls on the shoulders of a few unemployed people, while the remaining workers are concerned primarily with

[3] Cook, *The Start-up Entrepreneur*, p. 245.

keeping their jobs. It is better to trim costs by reducing wages and working hours for all employees, especially in a depression, when there are few alternatives. In any case, you need a contingency plan to trim overhead and operating expenses.

Diversification

Diversification is another area that deserves your attention. There are many reasons why you should branch out in a related business. Diversification is insurance against hard times caused by increased competition, unforeseen perils, or depressions. But even in the best of times, diversification pays only when it occurs in a related business. Acquisition of an entirely unrelated venture is risky, because you have to learn the new business from the ground up. It may also be costly and more difficult than spreading out in a related business. Facing the threat of an economic disaster soon, you certainly don't need to explore new areas.

The best candidates for diversification are retail stores, and the best activity to add to your basic business is some kind of repair capability. To your video store, you can add a video repair service; to your appliance business, you should add an appliance repair service; to your furniture store, you can add an upholstery business, and so on.

Another promising area of diversification is the used-consignment branch I have already mentioned. For instance, to a new-furniture business you could add used furniture, which could be taken on consignment or as trade-in. You may hate to mingle the old with the new, especially if you carry quality and high-cost goods. However, auto dealers do it all the time, and there is no stigma attached to the practice. In Cook's words, "The ideal diversification would be totally recession-proof and impervious to the business cycle. Such a company probably doesn't exist. Next best would be a venture that offset the cyclical nature of your main business."[4]

Diversification into a related area is probably a good idea regardless of the nature of your basic business. But make sure that branching out won't be too costly and won't take a long time to materialize. Remember again that you don't have much time to plan. And if you decide to spread out in a service area, then you must find skilled employees to provide a quality product, even if this means expanding your payroll. Invest in good people now, because the effectiveness and profitability of your service operation will depend upon you and your employees.

Retrenchment

Retrenchment is the opposite of diversification. If your business has branched out in an unrelated area, chances are that your new venture is either losing money, barely breaking even, or earning an unsatisfactory return. You may also be saddled with large debt incurred in business acquisitions. There has been a great wave of mergers during the 1980s, and many companies acquired large debt in the process of taking over another corporation or defending themselves from a takeover. Between 1984 and 1986 alone, merger-related debt jumped by over $200 billion.

If the debt load is high or if a new venture is a burden to the overall profitability of your main business, it is better to unload now and reduce your debt. Don't wait for good times in the 1990s to bail you out. Depressions are very hard on debtors. Retrench now while there is time, and focus on those activities which are related and in which you have already achieved success.

[4] Ibid., p. 236.

Cash Management

When business is good, companies tend to neglect cash management. Other matters, especially those dealing with expansion, seem to be more important. But effective cash management is an integral part of business success. In a crisis, it can make the difference between survival and bankruptcy.

A business can go bankrupt even with a positive net worth—that is, even if its assets exceed its liabilities—if it does not have enough cash to pay for operating and unforeseen expenses. This is because bills must be paid with cash, not capital equipment or illiquid assets such as accounts receivable, new orders, and inventories. These items, of course, can be used as collateral to borrow money from banks, but ultimately you need cash to conduct your day-to-day operations.

There are two kinds of cash, argues Leon Wortman— working cash and capital cash.[5] Funds needed to pay for inventory, wages, rent, utilities, and day-to-day operations are included in working cash, whereas the funds needed to replace fixed assets such as plant and equipment are part of capital cash. The difference between the two types is that a successful business generates working cash from its daily operations but may, if necessary, borrow to pay for capital requirements.

In a business downturn, cash should be conserved and long-term projects requiring new technology or capital improvements should be postponed. Your main concern at that time is survival, not progress. Anticipating a major downturn, you should now maximize your working cash and minimize your requirements for capital cash. Don't borrow for new projects, unless it is for diversification into a repair service or a business in second hand products.

[5] Leon A. Wortman, *Small Business Management* (New York: American Management Association, 1976).

And even there, try to minimize your debt as much as possible.

First you need an estimate of your cash requirements on a monthly basis. In the early months of the coming depression, you won't be able to chop off all your overhead expenses. You will have to pay the same rent, utilities, wages, and taxes while your sales begin to decline. Your cash needs could be unchanged, while cash receipts fall.

In order to stay afloat, you need to have a bigger cushion of cash in the coming downturn than in usual recessions. You may think you could borrow even to meet needs for working cash, but banks in the future might not lend you enough, if anything, in an uncertain and declining economy. You need to generate more cash now by offering cash discounts, reducing your sales on credit, or simply selling some assets. Reduced credit offerings could cost you some in sales, but the strategy could pay dividends in the future by increasing your current cash base.

When you purchase inventory and increase hiring to expand sales, you have to pay in cash; but when you sell on credit, you are taking a risk of nonpayment. In boom periods, such risk may be justified—your customers are likely to make payments on time. But when you anticipate trouble ahead, it is wise to cut back on credit operations even if you have to forgo a large contract.

Monitor your list of new orders in the same vein, because they can quickly disappear in a sharp downturn. If possible, ask your customers for a down payment equal to the cost of inventory or raw materials, especially if it takes a long time to meet the order. If you dislike reducing your customers' credit, you can at least tighten your credit terms. Instead of giving your customers sixty or ninety days to pay you can ask them to pay within thirty days. In return, you may offer them generous cash discounts up to 3 percent.

Billing customers is another practice that deserves your

attention. As much as possible, your bill or invoice should be enclosed with your shipment, or sent simultaneously, neither before nor long after the actual delivery of the product. If the invoice arrives too early, the customer is unhappy, and if it arrives too late, you have unnecessarily delayed your inflow of cash.

When customers fall behind in their payments, send them a timely but courteous reminder. This way you can stay on top of your cash receipts, keeping your company as liquid as possible.

Export Sales

Since the Second World War, there has been a sharp rise in international trade, but American companies have been slow to explore overseas markets even though these markets have grown faster than the U.S. markets. Competing abroad is tough and time-consuming, and the United States is still the largest market in the world. For these reasons, most American companies have focused on domestic sales and neglected opportunities abroad.

In the coming depression, international commerce is likely to collapse, perhaps much more than any other area of the world economy. In view of this, it would seem that I should advise you to reduce your reliance on overseas sales and expand your base at home. For American companies, however, this advice does not make sense. It is fine for businessmen in Britain, Canada, Japan, West Germany, Australia, Hong Kong, Singapore, and Taiwan, among other countries, which depend so heavily on foreign trade, but not for U.S. businessmen.

The U.S. currency has been depreciating since February 1985, and by the end of 1987 had fallen as much as 50 percent against the currencies of Germany and Japan. This has made American goods cheaper abroad and foreign goods dearer at home. For example, suppose the dollar-to-pound exchange rate is one to one—i.e., it costs $1 to buy a British pound. In this case an American shirt costing $10 at home would cost £10 in Britain, ignoring for the moment transportation and other costs. But now suppose the dollar falls in value by half, i.e., it takes $2 to buy £1. Then the same shirt would sell for £5 in Britain. In other words, American goods would become cheaper in Britain. Similarly, British goods would be more expensive in America, provided British businessmen keep their pound-denominated prices unchanged. They could, of course, reduce their own prices in proportion to the dollar depreciation, but in the process would have to accept lower profits or even losses. At some point of the fall in the dollar's value, British products would have to become more expensive than before.

The dollar has been falling steadily since 1985 and will continue to do so in the future. In fact, I expect it to fall drastically in 1989. This should open up many opportunities for American companies in foreign markets. Prices of U.S. goods will fall sharply abroad, although foreigners will find it very difficult to sell goods in America. In order to take advantage of such opportunities in the future, you need to develop and nurture contacts with foreign importers at this time. If you are already engaged in export sales, you should expand these operations, as they could prove crucial to your business survival. And to do so is much easier now than before.

Export sales can be more profitable than domestic business. Even small companies can be participants in such growing opportunities. You have to shed your "domestic only" thinking and do some exploring. This may be a real challenge, but it offers great rewards. One advantage you have is that English is spoken and understood in many other countries. Another advantage is that selling abroad is not much different from selling at home.

The U.S. government has a few agencies that offer invaluable help in the search for foreign contacts. The Bureau of International Commerce (BIC) of the Department of Commerce can assist you in finding buyers abroad. It has a list of foreign firms ready to represent U.S. concerns abroad and to help you get in touch with overseas agents, importers, distributors, banks, and customers.

The Department of Commerce also publishes many lists, directories, and magazines that can give you information you need about markets overseas. Some of these are as follows:

Commerce Today explores various foreign markets and sales opportunities. *Foreign Economic Trends and Their Implications for the United States* deals with individual countries and examines current economic trends and growth prospects. Other publications offering similar but detailed information are *Export Market Digests, Global Market Surveys, Market Share Reports, U.S. Trade Promotion Facilities Abroad, A Guide to Financing Exports, Overseas Trade Centers and Fairs,* and *A Basic Guide to Exporting.*

The sources listed above provide a wide range of business and market data for various countries. There are other services offered by the Commerce Department that give you information about the individuals or agents to contact overseas. There are, for instance, an export mailing list service, an agent distributor list service, and a new-products information service, among others.

The Bureau of International Commerce has many offices spread in the United States. These offices can help you develop your overseas market plan. As Leon Wortman points out, "It can be extremely valuable to contact them if you are (1) entering the field of export sales for the first time, (2) expanding your overseas sales, (3) trying to locate overseas sales agents or representatives, or (4) licensing your product for manufacture in a foreign country."[6]

[6] Ibid., p. 246.

There is no doubt that world commerce will dramatically decline in the coming depression. So will domestic commerce. But because of the plunging dollar, Americans will have a special advantage in world markets, Competition will be tough everywhere, but Americans will have an easier time competing abroad. If you can, you should now position your business to take advantage of future opportunities, and through export sales bring back some of the dollars which are now flooding the world. You may find it heartening to know that your government will help you in this endeavor, and for a vast majority of products and services, you are free to sell abroad without any special license.

Some Precautions

While I strongly urge you to diversify into export sales, you should keep in mind that the road to foreign sales is fraught with peril, especially when dealing with the less developed countries, or LDCs. You have to proceed with caution. You must know who you are dealing with before signing a deal. You should not ship your goods until you receive a confirmed letter of credit through a reputable international bank, preferably one with branches in America.

Some of the Third World countries are growing rapidly and can provide lucrative markets. But you have to beware of political and commercial risks. Currency conversion is the most common irritant. Third World countries face critical shortages of foreign exchange and are reluctant to part with foreign currency. Sudden currency devaluations further complicate the problem. The best way to deal with these situations is, as I have already suggested, to secure a confirmed letter of credit through a bank located in the United States. You receive payment as soon as your product lands abroad.

You can also take out insurance to cover various risks stemming from possible confiscation of property, physical damage to your property, and currency inconvertibility, among others. Despite all the difficulties, however, exporting can be a rewarding venture with handsome profits. Just proceed with caution.

CHAPTER 5

Job Prospects and Earnings

HISTORY IS A RECORD of human behavior under a variety of circumstances. Even if our institutions today are very different from those of both the recent and the distant past, faced with a similar situation we might behave in the same way as our forefathers. That is why society and its institutions move in cycles. As circumstances repeat themselves, human behavior also repeats itself. This is precisely why a study of history is so important. Its lessons should never be forgotten.

One lesson history teaches is that when economic institutions change to permit a limitless expression of greed, which is always present in society, severe depressions inevitably occur, leading to massive unemployment and loss of earnings. The Great Depression affected various types of jobs, professions, and their earnings in the 1930s, and we can expect the same thing to happen in the depression of the 1990s. You need not be taken by surprise. There is still time to prepare.

At various times in your life, you have to face a number of questions about your career. As a teenager, finishing high school, you have to decide whether to go to college or take a job; as a college graduate, you have to decide whether to find employment or go on to earn an advanced degree. Among various categories of jobs, you have to decide which one is right for you, offering you security or high earnings, or both. And finally, there are decisions that must be made when you seek advancement in your job, when you are looking to change jobs or even careers, and when you are fired or temporarily laid off.

These are perplexing decisions that test your mettle even in the best of times. In bad times, however, they become crucial for survival. These decisions will be easier to make if you know where the jobs are likely to be in the near future, what you should now do to hang on to your job, and how you can cope in case you are laid off.

Hardest-Hit Jobs

Let us first develop a criterion for the jobs and earnings that will be hardest hit in the coming depression. Table 10 displays figures for employment, unemployment, and earnings in 1929 and 1933. It is clear that during the worst phase of the previous depression, employment fell by 18

Table 10
Employment, Unemployment, and Earnings, 1929 and 1933

	1929	1933	Percentage Drop
Employed (thousands)	46,207	38,052	18
Unemployed (thousands)	1,550	12,830	−728
Rate of unemployment (percent)	3.2	25.2	−22
Full-time employee earnings (dollars)	1,405	1,045	26

Source: *Historical Statistics of the United States.*

percent, whereas the number of people without jobs jumped by 728 percent, generating an unemployment rate of 25.2 percent. Those employed suffered an income loss of 26 percent, but since the cost of living fell by 24 percent, their real earnings were essentially unchanged. Therefore, the brunt of the burden of depression fell on those who lost their jobs.

I have presented industry-wide data on employment and earnings during the Great Depression in the appendix to Chapter 5. Go through the appendix carefully, see which job category applies to you, and make preparations accordingly. These data show the national averages or yardsticks by which we can measure the job and earnings performance of various vocations and professions. Let us define the hardest-hit jobs as those in which employment fell by more than 18 percent or earnings declined by more than 26 percent. You will see the safest jobs were in government, both federal and state: employment here even went up, because the government sector in those days was small, and as the depression deepened, the government was called upon to help the unemployed, the homeless, and the elderly, who had neither Social Security nor pensions.

In the first two years of the Great Depression, thanks to Congress, public employees had to accept only token cuts in their salaries. However, in 1932 there was a vehement reaction against high public salaries, which were forced down initially by 10 percent and later by much more. A cabinet officer earned $15,000 per year in 1925, but only $10,900 in 1934, accepting a loss of 27 percent in nominal or money income. Similarly, congressmen had to live with a wage cut of 27 percent, as their salaries declined from $10,000 in 1925 to $7,260 in 1934.[1] As with the average full-time employees, however, their real income hardly changed. And as soon as business began to recover, politicians were the first to get back their 1925-level salaries and sharply improve their living standards in 1935.

In the coming depression, however, federal employees may have to accept huge cuts in real incomes to hold on to their jobs. My feeling is that federal employment will not fall sharply, but public real salaries will tumble, perhaps as much as 30 percent. Employees of state and local governments are likely to fare much better, because these governments don't have budget deficits. In fact, they have, on the whole, enjoyed large surpluses in the 1980s.

Other industries in which job losses in the early 1930s were not so high were finance, insurance, and real estate. Earnings losses were small in telephone and telegraph companies, gas and electrical utilities, education, and health care. In fact, in some of these industries, real incomes went up.

In manufacturing, production workers in book and newspaper printing suffered a money wage loss of only 5 percent, and union wages declined 13 percent. In other words, unions were able to protect the earnings of their employed members, though they suffered heavy job losses in many industries.

Among professions, college teachers enjoyed a real income gain, but physicians and dentists suffered surprisingly high losses in nominal incomes of 43 percent and 49 percent. Other hard-hit jobs were in construction, mining, agriculture, forestry and fishing, and metals. As you learned in the previous chapter, these are precisely the areas in which output and sales fell the most in the 1930s.

Most industries suffered heavy job and earnings losses during the Great Depression. Nevertheless, there were vocations in which real incomes actually rose, as money incomes fell less than consumer prices. Among services, repair jobs gained in employment, and so did legal services.

For some industries, the wage data are not available, but

we do have the payroll data. Since employment fell nationally by 18 percent and earnings by 26 percent, the total fall in payroll was the sum of these two, or 44 percent. These figures, not surprisingly, confirm that job and wage losses were the heaviest in durable goods industries, in which payrolls declined by much more than 44 percent, and were generally low in the nondurable goods sector.

Jobs in the 1980s

The rate of unemployment has steadily declined in the 1980s, reaching a low of 6 percent in 1987, when approximately 112 million people were fully employed, and another 20 percent of the labor force worked part-time. About 8.5 million people were officially without jobs and 1.5 million were classified as discouraged workers. The main reason why unemployment has declined in the 1980s, however, is a great slowdown in the growth of the labor force, which expanded at an incredible 2.3 percent annual rate in the 1970s and at only a 1.5 percent rate in the 1980s.

Employment has grown sharply in the 1980s, but much of this growth, as much as 75 percent, has occurred in the services-generating sector, with only 18 percent in manufacturing. Wages in services are usually well below those in other areas, especially the professions and goods-producing industries. Even without a depression, virtually all job growth in America in the next decade is expected to be in the service sector, which does not present a rosy outlook for the average worker. And in view of the expected depression, future job prospects are really dismal.

Average weekly earnings have already declined by 15 percent since 1973 and median household income by about 6 percent. College-educated or specially trained workers have not suffered such an income loss since the

1970s; some of them have, in fact, improved their lot. They are, however, a small fraction of the labor force.

The Bureau of Labor Statistics regularly publishes figures about jobs, earnings, and their future outlook. Many writers have analyzed these figures to reach a variety of conclusions. Their projections, however, assume that the economy in the 1990s will continue to follow the growth path it has followed since the war. If there is a serious depression, then many of these projections will turn out to be wrong. The fastest-growing occupations of today need not be those of tomorrow. The plum jobs of the 1980s could begin to decline or even disappear in the 1990s.

Fastest-Growing Jobs

I have prepared a list of the fastest-growing jobs during the worst years of the Great Depression. It is presented in Table 11. I think the job pattern of the 1930s will be repeated in the 1990s, with the one exception I have already mentioned. The federal government, because of its huge and persistent budget deficits, is likely to shrink in the 1990s, generating minor job losses rather than growth. If you take federal employees out of Table 11, you will have a picture of the areas in which jobs will actually grow in the next decade.

Table 11 shows that the maximum employment gains in the early 1930s occurred in gasoline service stations, which also employed auto mechanics to fix cars. If you add to this the job growth in miscellaneous repair services, you can see that repair-type occupations did the best during the previous depression and are likely to do so in the next depression.

State and local government employment also went up during the 1930s, and so did the number of teachers in colleges and public schools. As regards nurses, figures are available only for the numbers graduating from nursing schools. But they all must have found work, because the number of hospitals and of hospital beds soared at the time. Consequently, more doctors were working in 1934 than in 1929.

Bad times lead to increased litigation, so the number of those engaged in legal services also rose in the 1930s.

In view of my forecast of a great depression in the 1990s, Table 11 provides a better picture of the job outlook in the future than the estimates offered by the Bureau of Labor Statistics. In any case, competition for the limited number of jobs available is likely to be extremely intense in the near future. Employers will be very selective about whom they hire and keep on their payroll. Still, about 70 percent of the labor force will be employed, and whether or not you are one of the lucky ones could depend on the actions you take at this time. Perhaps never before in your life has career planning been so important. Anticipating a troubled economy, you may have to modify your goals and lower your expectations, at least for the first half of the 1990s.

General Career Guidelines

Between 1990 and 1994, the world economy will generally contract, and employers will be forced to fire millions of workers to keep their companies solvent. In deciding which employees to retain and which to terminate, a company will, of course, look at the records of their past performance. Whether or not you are retained could well depend on your image, work habits, productivity, and job skills. There are career guidelines which everyone should follow all the time to achieve success, whatever your job or profession. For the coming decade, however, these guidelines take on added importance, because if you are laid off, you may not be able to find a new job.

Table 11
Fastest-Growing Jobs During the Worst Years of the Great Depression, 1929–33

	1929	1933	Employment Gain	Percentage Gain
1. Persons engaged in gasoline service stations	245,278	328,263	82,985	34
2. State and local government employees	2,532,000	2,601,000	69,000	3
3. Persons engaged in repair services	264,000	312,000	48,000	18
4. Federal employees	533,000	565,000	32,000	6
5. College faculty[1]	82,386	108,873	26,487	32
6. Graduating nurses		25,312	25,312	
7. Persons engaged in legal services[2]	194,000	217,000	23,000	12
8. Persons engaged in liquor stores[3]	5,806	25,234	19,428	335
9. Public school teachers[4]	773,433	789,074	15,641	2
10. Persons engaged in secondhand stores	33,516	45,305	11,789	35
11. Physicians	152,503	161,359[5]	8,856	6

Source: *Historical Statistics of the United States.*

[1] Figures are for 1930 and 1934.

[2] Figures are for 1933 and 1935.

[3] Because of prohibition, which was repealed in the early 1930s, the liquor industry started with a very small base. It would not be able to repeat its past performance in the coming depression. In fact, it could shrink.

[4] These figures are estimated by dividing school enrollment by the pupil/teacher ratio for 1930 and 1934.

[5] This figure is for 1934.

Let me go over these guidelines one by one. The first and foremost is to keep your immediate superior happy with your work. Short of anything immoral, unethical, or illegal, you should do everything to please your supervisor.

What does your boss expect from you? He expects you to do your work and get it done on time. He expects loyalty, courtesy, and respect. And finally, he expects honesty and compatibility. Whatever your job or profession, you are usually part of a team, and no team can work effectively if one of its members doesn't pull his or her own weight and work well with other team members.

Don't consider any job beneath you if it is necessary to the successful operation of the team. Don't waste time and don't resent having to work overtime if that, too, is necessary. Look for any possible way to improve your job skills and your productivity. And last but not least, always present yourself and your work in the best possible light.

To improve your job-retention prospects for the years ahead, it may be necessary to lower your expectations for the time being. Some jobs offer great earnings and potential for growth, but are also risky. Given the choice between security and earnings, go for security, even if it means taking a cut in pay. During the coming depression there could be a decline in the cost of living, so that your real income may remain about the same. Hardest hit in the last depression were those without jobs.

A depression will bring about deep cuts in the ranks of middle management, especially staff positions that are not directly tied in to profit centers, as companies seek to streamline their operations. If your job falls into that category, it might be wise to look for ways to attach yourself more directly to your company's revenue source, thus making yourself more indispensable to company operations and your job more secure.

Should you change your job in anticipation of the coming depression? My answer, in general, is no. Suppose you are currently employed in an industry that will be hard hit. You are making good money, but are likely to be among the first to be fired as the depression hits. Should you now try to move to a job in a safer industry? No, because it is probably too late for that. Even if you are successful, you will have to learn new skills. And with the cutbacks and layoffs that inevitably come with a depression, last hired is usually first fired. Changing jobs at this time could merely increase your vulnerability. However, if for some reason you are so totally unhappy with your present job that you have to go, then don't wait too long. Act now while there is still time to make a move. But once again, changing jobs should be your last resort. If you are fired you should, of course, cut your expenses drastically and make every effort to find a new job as soon as possible.

Whatever your age or job experience, you will have to modify your career goals during the years ahead. Those of you already in the job market may have to resign yourselves to a period of lowered income and expectations. Those of you about to enter the job market may have to postpone your career dreams. In fact, everyone should brace himself or herself for the economic troubles ahead and be prepared for any eventuality. But most important, remember that the age of employers providing "womb-to-tomb" security is fast fading. Already Wall Street has been forced to fire thousands. Deregulation, mergers, and take-overs are adding hundreds and thousands to the unemployed lists. The depression may add millions. Remain flexible, remain visible, and be prepared to make lateral moves. But never count on a single company or corporation for your welfare. In short, think like an entrepreneur, even on salary.

There are also other ways that you can augment your salary, either by taking a part-time job or starting your own small business. But if you consider this latter option, do not assume (as many books suggest) that a current hobby or leisure-time activity will easily translate into a viable business during a depression. Instead focus on a service or product that requires little investment and will still be in demand in adverse times and also fill a market niche that will be too small to attract a large corporation. Such a business could generate much-needed income as well as generous tax deductions for expenses associated with the business. You can conduct your business from your home and even employ family members for further tax benefits. One of the best sources of information on starting and conducting your own small business is the Small Business Administration.

Whatever your source of income, it goes without saying that it is never wise to spend more than you earn. With the coming depression, it is imperative to live within your income. It is even more imperative to set aside money for savings and investment. Your savings today could be a lifesaver tomorrow.

CHAPTER 6

————————

The Safest Banks and Thrifts

WHEN AN ECONOMY is in the predepression stage, it invariably experiences deteriorating health in the financial sector. America and the rest of the world are now racing toward an unprecedented crisis. One symptom of the coming hemorrhage is the bleeding that has occurred in commercial banks and savings and loan associations during the 1980s. Savings and loans are also called S&Ls or simply thrifts. Banks and thrifts on the whole are now weaker than at any time since the 1930s.

During the 1970s, on average about ten bank failures occurred per year. They swelled to forty-two in 1982, to 130 in 1985, and to 184 in 1987. This is an eighteenfold increase, and is especially worrisome because it has occurred at a time when the economy is close to full employment. Such numbers were not seen even during the tumult of the 1973–75 recession, which was the worst since the Great Depression. Currently, the list of "problem banks" has grown to 1,500.

The thrift industry is limping even worse than banking. In 1972, the nation's S&Ls collectively had a net worth of $16.7 billion; by 1980 the industry had flipped and its net worth had become a negative $17.5 billion. By 1982, three-fourths of the industry, with 90 percent of total assets, was losing money. Between 1984 and 1987, 124 thrifts closed their doors, and an additional 74 merged with financially sound institutions. Another 387 were insolvent at the end of 1987, but were permitted to carry on their business.

It is not surprising, therefore, that many people are worried about the safety of their bank or thrift deposits. True, the financial sector today is operating with a cushion that didn't exist in the 1930s. Unlike then, our deposits are now insured—up to $100,000. And no insured depositor has lost a penny since deposit insurance began in the 1930s.

Yet the worry has valid grounds. Most commercial banks are insured by the Federal Deposit Insurance Corporation (FDIC), and most savings and loan associations by the Federal Savings and Loan Insurance Corporation (FSLIC). Both institutions have been designed to assure the public of the safety of deposits. There is a crucial difference, however. The FDIC is still solvent and has some $16 billion on hand, whereas the FSLIC became insolvent in 1986 and had to be bailed out by Congress with an infusion of $10.8 billion of new cash.

Are banks then safer than thrifts? Not really. There are almost fourteen thousand banks compared to fewer than four thousand thrifts in the nation, and bank deposits far exceed S&L deposits. The $16 billion in the hands of the FDIC is nothing compared to almost $2 trillion in deposits held by commercial banks. If banks begin to fail by the hundreds, the insurance fund will quickly vanish. Would the Fed print bushels of new money to bail out all the failing banks? Most likely not, because that would create hyperinflation and amount to deliberately wrecking the world economy—something I discussed in detail in Chapter 2.

Of course, the insurance funds can be stretched to the

limit by the regulators if they encourage the merger of an insolvent institution with a thriving bank or thrift. In such cases, the insuring agencies usually absorb a small loss from the bailout of depositors. Depositors also feel little impact from this kind of action. However, for a third of the banks that failed in 1987, no suitor came forth, a situation that can be inconvenient and costly. If you are caught in such a situation, you have to file claims quickly with the proper authorities and pray that you get all your money back. So far this system has worked, because the bankruptcies of financial institutions have been sporadic and the economy has not been tested by a depression. But with a depression now looming on the horizon, the safety of your money should be, if it is not already, paramount in your mind.

Relatively Safe Banks, S&Ls, and Credit Unions

Are there no safe banks in the world? No, there is no such thing as a 100 percent safe bank, but some are safer than others. During the carnage of the 1930s, thousands of financial institutions failed, but many thousands did survive and kept their doors open to their depositors. The crisis in domestic American banks in the future will be no worse than that in the previous depression; again, thousands of banks and thrifts will survive. But which ones? This is a critical question that must be answered for the sake of your future financial health.

A publication titled *Bank Financial Quarterly* and published by IDC Financial Publishing, Inc., provides a valuable service in rating the thousands of FDIC-insured commercial banks in the nation. It rates them with the help of five criteria embodied in a formula called CAMEL, which stands for capital, adequacy, margin, earnings, and liquidity.

Whenever you get into a business, you put your investment or capital at risk. The business of banking is lending money, and the risk comes mainly from the possibility of loan default. A bank with risky customers can lose a lot of money if they fail to pay back. That is why it is especially important to see if a particular bank has lent to Third World countries, many of which are unlikely to pay back their loans.

The first factor in the rating formula, CAMEL, is capital risk, which may be measured by the ratio of equity investment to total assets, of which a major portion usually consists of loans.

The second factor is capital adequacy, which compares the size of equity and loan loss reserves with delinquent loans.

The third factor, margin, is the difference between interest income and interest cost divided by the assets.

The fourth factor is a bank's earnings performance, which is measured by the return on equity capital.

Finally, the fifth factor, liquidity, is measured by the comparison of cash or near-cash assets with uninsured liabilities and nonearning assets.

CAMEL is a good formula by which to rate banks across the nation. It takes into account banking guidelines proposed by the Comptroller of Currency. Developed by IDC Financial Publishing, Inc., the formula generates a variety of ratios, weights them according to the size of assets, adds them up, and then comes up with a number for each bank. In this way IDC ranks some fourteen thousand individual banks, on a scale from 1 to 300. In IDC's opinion, any bank with a mark of 165 or more deserves an excellent to superior rating; with a mark between 125 and 164, it is just average; it is below average if its number ranges from 50 to 124, and it is in dire straits if the number is below 50.

IDC rating of a bank is based on a carefully devised and computed formula which is easy to understand. Of the 145 banks folding in 1986, 78 percent had an IDC rating below 50. Of the banks folding in 1987, 84 percent had a rating of just 1, 8 percent had a rating between 2 and 49, and the remaining 8 percent, a minuscule number, had a rating above 50. CAMEL seems to be a formula that works.

Of all the banks rated by *Bank Financial Quarterly*, seven thousand attained excellent or superior marks. Of these, I have selected some 1,500, each with assets of at least $100 million. I think large banks, with sound banking practices measured by high IDC financial ratings, have better chances to survive the coming depression than small ones.

These banks are listed in the appendix to Chapter 6, along with their rating and assets. Go through this list carefully and see which of them operate in your state and city. Money kept in these banks should have a large margin of safety.

Keep in mind that the higher a bank's rating and the greater its assets, the greater the chance of its weathering the looming storm. You may have noted that some of the largest banks in the nation failed to make my list. It may appear incredible to you that well-known banks with hundreds of billions of dollars in assets could actually go under or would be allowed by the Fed to go under.

I am not saying that huge multibank holding companies are certain to fail in the 1990s, but that the probability of their failure is fairly high. The biggest conglomerates, of course, will be the most difficult to rescue, especially when their foreign customers are in default. Banks certainly are not popular for lending billions to high-risk Third World countries. For political reasons, Congress may find it impossible to rescue banks that fold because of their loan losses to Third World countries, especially when during the depression there would be hundreds of demands on an already depleted federal Treasury. It's always possible that we could somehow muddle through, but I wouldn't count on it. The supply-side economists in 1981 made a similar argument. They recommended a huge pro-wealthy tax cut, saying that our budget deficit would somehow fall. It did not. Wishful thinking and self-serving policies are no substitute for hard realities.

Many people like the convenience of dealing with a neighborhood bank—convenience which could prove inconvenient in the future, if your bank fails and the government is unable to pay back the depositors. However, I have tried to list sound banks for every major city, so that most Americans can enjoy the more important convenience of a safety factor in their banking.

IDC Financial Publishing also rates S&Ls, savings banks, and credit unions, all of which are generally smaller in asset size than commercial banks. The rating procedure and criteria are the same as CAMEL. The lists in the appendix to Chapter 6 also include such financial institutions with a rank of 165 or more. These institutions usually have high liquidity, low cost of raising funds, high net interest income, and an excellent return on equity capital.

From the nearly two thousand financial institutions listed in the appendix, I have selected top-rated banks and S&Ls in major cities and listed them in Table 12. These institutions are not necessarily the best in America, but they are the best in large urban centers. (If any of the abbreviations used in Table 12 are puzzling, consult the appendix to Chapter 6; at the beginning of the appendix the abbreviations used by IDC in its lists are explained.)

Table 12
Top-Rated Banks and S&Ls in Major Cities
(alphabetically by state)

Name	City	Rank	Total Assets (millions)
First Alabama Bk	Montgomery, AL	202	4,112
First NB of Anchorage	Anchorage, AK	267	810
Arizona Commerce Bank	Tucson, AZ	243	111
Citibank of Arizona	Phoenix, AZ	277	915

Canadian Imperial Bk CMRC	Los Angeles, CA	230	612
Citicorp Savings, FS&LA	San Francisco, CA	212	6,939
Imperial Bank	Los Angeles, CA	221	1,603
Colorado State Bk	Denver, CO	269	115
First Federal Bank of Connecticut, FSB	New Haven, CT	240	1,628
Colonial NB USA	Wilmington, DE	251	1,171
Citicorp Savings of Florida, FS&LA	Miami, FL	274	2,718
Trust Co Bk of Cobb City, NA	Atlanta, GA	206	280
First FS&LA of America	Honolulu, HI	234	731
Citicorp Savings of Illinois, FS&LA	Chicago, IL	277	5,514
Northwestern S&LA	Chicago, IL	214	927
Bank One NA	Bloomington, IN	229	295
Davenport B&TC	Davenport, IA	209	1,477
First NB Iowa City	Iowa City, IA	200	260
First NB in Wichita	Wichita, KS	204	660
Mid American B&TC	Louisville, KY	257	682
American B&TC	New Orleans, LA	207	315
People's Heritage SVG BK	Portland, ME	237	1,623
Mercantile Safe Dep & TC	Baltimore, MD	203	1,315
First American Bk for Svg	Boston, MA	268	642
Merchants Bank Co-op Bk	Boston, MA	210	504
Midway NB of St. Paul	St. Paul, MN	230	244
Cass B&TC	St. Louis, MO	243	131
Investors Fiduciary TC	Kansas City, MO	235	330
First NB of Omaha	Omaha, NB	221	857
Citibank (Nevada) NA	Las Vegas, NE	248	2,959
Canadian Imperial Bk of Cmrc	New York, NY	225	756
Merchants Bk of NY	New York, NY	217	538
North Side Svg Bk	New York, NY	246	634

Table 12 (cont.)
Top-Rated Banks and S&Ls in Major Cities
(alphabetically by state)

Name	City	Rank	Total Assets (millions)
Sterling NB&TC of NY	New York, NY	218	782
Raleigh Federal Svg Bk	Raleigh, NC	245	478
First NB of Ohio	Akron, OH	215	1,814
North Side B&TC	Cincinnati, OH	211	201
Third FS&LA	Cleveland, OH	223	1,895
Allegheny Valley Bk of Pit.	Pittsburgh, PA	221	115
Prudential SA	Philadelphia, PA	216	141
Scotia Bank of Puerto Rico	San Juan, PR	217	441
Citizens' Savings Bank, FSB	Providence, RI	220	1,832
NCNB South Carolina	Columbia, SC	200	3,055
Citibank South Dakota NA	Sioux Falls, SD	205	10,775
Fidelity FS&LA of Tenn.	Nashville, TN	205	923
First FS&LA	Chattanooga, TN	245	613
Lockwood NB	Houston, TX	230	133
North Dallas B&TC	Dallas, TX	218	271
USAA Federal Svg Bk	San Antonio, TX	300	458
Jefferson NB	Charlottesville, VA	200	1,222
Washington FS&LA	Seattle, WA	227	1,871
Security S&LA	Milwaukee, WI	216	1,914

Source: IDC's *Financial Quarterlies*, February 1988.

My purpose in providing this short list of banking institutions is to underline the importance of the safety of your deposits in the coming depression. My list includes the names of those institutions that constitute the cream of the crop and is broad enough to include "safe" financial havens for most states and large cities and for small cities and towns. You should feel somewhat secure about funds deposited in these institutions. At least half of American banks and S&Ls would survive the coming disaster, and those included in my list are likely to be among them.

If your financial institution didn't make the list, it is not necessarily in trouble. I have used exacting standards. Many smaller banks and credit unions with quality ratings, have been left out. For a complete listing and analysis, you should consult IDC publications.

The address is:

IDC Financial Publishing, Inc.
P.O. Box 915
Hartland, WI 53029
1-800-544-5457

The publications are, however, expensive, costing $75 per issue. You might ask your local library to subscribe if it does not already do so.

Systems for rating banks and S&Ls change over time. But in the little time we have before 1990, that is not likely to happen. For the latest information, of course, IDC is the source to contact.

How Do You Select a Financial Institution?

In 1929 there were 25,568 commercial banks, and in 1933 only 14,771—a drop of nearly 40 percent. Similarly, the number of thrifts fell from 12,342 in 1929 to 10,596 in 1933—a drop of 18 percent. Clearly, the financial sector went through a carnage during the early 1930s, as thousands of banks and thrifts suspended their operations, and their depositors lost their hard-earned money. Millions of people became destitute overnight, because of the loss of their savings. I don't expect the financial sector to suffer the same carnage in the 1990s, because the Fed is supposed to have learned some lessons. There is also deposit insurance, and perhaps it would be enough to prevent a hemorrhage of the banking system.

However, despite our best efforts and wishes, calamity sometimes overtakes us anyway. Because of our past mistakes, we are forced to choose between necessary evils, and we select the least harmful alternative. A recent case in point was the tight-money policy that the Fed had to adopt in 1980 and 1981. Inflation was running amuck at double-digit levels at that time, and one way—possibly the only way—to restrain inflation is to leash the growth of money. This policy, however, invariably creates unemployment in the short run. The Fed knew this, but resorted to monetary restraint anyway, generating an unemployment rate of 11 percent by the end of 1982.

Something like this could happen in the 1990s to the financial sector. Nobody likes the nightmare of massive bank failures. But if the alternative is hyperinflation, then the nation may have to accept bank failures. Therefore, it is critical that you choose the right financial institutions at this time, because thousands of banks and thrifts could fail in the 1990s in spite of the Fed's best efforts to rescue them. The government could be forced to honor only a part of its commitment to depositors. But if your money is deposited in a sound institution, you may avoid this pain altogether.

Your choice of a financial institution depends on the city and the state in which you live. Agricultural and energy-rich areas in the United States have been hit hard by declining inflation and oil prices during the 1980s. The states affected include Texas, Oklahoma, Louisiana, Idaho, Wyoming, Montana, Mississippi, New Mexico, Alabama, Colorado, and Alaska. Not surprisingly, these states have suffered the most bank failures during the 1980s, with Texas leading the nation. These will also be among the worst-hit states in the coming depression. Their financial institutions have already taken a beating, and they are the most vulnerable to any new downturn. States heavily dependent on the construction and lumber industries will also be hurt badly. They include California, Florida, and

Oregon. Thus, residents of all the states I have just mentioned have to be especially careful in their choice of banks and thrifts.

If you live in a city dependent on one or two industries only, then your bank is also exposed to greater risks than banks located in cities with diversified economies. This is because diversification tends to lower risk in practically every activity.

The final factor in selecting a bank or thrift is the convenience, courtesy, and service it offers. With all this in mind, choose your financial institution in accordance with the following considerations:

1. If you live in a major metropolitan area outside the states mentioned above, then any institution listed in this chapter or the appendix and located in your area is a good bet. Otherwise, go with banks or S&Ls mentioned in Table 12, or with thrifts, savings banks, or credit unions ranked 200 or above, preferably with a large asset base. If you fail to find one with 200 or above rating in your area, then go with any that made my list.

2. If none of the quality institutions exists in your city, then go to the one with the nearest location.

3. Diversify your money into many federally insured financial institutions, so that if one fails, your funds in others are still safe.

4. If you cannot do without the convenience of local institutions not included in my list, then deposit with them only the small fraction of your funds necessary to carry out daily transactions. Place the rest in other healthy institutions, preferably inside your state, or else nearest to it. You may have to accept the inconvenience of banking by mail in order to safeguard your savings.

5. Don't entrust more than $50,000 to any one institution, even though the federal insurance is $100,000. Beware of lower-rated insititutions offering suspiciously high interest rates. Usually problem banks or thrifts have to pay higher rates to

attract deposits. Also avoid banks that offer you unsecured loans by mail.

6. Your safe deposit box, if possible, should be in a quality institution, so that it is easily accessible to you. If none is available, then go with the nearest institution in your state. Keep your receipt for the box in a safe place, and save the canceled check you wrote to pay for it. These will be your proof that you do own the box in the bank. The contents of your safe deposit box belong to you, and even if a bank fails, your assets in the box remain your property. However, the FDIC may deny you access to your belongings for up to ten days.

At this point you should note that many banks are owned by well-known but troubled bank holding companies. However, banks are independent of their parent corporations. If a bank holding company fails in one city, its individual banks in the same or another city need not. In future you should not panic if a bank holding company, parent of your bank, or a bank with the same name as your own bank fails in your city or another city. This rule does not apply to bank branches. While banks and their holding companies are different entities, all the branches fall as their parent bank falls. If for instance, bank X fails in another city, bank X need not fail in your city. My list takes this consideration into account.

You should find out if your financial institution belongs to a bank holding company or has several branches. If an institution included in my list has many branches, then go with any branch, as they all stand and fall together. But if it is part of a bank holding company, then go with only that subsidiary included in my list. Be careful. Some unrelated banks have similar sounding names.

One of the most important strategies for survival in the coming depression is to have a comfortable cash cushion when sources of income decline or dry up completely. It is only common sense to make sure that your savings are deposited in the safest possible banking institutions.

CHAPTER 7

Can You Count on Social Security?

IN 1935, with millions of Americans homeless, pension-less, and unemployed, President Franklin Delano Roosevelt signed the Social Security Act and laid the foundation of a system that has been a lifeline to the elderly ever since. The act created a program to ensure that in old age people would never have to starve. For the first time in American history, the government committed itself to offer the elderly the basic necessities of life.

The Social Security Act provided for a payroll tax designed to build a substantial fund and to make the program self-sufficient. The fund was to be used only to pay out benefits to the retired and to administer the system. The money was invested in Treasury bonds, and the interest income so generated was supposed to meet one-third of the total cost. The rest was to come from contributions from employers and workers. At first, the payroll tax was set at 1 percent on an annual income of $3,000, collecting a maximum of $30 from each worker and his employer. This way the government hoped to build a sufficient reserve to pay benefits over time. The system started out small. But today Social Security has the biggest appetite of all the government transfer payments to the economy, consuming $210 billion in 1987 from the federal Treasury. Its expense amounts to 40 percent of government spending on social programs.

In the beginning, Social Security benefits were modest; even in the 1960s the poverty level among the elderly was twice as high as the general poverty level in America. In order to cure this anomaly, President Lyndon Johnson launched his Great Society campaign. Helping the poor and the retirees was also good politics. In the late 1960s and early 1970s, Social Security benefits began to expand. For instance, in 1972 Congress approved a formula that linked the benefits with the rate of inflation and also automatically raised the annual income/benefits ratio. As a result, benefits began to rise faster than incomes and prices. By the 1980s the incidence of poverty among the elderly was lower than that among the entire population.

By the late 1970s, however, congressional generosity to the elderly had an unintended consequence: the Social Security system was rushing toward insolvency and payroll taxes had to be raised sharply. They are still rising and will keep rising until 1990. In 1987, for instance, the worker and employer each contributed 7.15 percent on wages up to $43,000, or a maximum of $6,263.40. The tax rate will jump to 7.65 percent in 1990, and the maximum taxable amount to $49,000.

Social Security works on a pay-as-you-go basis. This means that you pay while you are working and your contribution goes directly toward payments to retirees now. It is not set aside to ensure payment to you later. This method has worked so far, because each generation has outnumbered the one before it—that is, until the "baby boom" generation, which consists of the 77 million babies born between 1946 and 1964. The generation after that was a lot smaller, so much so that it was called the "baby bust" generation. This means that in 2112, when the first of the baby boomers become eligible for Social Security, there will be fewer workers to support them. Today, there are about 3.4 workers supporting a retired person. By 2025, this number will be reduced to 2.5 workers per beneficiary.

Another problem looming for the system is that there is growing poverty among the baby bust generation. So while the working population will still be responsible for the retired generation, it will also be responsible for the social programs necessary to aid its own underclass. To add to the problem, people are now living longer. The number of people older than sixty-five is growing three times faster than the population as a whole, and the number of people eighty-five or older is growing five times as fast. This means that by the time the baby busters reach retirement, there could be no money left for them. According to some estimates, Social Security taxes paid by a middle-income twenty-five-year-old will exceed his benefits by $40,000. Higher taxes will be required to support the baby boomers.

Social Security is a very good system for those who are on it now. Beneficiaries get back in less than nineteen months what they paid in over their lifetimes. Social Security is also need-blind. Thirty-three percent of benefits go to households with annual incomes above $30,000 a year, and another 33 percent of recipients also get money from pensions. There are 130,000 Social Security beneficiaries whose annual incomes are above $75,000.

The Emerging Dilemma

Both the young and the old face a dilemma. The problem is that because of constantly rising prices, lagging productivity growth, an aging population, and the slowdown of economic growth, Social Security benefits in the 1970s and the 1980s have been rising much faster than the national income. As Scott Burns, a business writer for the *Dallas*

Morning News, has noted, "While retirees benefit from both higher Social Security payments and higher interest rates on their savings, those who work must pay ever rising employment taxes on their work and make higher monthly payments on their house and car."[1] Using figures supplied by the Social Security Administration and the Bureau of Labor Statistics, Burns prepared a table, which I have reproduced as Table 13.

Table 13
Index of Retirees' Income and Workers' Income, 1970–87
(1970 = 1)

Year	Workers' Pretax Income	Consumer Price Index	Retirees' Spendable Income
1970	1.00	1.00	1.00
1975	1.37	1.39	1.75
1979	1.83	1.87	2.49
1980	1.96	2.12	2.89
1981	2.13	2.34	3.27
1982	2.23	2.49	3.55
1983	2.34	2.57	3.74
1984	2.44	2.67	3.65
1985	2.49	2.77	4.06
1986	2.54	2.84	4.17
1987	2.63	2.95	4.35

Source: Scott Burns, "The War Between Generations," *Dallas Morning News,* November 3, 1987, p. 13D.

From Burns's table, it is clear that the incomes of workers have lagged behind the incomes of retirees. From 1970 to 1987, the Consumer Price Index rose from 1 to 2.95, whereas the pretax wage index grew only from 1 to 2.63. On the other hand, the retirees' income index jumped

[1] Scott Burns, "The War Between Generations," *Dallas Morning News,* November 3, 1987, p. 13D.

from 1 to 4.35, far surpassing the price explosion. In addition, the payroll tax, 4.8 percent in 1970, soared to 7.5 percent in 1988. Thus the young workers have suffered a double-edged blow on their incomes: lower real wages plus higher taxes.

The dilemma for both the young and the elderly is real and cruel. No one would advocate lower living standards for the retired elderly. Yet if current social policies and high interest rates continue, the gap between the incomes of the young and the old will grow until it becomes unmanageable without some kind of dramatic reform.

Social Security Benefits in the 1990s

The conflict between the interests of the young and the old will really come to a head in the coming depression. According to legislation enacted in 1983, the retirement age will rise from sixty-five to sixty-six in 2009, and then to sixty-seven in 2027. The Social Security system had a reserve of $60 billion in 1987, which could grow to $150 billion by 1989. With rising payroll taxes and the new retirement age, the system is expected to "produce reserves of $12.4 trillion by the year 2030," as reported by Bernard Gavzer, among others.[2]

I don't know who originated this rosy figure, but to me it appears to be a figment of the imagination. Even in the absence of a depression, the U.S. economy, under the crippling weight of debts and deficits, is expected to slow down sharply in the 1990s and beyond. This will, at the least, retard the growth of Social Security tax receipts, as GNP growth declines. But in the event of the expected depression, GNP will drastically fall, and Social Security

[2] Bernard Gavzer, "How Secure Is Your Social Security?" *Parade,* October 18, 1987.

receipts will plummet. The reserve will quickly be wiped out, perhaps by 1992, thus setting the stage for a major conflict of interest between generations.

In spite of this gloomy assessment, the 40 million retirees have a brighter future than younger workers, who will be laid off by the millions, and whose unemployment compensation, meager and short-lived, will come out of a budget which, on average, has been in the red by $200 billion during the 1980s. The Social Security system at least has a reserve that should keep growing until 1989. If the system is managed properly, the elderly might not have to suffer undue hardship. For instance, if benefits were frozen now and the savings put in escrow to be paid out in case the depression fails to occur, then the reserve would grow even faster than otherwise and there would be a bigger cushion for the retirees when and if the depression does occur.

Even if the reserve is wiped out by 1992, Congress will be reluctant to cut the benefits. Given the numbers and the lobbying power of the elderly, Social Security will be the last to get the ax. Whatever cuts occur in the benefits will be minor, at least relative to those suffered by other social programs. Ironically, the elderly may then be in the position of helping to take care of their unemployed sons and daughters.

Don't, however, take your Social Security benefits for granted. Like any big government bureaucracy, the Social Security Administration can make mistakes in keeping its accounts. To make sure that your account is correct and up to date, request form OAR-7004 from your Social Security office. Complete and return the form and you will receive, at no charge, a copy of your Social Security records. Every three years you should make sure that your records are correct and up to date.

Medicare and Medicaid

After Social Security, Medicare and Medicaid receive the largest outlays in the government's social programs. These programs were launched in the Great Society's campaign to maintain and improve the health of those unable to afford doctors' bills. They also had a humble beginning, but began to grow sharply right from their inception. The two programs consumed some $110 billion of the federal budget in 1987.

These health-care programs serve a very useful purpose. Until 1966 about half of the elderly had no health insurance at all. Medicare changed all that. Before Medicaid took effect, the poor could not afford to go to doctors. That has also changed now. But the expense of these federal health programs has grown tenfold since the early 1970s, with no slowdown in sight. Attempts have been made by the Reagan administration to pass a bigger portion of the cost on to well-to-do recipients, but they have by and large failed. The increase in premiums to the beneficiaries has been minuscule.

With an aging population and rising doctors' and hospital bills, federal health-care expenses continue to expand. By the end of this decade, Medicare's Hospital Insurance Trust Fund is expected to be in deficit, which could grow to megabillions by the mid-1990s. Thus, while the Social Security reserves are in good shape and are expected to grow until 1989, health-care programs are already on the brink of deficits. In the coming depression, they will have to be pared in proportion to the overall trimming of government outlays, which will definitely hurt the poor and the elderly, and, of course, the newly unemployed, who will also be stripped of employer-sponsored health insurance. Careful planning is therefore essential to ensure that the government's social safety network works for those who need it the most, while waste and fraud are eliminated—something that will become indispensable during the difficult years ahead.

Can you depend on the government's social safety network to see you through the difficult years ahead? Obviously not. Unemployment insurance would probably not go very far toward covering your day-to-day living expenses. Social Security payments are small. And if you become ill or disabled and are no longer covered by a company-sponsored medical plan, your savings could be completely wiped out. As a first precaution, I would advise that you become fully informed about the benefits you may now have under your company plan. Many company plans fall far short of adequate coverage for long-term disability and benefits for dependents. If that is true in your case, it would be wise to augment your coverage with a private plan.

As a second precaution I would advise that you estimate the coverage you will need in the event that you are no longer employed. That coverage will include medical and disability insurance, particularly for catastrophic illness, along with coverage for hospital and surgical expenses for you and your dependents. You may also want to investigate insurance for long-term nursing-home care. These and other forms of insurance are offered in a bewildering variety by private insurance companies, and you should shop carefully and compare costs and benefits before you buy. As a general rule of thumb, you should be more concerned about adequate coverage for major illness or long-term disability than about coverage for lesser illnesses and routine medical expenses; the latter coverage dramatically increases the cost of the insurance, too. Careful planning and preparation now will enable you to take swift and informed action if it becomes necessary.

Careful planning is, in fact, essential in government, in business, and in our personal lives in preparation for the great depression which now approaches all but inevitably. A cataclysm such as a depression does not emerge overnight. It breeds on at least a decade of governmental mismanagement, which produces a slow, imperceptible festering of economic ills. There is no such thing as a trickle-down of prosperity, only a trickling down of disaster across the board. The depression of the 1930s had its roots in the prevailing classical economics, of which Reaganomics is a clone. We will learn in the near future, to our great sorrow, that whenever public policy permits an orgy of greed, depressions are the inevitable result. It is a simple dictum of history.

PART III

Investment Strategies for the 1990s

CHAPTER 8

Short-Term Instruments

THE U.S. ECONOMY has passed through all sorts of convulsions in its long march to prosperity. It has frequently suffered recessions and, occasionally, great depressions. Indeeed, great depressions are so rare that when one occurs the public is caught totally off-guard. Few people prepare themselves for a recession, much less for an economic disaster. But we are now in for a big one, and you cannot afford to be complacent.

You have already learned how the painful scenario is likely to unfold in the 1990s, whether the new depression will be inflationary or deflationary, and which jobs, businesses, and banks are safer than others. Now you are ready to take a further step and make financial plans to secure your future.

There are a wide and confusing variety of ways in which you can temporarily invest your money. Some of these investments involve a high degree of risk, which, of course, you should avoid. But you may want to consider other investments which are both relatively riskless and highly liquid—that is, in most cases you can withdraw your money at virtually any time. Let's begin with short-term investment vehicles offered by brokerage firms.

Asset Management Accounts

An asset management account (AMA) serves as a comprehensive financial package by bringing together a broad array of financial services that are usually offered in isolation. A typical AMA consists of a checking account, a brokerage account, a money market fund, a credit line, and a credit card. All these components are closely coordinated, and account transactions are listed in a single comprehensive monthly statement.

Asset management accounts offer a moderate degree of liquidity. Funds from the checking account and the credit line are, of course, instantly accessible. In addition, the AMA offers two other sources of credit. First, you may borrow up to the amount of cash and money market fund shares in the account. Second, you may borrow up to a certain percentage of the market values of securities held in the account, with the securities serving as collateral, often called the "margin" loan value of these securities. You also have access to a separate unsecured credit line that is not "tied" to any component of the AMA and that entails only the standard consumer loan rates.

In return for the services offered under an AMA, you have to pay an annual fee, ranging typically from $50 to $100. In addition, most institutions require an opening deposit of $10,000 to $20,000, and insist upon a minimum balance being maintained in the account at all times. Some, like Kemper "Money Plus," require an initial deposit of only $1,000 and no minimum balance.

Returns generated by an AMA are no greater than the yield on securities held in the account. That is, the AMA itself cannot enhance the return of its component securities. What it can do, however, is to improve the efficiency with which earnings are utilized. All cash proceeds from dividends, interest, and the sale of securities are immediately put back into the account's money market fund, where they start earning interest. Were these different services not coordinated under the umbrella of an AMA, this cash would lie idle until the investor decided how to utilize it. I will have more to say about money market funds later.

Beyond such advantages as ready access to credit and efficient disposition of returns, the biggest attraction of the AMA is its convenience. The coordination of a variety of financial services and the provision of comprehensive statements greatly reduce the effort and time you may have to put in managing your financial affairs. However, unlike accounts in banks or S&Ls, AMAs are not federally insured. They do carry some private insurance, which in today's uncertain times is not enough, and certainly will not be enough in the 1990s.

Commercial Paper

Commercial paper (CP) is short-term promissory notes issued usually by corporations but also occasionally by state and local governments. Maturities on commercial paper vary from as little as a week to as much as nine months, but usually average around thirty days.

Although commercial paper is sometimes issued in denominations of $50,000 or even $25,000, a typical issue is for $100,000 or more. Therefore, it is a feasible investment only for wealthy individuals or large institutional investors, such as brokerage houses and banks.

The secondary market for commercial paper is very limited. If you have to sell your CP all of a sudden, you may have some difficulty in doing so. However, because of the extremely short maturity on most CP, premature redemption is not a major concern. Moreover, issuing agencies will often buy back the paper at a discount if the investor finds himself in a must-sell situation.

Commercial paper usually offers rates of return that are higher than those of Treasury bills. The "spread" between the two varies with the maturity of the paper, but has historically averaged about 0.5 percent. CP issued by corporations usually offers a slightly higher rate than CP issued by state and local governments. However, the return on corporate CP is subject to state and local taxes, whereas government CP is, usually, exempt from such taxation. The tax liability incurred on corporate CP is a crucial determinant of its viability as a financial asset, because, depending on your tax bracket and the structure of state and local taxes, its after-tax return could be well below that available from government CP.

Although corporate CP usually offers higher rates than Treasury bills, it carries a higher risk, because typically the corporation does not back its CP with collateral. The risk of default is minimized by the rapid maturity of these instruments. However, there have been notable instances of default on payment by large corporations (e.g., Penn Central's default on $482 million of its outstanding CP). In order to attract investors, some companies back their CP with guarantees from insurance agencies or with credit lines at commercial banks. Moreover, information on the creditworthiness of an issuing corporation is easily available from the credit rating that Moody's Investor Service and the Standard & Poor's Corporation assign to CP. By contrast to corporate CP, the CP issued by state and local governments is generally considered riskless.

In summary, as an alternative to T-bills, commercial paper has both its attractions and its drawbacks. The primary attraction of corporate CP is, of course, the premium that it pays above the return offered by T-bills. However, you must ensure that this premium is high enough to cover not only the tax liabilities borne by the CP but also the additional risks it entails. In both these respects, governmental CP, which is partially tax-exempt and relatively riskless, offers an excellent alternative, especially for high-tax-bracket residents of high-tax states. An additional drawback of commercial paper is the high denominations in which it is offered, which place it out of the reach of most investors. Moreover, in the 1990s many large and seemingly healthy companies, debt-ridden as they are, could go bankrupt, taking their lenders down with them. The default risk of corporate CP will rise substantially.

Money Market Mutual Funds

Money market mutual funds offer the small and medium investor access to a number of short-term high-yield investment opportunities that would not be within his reach if he were to invest as an individual. A number of short-term securities, such as commercial paper, some corporate and bank CDs, and "seasoned" Treasury and federal agency notes, offer attractive yields but are inaccessible to the typical investor because of their large denominations ($50,000 and upward). A money market mutual fund pools the funds of a large number of small investors and uses these resources to acquire a portfolio of securities. Most money market funds diversify across a broad range of assets, but a few specialize in specific types of securities, such as U.S. government bonds.

Money market funds typically allow you to withdraw money at will, and some of them even permit limited checking facilities. In other words, money market funds are a highly liquid investment and, therefore, are ideal for temporarily depositing your cash before making any decisions on its longer-term disposition.

The earnings from most money market funds are subject to federal, state, and local taxes. A few funds are exempt from federal taxes, but as a rule the investor can avoid state and local taxes only if his fund specializes in bonds issued in his home state—a severe restriction, to say the least.

Earnings of a money market fund come solely from the yields on its portfolio. The return on the fund is periodically adjusted to reflect the current market yield on the portfolio; in other words, the fund's contributors are fully exposed to market fluctuations. If financial markets happen to be volatile, money market funds can be a very risky proposition. Typically, the money contributed into a money market fund by an investor is not insured, thus making him vulnerable to default and capital losses. Usually, money market funds sponsored by large brokerage firms minimize such risks by diversifying their portfolios broadly. Keep in mind that if some of the lesser known money market funds offer a higher yield, it is probably because they are working with a riskier portfolio. Another risk is that if, in response to a sharp rise in interest rates, a large number of the fund's members withdraw their holdings and move them elsewhere, you may have to wait before you get all your money back. And if there are capaital losses, you may receive only a portion of your investment.

When evaluating a money market mutual fund, you must weigh these risks against the advantages of earning higher market yields on cash without significantly forgoing liquidity. Another factor that you must evaluate is the average maturity of the portfolio upon which the fund rests. The longer this average maturity, the less liquid will your funds be. In view of the coming depression, the safest money market mutual funds will be those invested in AAA bonds of cash-rich companies, short-term T-bills, or AAA municipal bonds. (AAA signifies the highest Standard & Poor's rating.)

Money Market Deposit Accounts

The money market deposit account is the commercial bank's equivalent of the money market mutual funds offered by brokerage houses; like the latter, the deposit account is designed to provide smaller investors access to high-yield securities with very large denominations by pooling the deposits of a large number of investors.

Because it is based on essentially the same concept, the money market deposit account (MMDA) bears a close resemblance to its counterpart on Wall Street. The MMDA allows the investor to withdraw or deposit amounts at any time without incurring a penalty. In addition, these funds usually allow limited facilities for writing checks, or making automatic transfers to other accounts.

As is the case with the Wall Street money market funds, the rates of return on the MMDA are adjusted periodically —usually once a month, and sometimes as often as once a week—to reflect the current market yield of the underlying portfolio. At first sight, this appears to render the MMDA just as vulnerable to capital gains or losses as the Wall Street money market funds. However, it is on this point that the two accounts differ critically. Unlike the Wall Street version, MMDAs are insured up to $100,000 by the FDIC at most savings institutions, which gives the small investor an excellent opportunity to pursue attractive short-term rates of return without exposing himself to capital losses. However, like any other money market fund, the MMDA does not allow the investor to "lock in" the current interest rate. If the investor anticipates a drop in interest rates in the near future, this might prove to be a major drawback of the MMDA.

Despite being offered by savings institutions and being highly liquid, the MMDA is not a perfect substitute for a checking account, because the check-writing privileges on the MMDA are usually restricted to three checks a month. As a result, an investor should view the MMDA as complementing rather than replacing a regular checking account.

Another shortcoming of such accounts is that if for some reason an investor's balance falls below a prescribed minimum—usually about $1,000—the rate of return on the fund is lowered for that period.

In my view, among all the MMDAs, the safest ones are those offered by the financial institutions that are listed in the appendix to Chapter 6.

NOW Accounts

Negotiable orders of withdrawal—or NOW accounts, as they are popularly known—are accounts that offer a blend of the best features of checking and savings accounts. They usually pay interest of 5.25 percent and offer unlimited checking privileges. First authorized in 1980, these accounts have grown rapidly in popularity, and are now a staple feature of the services offered by savings institutions (banks, S&Ls, savings banks, and even credit unions).

In order to earn fully the attractive rates offered by these accounts, depositors are required to maintain a minimum balance, usually from $1,000 to $2,000. The penalty for allowing the balance to fall below the minimum is a service charge (ranging from $3 to $8), which, depending on the size of the balance, can cut significantly into interest earnings. Some banks go to the extent of suspending all interest payments on the account for the relevant period (e.g., a month) if the balance falls below the minimum during that period. The return on NOW accounts is also offset partially by fees that banks often charge to service the accounts—fees that are perceptibly greater than those on ordinary checking accounts. Finally, NOW accounts, like all bank accounts, are insured up to $100,000 by the FDIC and have therefore been considered riskless.

A NOW account is an attractive option only for those who routinely maintain more than $1,000 in their checking accounts. Purely as an interest-earning investment opportunity, it does not have much to offer, since its usual rate of 5.25 percent is less than that of other short-term interest-bearing investments, such as money market funds, CPs, and CDs. Its drawing card is its combination of modest interest earnings with unlimited liquidity. Of course, in order to reap all the benefits, you have to ensure that bank fees don't eat too deeply into your earnings and that you are able to maintain the minimum stipulated balance, thus avoiding potentially large service charges. As with MMDAs, the best NOW accounts are those offered by relatively safe banks and S&Ls.

Credit Union Accounts

Credit unions are financial cooperatives that are operated on a nonprofit basis by large corporations, professional associations, churches, etc. These cooperatives are designed to offer their members a basic range of financial services, while at the same time trimming down the high operating expenses and profit margins that characterize a commercial bank. The resultant savings are passed on to the members in terms of higher yields on deposits or lower interest rates on loans.

Credit unions vary dramatically in the range of services they offer. A typical credit union restricts itself to accepting deposits, offering consumer and mortgage loans, and operating a range of payroll deduction plans. However, a growing number have begun broadening their horizons by offering interest-bearing checking accounts, traveler's checks, IRAs, and even accounts that operate like money market deposit accounts.

There is a technical difference between a deposit in a commercial bank and a deposit in a credit union. A person who holds a deposit in a credit union is technically an owner of that union; his deposits are treated as contributions of equity capital, and his returns on these deposits are designated as dividends. However, for operational purposes this distinction is currently irrelevant. Dividend earnings are treated just like interest earnings in computing taxes. Credit union deposits are almost always insured to the same degree that bank deposits are. For borrowers, credit unions offer loans at lower rates than commercial banks, finance companies, or S&Ls. Moreover, the criteria for loan qualification are less stringent.

Credit unions are not without their disadvantages. While some of the savings described earlier are obtained by eliminating the profit margin charged by banks, a significant part comes at the expense of the range and quality of financial services. Few credit unions provide the range of services offered by banks and other financial institutions. Frequently, their deposit accounts or their loans lack the flexibility of similar arrangements in banks. Finally, the service provided by the staff at a credit union tends to lack the professionalism offered by the staff at other commercial institutions.

When evaluating a credit union, it is important to determine the extent to which you are sacrificing service levels and convenience. As an example, both a credit union and a commercial bank may offer a checking account, but the credit union may have no arrangement for returning canceled checks. Another pitfall that sometimes awaits the unwary credit union member is that although the union offers a higher interest rate on deposits than a bank, it may compound its interest less frequently, thus making its effective yield actually lower than that of the bank. A credit union is a useful facility in conjunction with a full-service financial institution; in isolation, its limitations may well exceed its benefits. For a list of "safer" credit unions, see the appendix to Chapter 6.

Treasury Bills

Treasury bills are short-term obligations of the U.S. government issued in denominations of $10,000 and more and bearing maturities of three, six, or twelve months. Treasury bills are probably the best-known short-term securities available in the financial market, and certainly one of the most popular. Their main attractions are that they are considered practically riskless, they are exempt from state and local taxes, and they are easily traded and hence liquid.

Treasury bills don't offer a regular stream of interest payments. Instead, they are sold to the investor at a price that is less than the redemption value of the bill, and the difference between these figures is the interest payment received by the investor in advance.

Another distinctive feature of Treasury bills is the manner in which they are sold. Newly issued three- and six-month bills are sold at a weekly Treasury auction, whereas fifty-two-week bills are offered once a month. As at any other auction, the sale price of these bills is determined through a bidding process.

There are two ways in which a regular investor can acquire a T-bill. He can either directly place a bid for it, or he can purchase it through a broker or a bank for a fee. If he opts for the former, the safest strategy is to submit a "noncompetitive" bid, which means paying the average market rate at the auction. Besides the auction market for new bills, there is an active market for bills that have already been issued, but have not yet reached maturity. The trading in this market is very active; therefore it is easy to dispose of a T-bill before its maturity date. The price that is obtained on such a bill depends on the going interest rate and the duration to maturity of that particular bill.

In addition to their high liquidity, T-bills are also considered to be completely riskless because they are fully backed by the credit of the U.S. government. Such backing does not, of course, protect the bill-holder from a capital loss if he tries to sell his bill prematurely in a climate of rising interest rates.

Because of their complete risklessness and almost complete liquidity, the return on T-bills is usually treated as a benchmark against which all other lenders or borrowers adjust the return on securities they buy or sell. The rate of return on a T-bill is simply the dollar value of the discount expressed as a percentage of the price of the T-bill. For example, if a one-year $20,000 bill is sold for $19,000, the rate of return on the bill is

$$\frac{20,000 - 19,000}{20,000} \times 100 = 5\%.$$

The interest income earned on a T-bill is subject only to federal taxes.

T-bills can sometimes be used to defer tax liabilities into the next year, because the interest income is subject to taxation only in the year in which the bill matures. Therefore, by withdrawing money from a NOW account or a money market fund, where interest accrues daily, and moving it into a T-bill maturing in the following year, the investor can defer taxes by a year. In addition to their safety, the return on T-bills compares favorably with money market mutual funds and deposits. However, bank CDs usually outperform them, except in states with very high state and local taxes, where the story may be quite different. Because T-bills are exempt from these taxes, their after-tax yield may actually be higher than those on CDs.

Despite their unmatched soundness and liquidity, T-bills are not quite the ideal short-term investment for a typical investor. Their biggest drawback is that they require a fairly substantial outlay of funds—a minimum of $10,000—and the typical small investor may be either unwilling or unable to make such a large commitment. In fact, it is precisely in response to this problem that money market funds and deposits came into being. In addition, if T-bills are bought directly from the government, the purchaser is not allowed to sell the bill within twenty days of purchase or twenty days of maturity, and this limits the liquidity of the bill. On the other hand, buying from a bank or broker, while preventing this loss of liquidity, entails a fee that eats into yields.

Even though T-bills are traditionally regarded as riskless, they are not as risk-free as they were until the 1970s, when the federal debt was below $1 trillion and the budget deficit below $100 billion. Although it is unlikely that the federal government would default in the coming depression, it could alter the terms of repayment on outstanding obligations.

Treasury Notes

Treasury notes are, in most respects, the medium-term equivalent of T-bills, which are short-term. The maturities on Treasury notes usually range from two to ten years, thus placing them in an altogether different class from the short-term securities we have been considering so far. Like T-bills, Treasury notes are regarded as completely free from default risk. However, they are vulnerable to capital losses in the event they have to be sold before maturity.

Again like T-bills, Treasury notes are traded in very active markets, thus making them very liquid. Treasury notes are also sold in auctions, and the investor who wishes to purchase them has exactly the same options as he has with T-bills. The major difference between T-notes and T-bills, besides maturity period, is that T-notes are available in much smaller denominations, starting at $1,000. Notes maturing in less than four years usually come in minimum denominations of $5,000.

Treasury notes offer returns slightly higher than those available from T-bills. Once the price of the note is settled in auction, the rate of interest on the note is automatically determined, and the Treasury pays the investor a fixed rate at half-yearly intervals until the day of maturity. Therefore Treasury notes offer an excellent means to lock in a high interest rate for a long time. Interest earnings are subject to federal taxes, but exempt from state and local taxes.

In addition to the safety and liquidity advantages, Treasury notes have the attractive feature that they come without a call provision, which means that the issuer (here the Treasury) cannot force the investor to redeem the bond before its maturity. The investor has complete freedom over its disposition.

Certificates of Deposit

Banks, thrifts, and even credit unions offer a certain type of account called a certificate of deposit (CD) with which you can lock in high yields for a few months or years. These savings instruments are highly flexible. They are usually issued in maturities of six to twelve months, but many banks will tailor them to suit your needs. CDs with longer maturities, of course, earn higher interest rates.

The denomination of CDs is also flexible. Savings institutions offer them in amounts from $1,000 to $100,000, federally insured up to the full amount. Large-denomination CDs, those larger than $100,000, are also available, but the higher amounts lack the safety of federal insurance. They do pay higher rates than smaller CDs. Big institutions, including money market funds, are the main buyers of large certificates.

Although some CDs pay rates higher than even Treasury bills and are also very safe, they do impose a penalty for premature withdrawal. The penalty varies from a month's to three months' interest, even if interest has not been earned. Unlike Treasury bills, income from CDs is subject to all taxes. In order to remain liquid and still earn the higher rates offered by CDs, I suggest you go with one- or two-year maturities offered by safer banks.

Investment Strategies in the Coming Depression

In times of economic uncertainty and upheaval, there are three general rules that always apply. The first is that to the degree possible, your assets should be kept in cash or so-called cash equivalents. This does not mean, of course, that you should bundle up $20 bills and stuff them in your mattress or hide them in the back of a closet. The second general rule is that you should take every possible precaution to safeguard your cash assets. The concept of risk is key to both these rules. You must avoid the risk of actual loss or theft by keeping your cash in an account in a bank or some other type of financial institution. And you should choose very carefully the *kind* of account in which you deposit your assets in order to avoid the risk of a loss in their value. Finally, as the third general rule, wherever and however you deposit your assets, they should be in a highly liquid form; that is, they should be immediately available to you.

Simple checking and savings accounts in banks or other financial institutions fulfill all three of these general rules: safety, security, and liquidity. Such accounts also pay a moderate rate of interest. There is, of course, the possibility that the institution will fail, in which case accounts up to $100,000 are fully insured by the federal government. And you can further guard against failure by choosing among those banks and financial institutions listed in Chapter 6 and its appendix. I would also suggest that you consider keeping enough cash in the form of traveler's checks to cover your expenses for at least one month. If a bank should fail, it could take that long to recover your savings through the FDIC. Cash kept in traveler's checks or deposited in banks today may possibly be worthless in terms of buying power in the years ahead if our economy goes into an inflationary spiral. But in all probability, the 1990s will experience stable prices and the buying power of your cash will not change much.

A big question is whether federal instruments are themselves safe. As long as the politicians say so, we should trust the government. In considering investments above and beyond the funds you keep as cash or cash equivalents, again the rule is safety, security, liquidity. Treasury bills and notes fulfill these requirements, but just what will the government do during an emergency, when it simply does not have enough money to pay its bills? Nobody really knows. Debt default, however, would be the last resort of the government. If the government's financial predicament makes you uneasy, then you should go totally with safe banks, S&Ls, and credit unions, maintaining accounts suitable to your needs, such as NOW accounts or one-to-two-year CDs.

I suggest that you steer clear of the asset management accounts offered by brokerage firms because of their lack of federal insurance. They do have private insurance, but who is going to insure the private insurer? Moreover, you may be unable to reach your broker in times of panic, as happened on Black Monday in October 1987. Corporate CP is also very risky. There is a good possibility that many corporations, as well as brokerage houses, will fail in the coming depression. My thinking is that in hard and uncertain times, one should err on the side of safety and invest conservatively. If there was ever a time to be conservative with your investments, it is right now.

Finally, for use in emergencies, you may want to consider obtaining a standing loan from a banking institution. Many banks today will give you an unsecured credit line of up to $50,000, depending on how much debt you already have. Because of economic troubles, this source may dry up in the future, so try to secure the credit at this time. The credit line is costless until the funds are actually used.

CHAPTER 9

Stocks

THE CRASH THAT THUNDERED in the New York Stock Exchange on October 19, 1987, was heard all around the globe. Thus emerged a phenomenon which I had predicted as early as 1978—that toward the end of the 1980s, after rising feverishly for several years, the stock market would enter a volatile phase, eventually triggering a collapse of the world economy.

The October "meltdown" has created a new reality for investors in the stock market. How this reality will fit into the painful scenario of the 1990s is a question I have been asked time and time again. Before I give you my reply, let me first introduce you to the complex world of stocks and related investments. You should know a bit about how markets move—up or down.

Stocks have traditionally been one of the best-known and most widely discussed instruments of individual and institutional investment. When you purchase stock in a corporation, you are essentially acquiring a share in its ownership, and your earnings, called dividends, are, in fact, your share in the company's profits. Thus the ownership of stock is fundamentally different from the ownership of bonds, which are treated by the company as debt and which, therefore, make the investor a creditor to the company.

The most important determinant of the price of a stock is the performance of the underlying company itself. Since a share in a company is nothing but a claim to a portion of its net asset value—i.e., the present value of its assets less the value of its liabilities—the amount that a sensible investor pays for this share should not be grossly out of line with net asset value. Investors constantly seek out fresh information that will affect the earnings prospects of various companies and hence their net asset value. The moment such information is received, new expectations may be formed, and the market price of the share will adjust to reflect the reassessment. Good news encourages investors to buy, and the price of the stock rises with demand. Bad news influences investors to sell, and with lack of demand, the price of the stock falls. In general, every action or decision taken by the company is eagerly watched and instantly judged by the market. It is in this sense that the market price of a company's stock reflects its current and future prospects.

A company's prospects can also be affected by factors that are well beyond its control. For example, an economy-wide slump would make the demand for automobiles, industrial equipment, etc. sluggish, thus causing a fall in the price of stock in companies involved in such products, and the reverse would occur in a boom. Therefore, in evaluating a stock investors have to consider not only the value of the company but also fluctuations of the economy as a whole.

Does the price of a company's stock at all times faithfully reflect the true value of the firm? No, not always. Efficient as it may be, the stock market cannot always acquire and act upon fresh information instantaneously. This problem is particularly acute with smaller and less-known companies whose performance is not subjected to the same kind of scrutiny as that of the bigger companies. However, mis-evaluation caused by lack of information is usually short-lived; there are so many professional investors hunting for undervalued stock on which to make a killing that these opportunities do not remain hidden for long. In fact, cor-porate takeovers are usually an attempt on the part of investors to pick up at low price a company whose stock has been undervalued. Needless to say, in the case of larger corporations, undervaluation because of lack of in-formation evaporates almost as soon as the information is revealed.

A more pervasive source of misevaluation, one that can last for a long time, is a form of inertia that develops in investors' minds when forming expectations about the general economic climate. A period of prosperity creates a systematic upward bias in these expectations; investors begin to believe that the only way for stock prices to go is up. In this kind of bullish market, the optimism of inves-tors, quite often unjustified, inflates stock prices well above their intrinsic value. However, during a downturn, espe-cially of the kind expected in the near future, a stock's price may plummet even with the best of news about the company's prospects.

Since stock prices may deviate significantly from their intrinsic values, at least in the short run, many market analysts prefer not to rely on fundamental factors such as projected earnings, market share, etc. when evaluating a company's stock. Instead, they study historical trends in such things as the price of the stock and its volume traded, in the belief—more often in the hope—that there may be systematic patterns in the movement of these variables over time. Unfortunately, this approach—sometimes called the technical approach—to forecasting stock prices has not proved to be significantly better than fundamental analysis; nor has it proved to be significantly worse.

Despite the great variety of stocks, they can be broadly classified into two categories. First, there are those issued by large, well-established corporations which have developed a stable market for their products. These stocks pay dividends that are both durable and high in comparison to those paid by other stocks. However, the corporations themselves may have exhausted much of their growth potential, and this, in turn, limits the possibilities of an increase in value of both their assets and their stock. Such stocks are sought out primarily for the attractive dividends they currently yield and are therefore described as income stocks.

In contrast, there are the stocks issued by corporations that are relatively new in the market, or that are operating in an exploding or volatile industry. These stocks don't look overly attractive at the present; their dividends are low and erratic. Their major draw is that the underlying corporation and industry have not yet exhausted potential for growth, and thus there is the possibility of a significant increase in value for their stock. Such stocks, called growth stocks, are obviously much more speculative than income stocks.

As part of an investor's portfolio, stocks have a number of attractive features. They are highly liquid. The trading on stock markets is so active that, as a rule, an investor will have little problem acquiring or disposing of a stock. However, it should be emphasized that for those looking for safe and solid returns, stocks should not be the preferred investment. No matter how stable the underlying corporation, there is no guarantee that your investment in a stock is safe; even prices of the most established stocks fluctuate. As for dividends, neither the level of these payments nor their regularity is guaranteed, as they would be with payments on a government bond or a highly rated corporate bond. Stocks should be considered only by those investors who already have sufficient savings invested in securities like insured bank deposits and Treasury bills that have traditionally been regarded as riskless. In view of the coming depression, stocks have to be approached, if at all, with extreme caution.

Options

An option is an instrument that provides the investor an opportunity to gain from fluctuations in the market value of securities without actually owning the securities. An investor who buys an option is merely purchasing the right to buy (or sell) one hundred shares of some stock at a designated price, called the "strike" price or exercise price, during a specified period of time—the "life" of the option. Options come in two varieties: "call" options, which are options to buy the security, and "put" options, which are options to sell. Options, as the name suggests, entail no coercion; the holder is perfectly free to let his option expire without exercising it.

How do options work? Consider a simple scenario. Beta Toys, a leading manufacturer of children's toys whose shares are currently selling for $50, announces a new line of talking dolls. The market responds very coolly to this announcement. However, Bonnie Smith, an individual investor who has raised four daughters and believes she understands little girls very well, thinks the dolls will be a huge success. She can act on this conviction and buy a "call" option on one hundred shares of Beta stock at, for example, an exercise price of $52 and with a "life" or maturity of three months. The dolls are released in the market. If Bonnie is right and the dolls are a big hit, the price of Beta's stock will immediately rise. If, at any time during the next three months, Beta stock rises above 52, Bonnie can instantly exercise her call option and buy one hundred shares at $52. She can then turn around and sell them in the market for the going price—say it's $55—and reap a gain of $3 on each share. If it turns out instead that Bonnie guessed wrong and the stock price never rises above $52, she can let her option expire, losing in the process only what she paid for the option.

Put options work on the same principle, but in reverse. If, in the above example, Bonnie decided that the dolls will be a disaster, she could buy a "put" option, which would give her the right to sell one hundred Beta shares at, say, $48 at any time during the next three months. Now if Bonnie is right and Beta stock plummets to $45, she can profit by buying on the market at that price and exercising her option to sell at $48. To summarize, call options are for the optimists who believe that the stock price will rise, while put options are for pessimists who expect the stock price to fall.

Although options are instruments of speculation, they can also be used for other purposes. For instance, if you already own stock in Beta Toys, you can purchase a put option on your shares to insure yourself against an excessive fall in the price of your stock. If your Beta stock is currently worth $50 a share, you can insure yourself against capital depreciation of more than $10 a share by buying a put option for $40. Of course, this insurance comes at a price—the price of the option. You can also write put or call options on stock you already own in order to enhance the capital gains that you earn on your stock. Such options are called covered options, to distinguish them from options on stock you don't own—which are called naked options.

Although options can be written for maturities up to nine months, most are for periods of less than three months. All options bear a specific expiration date, and can be purchased at any time before that date. Therefore, a more convenient way to capitalize on having bought the "correct" option, the one reflecting the correct guess, is simply to sell the option itself at a premium over your purchase price.

Options are an attractive alternative for investors who want to speculate on the fluctuations of stocks, but who don't have the financial resources actually to buy a sufficient number of shares. In our previous example of the call option, if Bonnie Smith tried to speculate by actually buying one hundred shares of Beta Toys, she would have to invest $5,000 for an indefinite period of time in that stock. By purchasing an option instead, she can reap exactly the same capital appreciation on the underlying stock simply for the price of the option. Options are currently available on most of the major stocks that are actively traded; in fact, options are now available even on portfolios consisting of a number of assets

Stock prices will fall dramatically in the depression ahead, and knowledgeable investors may seek to use options as a means of profiting from the decline or limiting the loss on investments they already own. However, options are very risky even in the best of times. You can make a killing, but you can also take a beating. Options essentially represent a gamble, and in today's uncertain economy, the odds are heavily stacked against you.

Margin Trading and Short Selling

Stocks, when viewed as a means for speculative gains, appear to have one major drawback. To make large profits, the investor has to deal with large quantities of stock, and that may require a significant amount of cash, which he may not have at his disposal. However, there are a few ways in which an investor can capitalize on stock price fluctuations without actually paying in full for the stock. One of these you have already seen—options. There are two other major strategies designed to maximize profits from stock trading, namely margin trading and short selling. Both involve some sort of borrowing, which is what distinguishes them from the use of options.

Margin trading is simply buying stocks on credit. The buyer has to pay only a certain percentage of the stock price in cash to the broker. The rest is treated as a loan from the broker to the buyer, to be redeemed upon the sale of the asset. In addition to enhancing the volume of trading, borrowing on margin can also magnify the gains and losses from speculation. To see how this works, consider an example. An investor has the opportunity to buy one hundred shares of Beta Toys at $50 each. If he had to pay the whole purchase price up front, he would have to invest $5,000. But suppose his broker allows him to borrow 50 percent of this sum on margin. Now the investor pays only $2,500 plus interest on the loan to the broker. Shortly after this transaction, Beta stock rises to $100, and the investor decides to sell his stock. If he had paid the full price of the stock up front, his capital gain would have been 100 percent; however, because he had to pay only $2,500 in cash initially, his capital gain is now 200 percent. Of course, if the Beta stock price crashed to $25, the reverse would be true and his loss would be magnified.

In addition to the magnification of his losses, the investor runs another risk when he trades on margin—the risk of a "margin call." Following the crash of 1929, for which rampant margin trading was held to be the culprit, the Fed mandated that the amount borrowed on margin can never exceed 50 percent of the current market value of the stock. Going back to the Beta Toys example, if the price of Beta stock goes down to $25, the market value of one hundred shares becomes only $2,500, of which 50 percent is $1,250. This is all the broker can now lend to the investor. However, the broker has actually loaned $2,500. Therefore, he is forced by law to demand $1,250 from the investor. This is a margin call. If the investor cannot meet this sudden request within three weeks, his stocks are sold at a loss. Margin trading requires strong nerves and ample financial reserves, and is best avoided by the inexperienced or small investor. In today's uncertain milieu, margin buying of stocks is inadvisable.

Short selling, like the put option, is based on the gamble that market prices will go down. The idea here is to borrow shares from someone who formally holds ownership of those shares, with a promise to return the shares at a later date. A broker serves as an intermediary for the transaction. Having borrowed the shares, the investor immediately sells them at the going price. If he is right and the price of the stock actually drops in the immediate future, he can buy them back at that price, return them to the original owner, and keep the profit. Of course, the investor may well prove to be wrong; the price may not fall, or may even rise, after he has sold the borrowed shares, in which case he will have to buy back the stock at that market price, thus taking a loss. Once again, in most markets, and especially in times foreshadowing a depression, short selling is risky, to say the least, and should be avoided by inexperienced investors who do not have the time to monitor stock prices constantly and act within minutes.

Mutual Funds

In a mutual fund, the financial resources of a large number of individual investors (typically of small or medium scale) are pooled together and held in a portfolio of assets monitored by a team of professional managers. An investor can buy into, or sell out of, a mutual fund simply by purchasing or selling shares in that fund. The shareholders of the fund receive dividend payments on their shares that are periodically generated by earnings on the underlying portfolio. In addition, any capital gains that accrue from the sale of securities in the portfolio are distributed among shareholders annually.

The performance of a particular mutual fund is determined entirely by the composition of its underlying portfolio. This can vary significantly among mutual funds according to their investment objectives. Funds that seek to maximize current dividend income on their shares—typically called income funds—stack their portfolios with stocks and bonds that currently offer high yields. Other funds may be interested more in the opportunities for growth via capital appreciation. Such funds, called growth funds, look for stocks that offer promising prospects of capital appreciation even at the expense of current dividends. Some funds prefer to stick exclusively to bonds because of the greater safety they offer. Others go entirely for stocks because of the possibility of capital gains, while some others—called balanced funds—conservatively blend these strategies. Finally, some funds try to develop a greater expertise with their portfolio base by restricting themselves to a few types of securities—the so-called specialized funds—while others go for the greatest possible degree of diversification. Every mutual fund offers a prospectus which details the investment goals of the fund.

Mutual funds offer many attractions to the small and medium-scale investor. To start with, a mutual fund offers access to short-term securities that pay high yields, but that come in denominations too large for an average investor to afford individually—e.g., $100,000 corporate commercial paper. Moreover, its large financial pool allows a mutual fund to achieve a much greater degree of diversification than the individual investor would ever be able to achieve on his own. Finally, for those investors who lack the expertise to handle portfolios efficiently or the time to acquire this expertise, the professional management of mutual funds is a major draw. Investors no longer need to spend hours researching their potential investments. This convenience comes at a price, however.

The individual shareholder has no control over the manner in which his finances are used within the fund. If he disagrees with the portfolio investment decisions of this fund, his only option is to sell out—a poor option if the fund is doing badly, since it will probably entail a capital loss. This fact merely emphasizes the importance of finding a fund whose objectives and attitudes toward risk most closely match your own. Fortunately, the number and the variety of mutual funds available in the market is so large that such a matching should always be possible, provided the investor searches carefully enough. In my opinion, a conservative, well-managed mutual fund with a proven track record is by far the best way to invest in the stock market, provided that you have enough assets in liquid and relatively risk-free investments to see you through the troubled years ahead.

Advice to Stock Owners

The October 1987 stock market crash foreshadows a major calamity in the near future. Many puzzles have arisen in the wake of that crash. What caused it? What are its lessons?

I will answer these questions in detail in Part IV. Here suffice it to say that stock markets all over the world were overheated and finally succumbed to a variety of pressures on that fateful day in October. The decade of the 1980s saw a huge speculative bubble that began in 1982 and kept expanding until it finally and inevitably burst. This was, however, a minicrash—a mild preview of things to come. Before a hurricane hits, there are always a few storm warnings. The October crash was the first such warning. Another crash occurred on January 8, 1988, when the

Dow Jones Industrial Average fell 140 points. That was the second warning. There will be at least one more before the final crash occurs in 1989 or 1990.

The main difference between a minicrash and a final crash is that from the latter there is no recovery for several years, because by that time various governments have exhausted all their defensive options. As far as the stock market is concerned, a final crash is not necessarily worse than the preceding minicrashes, but its economic repercussions are devastating.

A look at the 1920s illustrates my argument. In that decade, a speculative stock market bubble began and kept expanding until 1926, when it experienced its first minicrash—a decline of 10 percent. The markets quickly recovered, but nose-dived again a year later in October 1927 —this time a plunge of 12 percent. That is when the U.S. government used its first defense by lowering interest rates. The speculative bubble got a new life and share prices soared again. However, two more minicrashes occurred before the stock market finally collapsed in October 1929. By that time world governments had used their other main defense against the final crash, artificial stabilization of the pound, the principal international currency of the time.

Let us now take a look at the 1980s, sixty years from the 1920s. In 1982 the stock market began to surge in another speculative bubble and experienced no major correction until October 1987. There was no minicrash in 1986 corresponding to the one in 1926. Hence, the crash of 1987 combined two minis into one. But as in 1927, the government responded by lowering interest rates, which, in fact, fell worldwide.

When the stock market crashed again in January 1988, the so-called Group of Seven world governments responded by resolutely defending the dollar. This action stabilized the security markets—once again. The stock market crashes of October 1987 and January 1988 turned out to be mere minicrashes, because the Group of Seven have not yet exhausted all their defenses against the final crash. But by the end of 1989, these governments will have used up all their defensive options. By then interest rates will be irreducible, and the dollar indefensible. It will fall freely against major currencies such as the yen and the mark, and speculative bubbles will then burst in Japan and Germany, quickly engulfing the world. If, on the other hand, the U.S. government raises interest rates to defend the dollar, the American stock market will collapse, crippling the markets everywhere else.

We are now in the final stage of the speculative bubble of the 1980s. Such bubbles usually last about seven years before collapsing. Being in this final stage, stock markets all over the world have become highly volatile. Weekly and monthly share price fluctuations are now much larger than ever before. In such a bullish but erratic market, you need nerves of steel to make money. When the Dow can drop 508 points in one day, who has the nerve to stick around and wait for long-term gains? Yet that is exactly what is usually needed to make money in the stock market.

In my book *The Great Depression of 1990*, I advised readers to set aside at least $44,000 in relatively risk-free assets and invest no more than 25 percent of their remaining assets in stocks. Since less than 10 percent of Americans have more than $44,000 in savings, in effect I advised the vast majority of people to stay away from Wall Street—this in spite of my belief that the Dow could rise every year after 1982 until its final crash, except in the last quarter of 1987 and the first quarter of 1988. The meltdown in October 1987 and the January 1988 crash show that my caution about stocks, despite their generally bullish trend, was fully warranted. Even though between 1982 and 1987 the Dow closed higher each year, thousands of investors, especially the latecomers, lost a lot of money on Black Monday, and in its aftermath.

Even though I don't expect the depression to begin until

the end of 1989, I suggest that you stay away from investing in common stocks, and sell any that you may now own
by the presidential election in November 1988. Note that
even after 1989, stocks will not drop in a straight line.
Nothing ever moves in a linear fashion. But the trend
would be downward, with the Dow plummeting by as
much as 80 percent over two to three years.

Anticipating this, you may be tempted to sell short or
buy put options, but I won't. Even the most experienced
investors have been caught by market fluctuations. You
can lose money in the short run even if you correctly anticipate the market direction. But if you insist on investing in
a falling market, first set aside enough cash and liquid
investments to help you survive the depression. Only then
invest in put options, where you know what your maximum loss could be. With short sales the loss is uncertain
and can be enormous. But never gamble beyond your
means.

To give you an idea of how stocks behave during a pro-
longed downturn, consider Chart 2 and Table 14. Chart 2
plots the quarterly averages of stock prices in three categories indexed by Standard & Poor's: utilities, industrials,
and a composite group. It is clear that all these groups
jumped in the first half of 1929, then plummeted in the
second half, recovering a bit in the first half of 1930, and
then dropping again virtually unchecked until mid-1932.
This is what a great depression does to common stocks. In
fact, from their high points in 1929 to the 1932 close, the
Dow Jones Industrial Average fell by 77 percent and the
S&P industrials by 80 percent. The same type of carnage
could occur in the 1990s. The Dow could drop to the
600–700 range before consistently rising again.

There will, of course, be some rising spells even in an
ultra-bear market. But they will be short-lived, and unless
you can constantly examine stock prices, you could be
courting disaster with premature investments in stock.
Once the Dow has bottomed at around 650, you may

safely reenter the stock market. Buy with caution, however, because stocks could depreciate again in 1994. After that the danger to stocks would be gone for all practical purposes, although the depression could linger on until 1996–97.

What will be the best stock buys in the 1990s? Table 14 provides the answer. It displays the lists of the biggest and smallest losers during the Great Depression. Between the

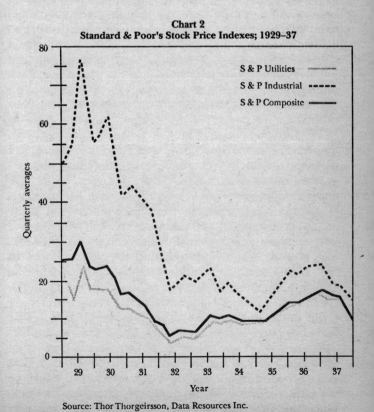

Chart 2
Standard & Poor's Stock Price Indexes; 1929–37

S & P Utilities
S & P Industrial
S & P Composite

Quarterly averages

Year

Source: Thor Thorgeirsson, Data Resources Inc.

1929 stock market peak and the close of 1932, the S&P industrials dropped by 80 percent. This figure serves as my benchmark. Stocks dropping more than 80 percent are the biggest losers and those dropping by 80 percent or less may be classified as the "smallest" losers.

Table 14
Biggest and Smallest Losers
During the Great Depression

Standard & Poor's industrials with the biggest and smallest percentage loss in stock prices from the 1929 high to the closing price in 1932, and their subsequent percentage gain from 1932 to 1936.

Biggest Losers	Percentage Loss, 1929–32	Percentage Gain, 1932–36
Machine tools	95	994
Motion pictures	95	275
Paper	94	1,000
Copper	93	900
Aerospace	91	240
Investment companies	90	130
Tire and rubber	89	280
Automobiles	88	400
Electrical and electronic	88	288
Office and business equipment	88	285
Steel	88	324
Building materials	87	490
Home furnishings	85	415
New York City banks	84	17
Finance companies	81	660

Smallest Losers	Percentage Loss, 1929–32	Percentage Gain, 1932–36
S&P industrials	80	218
Retail stores	80	150
Air transport	80	133
Textiles (apparel)	77	202

Drugs	76	88
Oil	75	149
Property-liability insurance	74	162
Foods	68	45
Electric utilities	68	0
Telephone and telegraph	67	61
Metals and glass	64	150
Soft drinks	62	550
Tobacco products	50	84

Source: Prepared from data supplied by *Standard & Poor's Trade and Securities Statistics*, 1976 edition.

The list of biggest losers contains few surprises, because they belong to what I have earlier termed the worst-hit industries (see Chapter 4). Some of these stocks lost as much as 95 percent of their peak value reached in 1929. What is more interesting is that, in general, the biggest losers also turned out to be the biggest gainers when the market began to recover in 1932 and steadily rose until 1936. Except for investment companies and New York banks, all stocks that lost big also rose mightily during the 1930s. While the S&P industrials climbed by 218 percent between 1932 and 1936, some of the loss leaders jumped by several hundred percent. Will that be true in the coming depression? Most likely. In any case, you will not lose by again investing in such stocks once the Dow has troughed. Note that most of these loss leaders also lost big on Black Monday and its aftermath.

In the smallest-losers category are industries such as electric utilities, tobacco products, and telephone and telegraph. The only surprise in this group is the metals and glass industry. Others are among the least-hit industries mentioned in Chapter 4. You can see, however, that most of the small losers were also small gainers when the market recovered, except for the soft drink industry. Electric utilities seemed to gain nothing during the recovery. Actually, this group troughed in 1934 rather than 1932, and rose moderately thereafter. It is noteworthy that most industries in the second list of losers were also relatively small losers on Black Monday.

Did any stock benefit from the Great Depression? Yes, gold-mining stocks did after dropping initially in the carnage of 1929. Consequently, gold production rose steadily throughout the 1930s. All in all, we can draw the following conclusions about the behavior of the stock market during a depression:

1. Stock market crashes precede the onset of the depression by two to three years.
2. Most, if not all, stocks may plunge uncontrollably before and in the early years of the depression.
3. Utilities, foods, and other necessities fall less than capital goods, commodities or raw materials, transportation, and leisure-time products.
4. Once the market has bottomed out, most, if not all, stocks record sharp gains long before the depression is over.
5. The biggest losers are in general the biggest gainers.
6. Gold mining is perhaps the only industry that steadily gains after a depression is underway. You should therefore consider investing in gold stocks shortly after the depression has begun, provided they have also fallen sharply.

These stock market trends and the behavior patterns of the industries listed in Table 14 can be a useful guide when the time comes to reinvest in stocks. But even in a recovering market, stock prices will be volatile and caution should be the rule. If your job and income are secure, you might consider dipping into your cash cushion to make more profitable investments. But I recommend that you retain at least 40 percent of your assets in relatively risk-free and liquid instruments—surviving money market mutual funds and bank CDs, for example.

The money available to invest in stocks, for the sake of diversification and good management, could then go into stock mutual funds rather than into individual stocks. As we have seen, these funds offer a variety of investment options and specialties, and you can choose those that best suit your needs for income, growth, and safety. But the recovery of the market will be slow, and quick profits for the small investor are a thing of the past. Therefore, I suggest that you invest conservatively and for the long haul.

CHAPTER 10

Bonds

HOW DO BONDS BEHAVE during a depression? To some the answer is obvious: bonds consistently appreciate during a downturn as business activity declines and interest rates fall. This, while generally true, is not always the case during a depression, especially a great depression.

A bond is essentially an instrument of debt: the buyer of a bond lends a sum of money—equal to the par value of the bond—to its seller. This loan is made for a specified period, at the end of which the principal is returned to the buyer. In the interim, the buyer (who is the lender) receives regular and prespecified interest payments—referred to as coupon payments—on this loan. The bond itself specifies all the terms of the loan—the time to maturity, the size of the coupon payments, and the intervals at which these payments will be made.

Bonds are issued almost entirely by governments—federal, state, and local—and private corporations. To the individual investor their biggest attraction is the degree of safety they offer. Except when the issuer goes bankrupt before its maturation, a bond leaves the investor in no doubt as to his interest earnings and the duration for which the loan is "alive." However, this very inflexibility can turn against the investor, especially if he is holding a corporate bond. The rigidity of the terms of the loan does not allow the bondholder to participate in any growth that the company may experience, whereas a stockholder does participate in growth.

Although the safety of a bond is its most publicized and popular feature, there is one type of risk to which even the bondholder is vulnerable: the possibility of capital loss if the bond has to be cashed in before its maturity. Consider an investor who purchases a $10,000 bond which is to mature in five years and whose coupon payments represent an interest rate of 6 percent. Unfortunately, some financial emergency forces this investor to "cash in" (i.e., sell) his bond after only three years. During this period, interest rates have moved up to, say, a 10 percent return, and the investor can succeed in selling his 6 percent bond only if he is willing to accept less than $10,000 for it. Therefore, he is forced to accept a loss on his principal, i.e., a capital loss. This example also illustrates a general principle about the prices of bonds: *they move inversely with the interest rate*. Therefore, an investor who purchases a bond in a period of rising interest rates is vulnerable to the risk of capital loss if he has to sell it before maturity.

By the same token, a period of falling interest rates is risky to the issuer of the bond. When you sell a bond, you commit yourself to paying an interest rate for a certain period. If in the interim the rates come down, you still have to pay the old higher rate. This risk is especially great when the market rate is significantly above the historical norm, as was the case from 1979 to 1982. To mitigate this danger, the borrower frequently adds a "call-back" provision into his bonds, allowing him to redeem them at any time after a specified date, but before maturity. Prior to this date, the investor is protected from a premature call on his bond; but any time after, if interest rates plunge, the issuer can redeem (or call in) the bonds currently outstanding, and issue bonds of a similar par value at the lower rate of return prevailing currently. In return the investor is usually offered a "premium," e.g., one year's interest.

In recent years, the tremendous volatility of interest rates has actually made bonds a viable instrument of speculative gain. Recall that volatility in interest rates means a corresponding volatility in bond prices. However, the major draw of bonds still is the insurance they provide against vagaries of the market—a function they generally perform better than stocks.

Bonds can be found with maturities ranging anywhere from one to thirty years. Therefore an investor seeking out bonds for their safety features should be able to find a maturity matching his financial needs. Bond prices are usually quoted at 10 percent of their face value. For example, a bond quoted at 82.5 has a purchase price of $825. Bonds are most often found in denominations of $1,000 and $5,000. Exceptions to this rule are U.S. savings bonds, which sometimes go as low as $25, and zero-coupon bonds, which we shall discuss later.

Depending on the issuing agency, we can distinguish among three classes of bonds, each with its own inherent advantages and disadvantages. First, there are the bonds issued by the federal government, i.e., the Treasury and a few other designated federal agencies. Second, there are the municipal bonds issued by state and local governments. Finally, there are the corporate bonds issued by a large number of private corporations. Before exploring how bonds behave during a depression, let us see what properties various bond categories have.

Federal Government Securities

The most important among this class of securities are those issued by the Treasury Department to meet its short-

and long-term spending requirements. It is generally believed that the Treasury Department, because of its virtually unlimited powers to borrow money, can always
avoid bankruptcy. Therefore any bond issued by the
Treasury is considered to be about as riskless as any asset
can get, and forms the benchmark by which the riskiness
of all other assets is measured.

The Treasury puts out two types of bonds: Treasury
bonds and U.S. savings bonds. Treasury bonds are designed to meet the long-term borrowing needs of the
Treasury, and therefore usually bear maturities of ten to
thirty years. Whenever the federal government runs a
budget deficit, it has to be financed through borrowing, of
which Treasury bonds are the major instrument.

In addition to virtually guaranteeing the principal,
Treasury bonds also provide excellent protection against
capital losses that can occur with a premature call. Only
thirty-year T-bonds carry a call provision, and even on
those the provision cannot be exercised before twenty-five
years. Therefore, if the investor purchases a T-bond in a
period of high interest rates, he can "lock in" that rate for
a very long time. Thus, for sheer safety, Treasury bonds
are unbeatable. At the same time, if the investor chooses
to do so, when interest rates go down he can sell the bond
and reap any capital gains that accrue.

The interest on T-bonds is paid twice a year and tends
to rise with maturity. T-bonds can be purchased in denominations of $1,000, $5,000, $100,000 and $1 million.
The interest on T-bonds is not exempt from federal taxes
but is exempt from state and local taxes, a fact that makes
them attractive to investors residing in high-tax areas.

Another way the federal government borrows money
from the public is by issuing U.S. savings bonds, which
have traditionally been popular with small investors. Savings bonds, which usually bear a maturity of twelve years,
can be obtained in denominations as low as $50 and as
high as $10,000. Having first emerged into prominence

during the Second World War, savings bonds have always
been associated with patriotism, which has ensured a
steady demand for them over the years. In the 1970s,
however, the yield on these instruments dropped relative
to that from other bonds, and patriotism alone could not
shore up their sagging demand. In response, the Treasury
created a special class of savings bonds, the series EE. The
distinctive feature of this series is its variable yield. The
interest rate on the EE, unlike that on T-bonds, which
have a fixed rate, is adjusted every six months to reflect
the current yield on five-year Treasury notes. At the same
time, however, the Treasury guarantees the yield on these
bonds to be at least 6 percent if you hold them for five
years, irrespective of how interest rates fluctuate in the
interim.

The interest on EE bonds is not paid semiannually, but
instead accumulates until the time of maturity of the bond,
at which time it is returned along with the principal. As
with the T-bond, the yield on EE bonds is exempt from
state and local, but not federal, taxes. Although the series
EE is the only class of savings bonds being sold today, the
holders of EE bonds have access to another class of savings
bonds, called the series HH. Series HH bonds can be acquired only in exchange for at least $500 worth of EE
bonds. In contrast to EE bonds, HH bonds pay semi-
annual interest at a rate of 6 percent per year.

As Gary Klott notes, EE bonds, because of their interest
deferral, have an interesting tax implication.[1] One of the
added wrinkles of the current tax laws is that children
under fourteen with investment income exceeding $1,000
are liable to be taxed at the same rate as their parents.
Children over fourteen are taxed at their own rate. Now
suppose the parents are in the 33 percent bracket; the
child, provided he doesn't have other sources of invest-

---

[1] Gary Klott, *Personal Investing* (New York: Times Books, 1987), p. 134.

ment income, is likely to fall into the 15 percent tax bracket when he becomes fourteen. If the child's parents bought EE bonds in the child's name when he was five, by the time the bond matures, he will be seventeen. Even though the interest has been accruing over the years, he has to pay taxes on this cumulative amount at only 15 percent, instead of paying 33 percent on it through most of his childhood.

In addition to the tax break that they confer on a family's investment for children, series EE bonds are attractive for other reasons. Their issuance by the Treasury makes them virtually riskless, like T-bonds. The many small denominations in which they come may be more congenial to the small investor's budget. If held for a minimum of five years, the yield on EEs approaches the market rates. There are no commission charges for buying or selling these bonds, and the interest they pay is, of course, exempt from state and local taxes.

In addition to the U.S. Treasury, a number of other government-controlled and government-sponsored agencies enjoy congressional authority to issue their own bonds. These bonds also, for the most part, offer the tax exemptions (state and local) that T-bonds do; they are also well protected against premature redemption. However, unlike T-bonds, most such bonds are issued by agencies lacking the full credit of the federal government. Consequently they do bear a slight element of risk. Since it is very unlikely that any administration would court the serious loss of credibility that would accompany the forfeiture of any of these debts, the risk has so far been considered minimal. However, it does manifest itself as a perceptible premium in the interest rate paid by these bonds. Federal agency bonds also offer the investor a wide choice of maturities, ranging from one to thirty years.

One group of agencies issuing these bonds are those fully owned by the government—for example, the United States Postal Service, the Farmers Home Administration, and the Export-Import Bank (EXIM). The other group of such agencies are those that were once under government control through majority ownership of common stock, but are now in public hands. Among these are the Federal Home Loan Bank and the Federal National Mortgage Association. In addition, this group includes three major international sources of developmental aid: the World Bank, the Asian Development Bank, and the Inter-American Development Bank. These international agencies bear only an indirect guarantee from the federal government, via the obligations that member nations (the United States included) have with respect to meeting the debt obligations of these organizations.

When estimating his return from buying or selling these securities, the investor must allow for the commission costs, which usually range from $5 to $25. Furthermore, not all federal agency bonds are exempt from state and local taxes. The bonds issued by the Federal Home Loan Mortgage Corporation, the EXIM Bank, the Federal National Mortgage Association, the Farmers Home Administration, the Federal Housing Administration, and the Government National Mortgage Association are all subject to these taxes.

Traditionally, Treasury bonds have outranked federal agency securities in the eyes of the investor. The reason for this is not the difference in the risk factor; this difference is negligible and in the case of bonds issued by the EXIM Bank, the Farmers Home Administration, and the Government National Mortgage Association is nonexistent, as they are fully federally backed. The real reason is the difference in their liquidity. The market for Treasury bonds is larger and much more active than that for federal agency bonds, thus making Treasury bonds easier to sell.

Mortgage securities are a particular class of federal agency securities that deserve special mention. The basic idea underlying these securities is to bring to the ordinary investor the benefits of high interest rates that mortgages have been generating since the early 1970s—benefits that hitherto were enjoyed only by large banks.

Mortgage securities are simply those supported by an underlying portfolio of mortgages. Each security holder receives his share of the interest earnings generated by this portfolio. In essence, mortgage securities are like a mortgage-based mutual fund. What sets them apart is that the primary backer and organizer of this fund is the federal government. The most prominent mortgage security operation is run by the General National Mortgage Association, GNMA, or Ginnie Mae as it is commonly referred to. Ginnie Mae puts together a portfolio of mortgages that are fully insured by the Federal Housing Administration and the Veterans Administration, so that the principal of any contributor to this pool has so far been safe. Moreover, Ginnie Mae guarantees regular payment of the fixed interest to each security holder, even if some of the underlying mortgage payments have not been made on time. Finally, these securities, not surprisingly called Ginnie Maes, are fully backed by the credit and the credibility of the federal government.

At first sight, there appears to be a lot in common between Ginnie Maes and T-bonds. Both pay a fixed interest, and both experience price appreciation when interest rates fall. However, the similarity ends there. Ginnie Maes pay returns each month instead of every six months as T-bonds do. Further, the monthly payments from a Ginnie Mae consist not just of interest payments, but also of a portion of the principal, because this is the manner in which the underlying mortgages are paid off. This technicality has an important implication. In periods of low interest rates, homeowners may try to get rid of their high-interest loans early and refinance them at lower rates. Therefore, the Ginnie Maes start maturing much more rapidly. Thus if in a period of declining interest rates an investor bought a Ginnie Mae instead of a bond, he would find his asset expiring faster than he expected. The fluctuating lifespan of the Ginnie Mae does not allow him to lock in a high rate of return for a specific period, as a T-bond does. Ginnie Maes thus can miss out on the capital appreciation that accrues to T-bonds when interest rates decline.

Besides the Ginnie Mae, there are two other popularly used mortgage-based securities, one issued by the Federal Home Loan Mortgage Corporation, FHLMC or Freddie Mac, and the other by the Federal National Mortgage Association, FNMA or Fannie Mae. Both operate on the same principle as the Ginnie Mae, but with one important difference. The mortgage pools of these securities consist of conventional mortgages, not the FHA-insured or the VA-insured ones. The securities in these pools are covered by private mortgage insurance, with spillover losses being covered by the respective internal resources. In short, neither Freddie Mac nor Fannie Mae has the same unconditional government backing as Ginnie Mae, and their securities are, to that extent, riskier.

Because of the uncertainties in the maturity of Ginnie Maes, they traditionally offer a return that is a couple of percentage points above that of a T-bond. Freddie Macs and Fannie Maes offer even higher yields because of their additional risk. And unlike the interest on T-bonds, the yield on these mortgage-based securities is subject to state and local taxes.

Municipal Bonds

Municipal bonds, sometimes called munis, are the major borrowing instruments of state and local governments. Their traditional draw had been their exemption not only from state and local taxes but also from federal taxes. Taxable bonds, such as corporate bonds, would have to offer significantly higher yields merely to provide the same after-tax returns. However, the Tax Reform Act of

1986 has muddied the waters. While the munis still remain exempt from state and local taxes, not all of them are exempt from federal taxes. In fact, this act has stratified the municipal bond market according to whether the bonds are (1) fully exempt from federal taxes, (2) subject to the alternative "minimum tax," or (3) fully subject to the federal tax.

1. Bonds that are issued to finance regular governmental operations and to construct general infrastructural facilities such as roads, bridges, and schools are fully exempt from the federal tax. This category still accounts for a substantial segment of municipal bonds issued every year.

2. Municipal bonds that are issued to finance expenditures targeted toward a certain segment of society—a specific industrial development project, student loans, etc.—are subject not to a federal tax, but to an alternative minimum tax.

3. Bonds that are issued to finance such projects as sports stadiums and convention centers are fully subject to the federal tax. These are the so-called taxable municipal bonds.

Differences in their tax status are, of course, reflected in the yields offered by these three classes of municipal bonds. Another important difference among municipal bonds is in the source from which their interest and principal payments are met. Some securities are backed by general finances of the government; these so-called general obligation bonds are the securities for which the government will raise revenue by one means or another, the only constraint being that enough money is raised. In contrast, some bonds are supported only by a limited portion of the government's taxing power—the so-called limited-tax general obligation bonds, an extreme but not uncommon case being a special tax bond whose repayment is tied to one particular tax. In addition, there are revenue bonds, which are financed out of the revenues generated by the project for which the loan was taken, and industrial revenue bonds, whose repayment is financed by leasing out the newly constructed project to a private enterprise and using lease funds to meet bond repayment. Clearly the viability of an industrial revenue bond rests with the viability of the lessee.

Municipal bonds offer a number of attractions to the ordinary investor. As mentioned earlier, despite the new tax law, a large number of municipal bonds are still exempt from state, local, and federal taxes. They are shielded for at least ten years after issuance from premature calls. They are fairly liquid because of the heavy trading that occurs in these bonds. And finally, they offer excellent diversity, with many different maturities and terms.

However, within this class of bonds, there are varying degrees of risk. Revenue-financed bonds are subject to the risk that the project may not prove as lucrative as anticipated. Industrial revenue bonds could easily be hurt if the associated private enterprise fails to do well. Sometimes municipal bonds are privately insured, but this does not completely eliminate the risk from the loan. The private insurer itself could run into financial trouble.

An additional problem with municipal bonds these days is their labyrinthine tax treatment. With heavy investment in the munis, you can easily make a mistake in your tax return and be unexpectedly hit by a large tax bill from the IRS.

Corporate Bonds

Corporate bonds are usually considered the riskiest of the three categories of bonds. Even a bond from IBM carries some, albeit small, risk of the loss of principal. Not surprisingly, then, corporate bonds also offer the most attractive returns, and, needless to say, the more attractive the return, the greater the risk.

Clearly the single most important prerequisite for investing in a corporate bond is the creditworthiness of the issuing company, and the task of assessing this creditworthiness is complex and formidable. Fortunately, the individual investor does not have to undertake it on his own. There are independent credit-rating services, such as Moody's and Standard & Poor's, that rate the credit risk of different bonds, with brief descriptions of the pluses and minuses of the issuing corporations. The S&P ratings are AAA, AA, A, BBB, BB, and so on; the equivalent Moody's ratings are Aaa, Aa, A, Baa, Ba, and so on. Any bond with an S&P rating of BB or below is less than solid and ought to be regarded as definitely speculative. In fact, the conservative investor would do well not to go below the As in normal times and AAAs during periods of turmoil.

Apart from the risk of losing principal, there is a less dire, but perhaps more common, threat of capital loss with bonds bought at premium—the threat of a premature call, which is the greatest with corporate bonds. Utility companies usually reserve the right to call back after just five years, and industries do it within ten years. The premium of one year's interest payment that sometimes goes with a recall to sweeten the deal may not prove to be adequate compensation if interest rates fall rapidly.

With so many strikes against them, why are corporate bonds still so popular? Mainly because the premium they pay over the more staid T-bonds is large enough to make them attractive. Corporate bonds, especially of an AA or AAA variety, offer the best of two worlds—considerable safety along with a genuine chance to make a significant capital gain. This is because prices of corporate bonds tend to be much more volatile than those of, say, T-bonds.

Moreover, corporate bonds are highly liquid, a prerequisite not only for making a profit on their sale, but also for a timely resale, if necessary.

Zero-Coupon Bonds

There are some bonds that pay no interest until redemption. They are called zero-coupon bonds and are offered by the federal government, brokerage houses, and some corporations. Most of the zeros are very long-term bonds, and since they pay no interest until maturity, they sell at a deep discount. They are most suitable for retirement accounts, but they are highly volatile, more so than other bonds of comparable risk. Moreover, in troubled times, an investor should not be locked into very long-term investments, which may not come to fruition. Long-term zeros, regardless of their source, carry special risk at this time.

Advice to Bondholders

Even in normal times, bonds are safer than stocks and stock-related investments. This certainly holds true for the near future. Among the various types of bonds available, I suggest you go with AAA corporate bonds, especially those of cash-rich companies, which, in descending order, are Ford, IBM, Exxon, Shell Oil, and Chrysler. I have selected these companies not only because of their huge cash hoards, but also because of their low long-term debt relative to liquid assets.

Another important question is when to buy. I expect interest rates to stay flat in 1988 and move up in 1989. The outlook for 1990, the first year of the coming depression, is extremely uncertain. You can start buying bonds after the middle of 1989, and become more aggressive in 1990, especially if there is a free fall of the dollar at the same time. The perfect time to buy bonds would be after the dollar has reached its bottom, which is likely to occur in 1990. Even if the stock market crashes, AAA bonds, especially of cash-rich concerns, will be safe.

What about government bonds? They will not be as risk-less in the future as they have been so far. Between the AAA municipals and Treasury bonds, I prefer the munic-ipal bonds. The federal government may well have diffi-culty meeting all its obligations in the years ahead. Among the municipal bonds, the strongest are those issued by nonenergy and nonfarm states.

How do bonds typically behave during an economic cri-sis? A look at the past suggests that high-grade bonds gen-erally appreciate during the first two years of a depression, then depreciate for as long as six months before appreci-ating again and following the same pattern. Remember once again that nothing moves in a straight line, so all you can analyze is the trend path of a variable. Low-grade bonds generally depreciate, at least in the first half of a depression, as investors abandon them rapidly in their flight toward quality.

All in all, bond prices will stay flat in 1988 and fall in 1989. In 1990 they could fall further, but in 1991, high-grade bonds will rise, whereas low-grade issues and those belonging to *large* debtors could plunge. Following 1991, the high-grade issuers could continue to climb after a minor fall over a few months, all the way up to 1994. Eventually even the low-grade bonds of surviving compa-nies could recover their value as interest rates continue their falling trend. As the economy recovers, sometime after 1994, bond values will begin to decline as interest rates start to rise. All this, of course, could change if (1) the economic system is drastically overhauled in accor-dance with the reforms suggested in the final chapter of this book, or (2) the government is forced by the depres-sion to alter the terms applying to its long-term bonds.

During the 1930s many local governments defaulted on

their debt, but later honored their obligations in whole or in part. Many states did the same thing during the depression of the 1840s. The point is that governmental default on bonds is not unheard of during a depression. In view of this, my advice is that you should sell your bonds by the presidential election in November 1988, and then gradually buy AAA bonds of cash-rich companies or state and local governments in the second half of 1989. Once the recovery begins you might also buy shares in a mutual fund which invests in top-rated corporate bonds, thus ensuring greater diversification than you would have if you purchased individual bonds. And for both diversification and tax savings, you can purchase shares in a mutual fund that specializes in municipal bonds. One of the largest mutual fund families, Fidelity Investments, offers a number of "triple-tax-free" municipal bond mutual funds (free of federal, state, and local taxes) for residents of California, Connecticut, New York, New Jersey, Massachusetts, Michigan, Minnesota, Ohio, Pennsylvania, and Texas.

Corporate and municipal bonds are an attractive investment, however, only during periods of declining interest rates. Once the economy has begun to recover in 1994 and interest rates are on the rise, you can diversify your portfolio into mutual bond funds.

CHAPTER 11

Real Estate

EVER SINCE the Second World War, real estate has been the most popular form of investment, not just in America but also in much of the rest of the world. Owning a home is everybody's dream. During the 1970s, real estate provided a financial bonanza through dramatic price appreciation and handsome tax advantages. However, the market cooled down in the 1980s, largely because of a decline in the inflation rate and sweeping tax reforms. And in light of the coming depression, owning real estate could become a liability rather than an asset. The question is, what can you do now to lessen that liability? Should you sell? Rent rather than own? And is there any form of real estate investment that will be relatively depression-proof?

Homeownership

"My home is my castle," the saying goes. This was true in the past, is true today, and will perhaps be true in the future. In fact, in the coming depression, your home could really become a castle, a safe and solid haven against social unrest and crime, which soar during economic crises. If you own a home, provided it is affordable, you will always have a roof over your head at a time when thousands will be homeless.

Another advantage of owning your own home is that a part of your monthly mortgage payment goes toward equity, slowly increasing your stake. If you rent, your monthly payments go into your landlord's pocket. Moreover, rents can rise, especially in crowded cities or during periods of severe inflation, whereas your monthly mortgage remains constant, provided you have a fixed-rate loan. True, if property taxes rise, your residential costs will also rise; but so will rents, as landlords usually pass such taxes on their tenants. In a depression, however, property taxes are unlikely to increase.

With the passage of the Tax Reform Act of 1986, home-ownership became virtually the only tax shelter left for most people. It is unique in this respect. For most of you, the interest on your mortgage is the main deduction from your taxable income. Interest on other purchases and the variety of tax shelters available before 1986 either can no longer be used as deductions or are being phased out. Thus owning your residence offers a tax benefit which most other assets lack. Moreover, the appreciated value of your home qualifies you for a home equity loan, which could allow you, for example, to consolidate and pay off your existing debts at a lower interest rate than that of most credit card loans, automobile loans, and the like. Granted, a home equity loan is itself a form of debt, but used wisely it could help now and in the hard times to come, not only because interest rates are low, but because the interest is tax-deductible as well. Pending legislation indicates that up to $100,000 in interest payments will be tax-deductible.

Yet another advantage of homeownership is the option of renting out part of your home as a separate room or apartment. The added income could be a lifesaver in hard times. It may even be worth your while to make a few improvements now to create a rental unit.

Throughout America, home prices have sharply risen above their levels in the 1950s and 1960s. In some regions such as the East Coast and the West Coast, the appreciation has exceeded 1,000 percent. Annual gains were especially strong during the 1970s because of soaring inflation, and in some parts of the two regions just mentioned the gains continued well into the 1980s. But the real question is, will the past repeat itself in the future? To many, the answer is obviously yes. To me, however, it depends on your time horizon.

In the long run, perhaps home prices will continue to rise. After all, we are living on an unexpanding planet, while the world population grows every day, increasing the scarcity of land and housing. Inflation also seems to be built into the American and the world economy, and that alone should force a continued jump in residential values. I have no quarrel with the kernel of these arguments.

For the short run, however, I have a gloomy view of home values. During depressions, home prices tumble in most areas, especially in small-to-medium-size cities. In large cities, where good locations have already been taken, home prices may drop no more than 10 percent, but in smaller towns, they can plunge by as much as 50 percent. Even in crowded areas, expensive houses can depreciate sharply.

Texas provides a preview of what can happen to home values during a depression. Throughout the 1970s and until 1984, residential property there boomed in new construction as well as value. But since then, because of a severe drop in the price of oil, the entire state has gone into an economic tailspin, with home prices declining by as much as 40 percent in Houston, San Antonio, and west Texas. The same thing has happened to expensive homes in Dallas in spite of its well-diversified industry with only minor dependence on the energy sector.

In the long run, homeownership makes sense, but in the immediate future it does not. If you do not own your own home, there is no reason to buy a residence now, because you could get the same property at a much lower price in the 1990s. House purchase at this time will also make most of you illiquid. You may have to sink all your savings into the down payment to qualify for a mortgage loan. In fact, many Americans today cannot even qualify for a mortgage for a first home, because home prices in most areas of the country have increased faster than incomes. By the beginning of 1988 it became clear that the percentage of Americans who own homes is actually declining—for the first time since the Great Depression of the 1930s. Even if you can qualify for a mortgage now, you may lose your job in the future and not be able to maintain your monthly payments. The mortgage holder could foreclose on your property and sell it at a low price, and your savings sunk in the down payment could be wiped out.

Liquidity is the key to surviving depressions. And a home, which may take some time to sell and may even have to be sold at a loss, is not a liquid investment. You have to have the cushion of cash savings while going into the 1990s. That is why renting makes more sense at this time. Of course, if money is no problem, you can buy a residence. Look for safety and security today, with the expectation of a gradual appreciation in value at some time in the future.

Should You Sell Your House?

What if you already own a house? Not buying a house because of the expected depression is a much easier decision to make than selling your current residence. If you rent, the decision to postpone homeownership is very simple. But selling your house for fear of the coming depression is another matter. What if the crisis fails to materialize? You will have uprooted yourself for nothing, and whatever profit you make on the sale of your house could be cut by the cost of moving.

Emotional factors are also involved. Probably you and your family are attached to your home. You like the neighborhood, the school system, and the familiarity that comes with a long stay at one place. Selling your house for strictly financial considerations is an onerous decision—one that you and your family can make only after much thought. But there is one case where the decision is easy. Some people, fooled by the beguiling prosperity of the 1980s, bought expensive homes with high fixed-rate mortgages. A large portion of their take-home income now goes into the monthly mortgage, leaving next to nothing for saving. If you fall into this category, I suggest you immediately sell your house and move into a place with rent lower than your present mortgage payments. Give yourself a chance to survive the 1990s. The house sale will make you more liquid from the recovery of your equity and enable you to save more. You will no longer have to pay property taxes and home maintenance and repair costs, enabling you to save even more.

If you are reluctant to sell your home, you should consider refinancing a high fixed-rate mortgage (above 10 percent) into a variable mortgage by the end of 1989, when lending institutions will still be after new business and when your credit ratings will still be intact. Mortgage rates are likely to plunge in the 1990s, and with a variable rate your monthly payments could decline.

Other alternatives to selling your house are lease-back or equity-sharing arrangements. With the lease-back option, it is possible for a homeowner to sell his or her house to an investor and still live in it by leasing it back at an affordable rent. In an equity-sharing arrangement an investor becomes, in effect, a co-owner of your residence, assuming the burden of your monthly mortgage and thereby permitting you to live in your home rent-free. Upon the homeowner's death, or after an agreed-upon number of years, the co-owner is entitled to sell the property and obtain all or part of the capital gain. The equity-sharing option, however, is mostly for older people living on a fixed income.

Another consideration in your decision to sell your house is the cost of renting in your location relative to your monthly mortgage. In crowded cities like New York and Los Angeles, apartment rents are very high. If you bought your house years ago when interest rates were low, your monthly payments may be substantially less than the rent of an equivalent property. Even if you're willing to live in humbler quarters, the rent may be higher than your current monthly payment. In this case, you may well decide to keep your house.

In areas where house prices have fallen sharply, rents have also dramatically fallen, so much that they are far below monthly mortgages. In that case, of course, it will pay you to sell your house immediately, provided you can do so. For example, in many cities in Texas, Florida, and other areas hit hard by the current slump in the energy and construction sectors, apartments lease for much less than monthly mortgages. But it is also more difficult to sell your house in such localities.

While the decision to sell your house for strictly financial considerations is rather difficult to make at this time, you should at least postpone any remodeling you might have planned. There is no point in adding improvements to your property unless you are sure property values will hold in the near future. But don't confuse home improvements with creating a rental unit in your home or with necessary repairs and maintenance, which ordinarily should not be postponed.

All in all, you are the best judge of your individual situation. If you are comfortably placed, have a low mortgage, and also have sufficient savings or liquid assets, you should stay put and do nothing about your residence. But if your mortgage is large, your job future is risky or uncertain, or you have a large amount of equity sunk in your house and have very illiquid assets, then you should consider selling your house, renting at a lower monthly rate, and depositing your cash in safe banks until you decide what to do with it.

Rental Property

Next to homeownership, most people participate in real estate by owning rental property. The participation takes various forms. You may lease a room in your home, own a two-family residence and live in one side and lease the other, own a small or large apartment complex, or have a vacation home you use part of the year and lease out for the rest.

The advantages of owning a rental property are clear. You have rental income and a chance to make a profit from the sale of your property at a higher price than you paid. Until 1986 there were also huge tax benefits associated with real estate ownership. With the passage of the Tax Reform Act of 1986, however, they have been sharply scaled down, and for the wealthiest investors they amount to nothing.

If your adjusted gross income is below $150,000, the tax benefits associated with rental property, though not as large as before, can still be considerable. You can deduct all the costs of being in the real estate business, including depreciation of your property, from rental income, and even use losses of up to $25,000 a year to offset your income from other sources. The offset is 100 percent if your adjusted income is no more than $100,000, but partial if your income is between $100,000 and $150,000. Beyond $150,000, no deductions are allowed. Most rental properties generate smaller losses than the $25,000 cap, so the cap is generous. But it is reduced 50 cents for each dollar of your income exceeding $100,000, so that for those with adjusted incomes of $150,000 or more, the rental-loss offset drops to zero.

You must meet another requirement to claim rental deductions: you must actively manage your property. However, this requirement is easy to satisfy. All you need to do is to approve new tenants, decide on repairs, and approve rental contracts. You can still hire a management firm to look after your property.

Even in the best of times, there are a lot of headaches associated with rental properties, especially if you actively manage them yourself. Collecting rents, making repairs, and finding tenants are only a few of the many chores, and hiring professionals to do the job can be expensive. With some properties, rents barely cover the monthly mortgage payment and property taxes. On top of that, some cities have rent controls.

In a depression, property values fall sharply, and so do rents. It is true that people have to live somewhere, but those without jobs sometimes cannot afford housing and many move in with relatives, sharply reducing the demand for rental units. Other jobless people simply become homeless.

Just as I have advised against buying a house at this time, I certainly advise against buying rental property now. The main draw of such investments used to be a roaring inflation and tax benefits. Both have been reduced. Inflation has declined sharply in the 1980s and is expected to fall even further in the 1990s, whereas tax benefits have also come down, not only because of a cap over losses, but also because of tightened depreciation rules. In the past, you could write off your property over just nineteen years and use the accelerated depreciation method, which increased your deductions in earlier years of ownership. Now you must use a straight-line method to

depreciate the cost of residential property in equal installments over 27.5 years.

If you don't own a rental property now, don't buy one.
If you own a rental property now, my general advice for
most of you is to sell it and increase your liquidity. However, an inexpensive conversion of a room in your home
into a rental unit does not fall in the category of a separate
rental property. The decision to sell the former should be
based on the cost of your mortgage relative to your income
and savings.

If you own a rental property which is already paid off
or has a monthly mortgage substantially below its rental
income, and you also have enough savings or liquid assets,
then you should keep your property in the interest of
diversification. If your monthly mortgage payment exceeds or barely covers your rental income and other expenses, you should sell your property.

Land

During the inflationary 1970s, numerous people borrowed huge sums to speculate on farmland. With the decline of inflation, many dreams of quick profits have
turned into busts and a large number of investors have
been wiped out. "When people ponder the various paths
to riches, land is usually at or near the top of their list,"
says Gary Klott, financial writer for *The New York Times.*
"But while success stories abound in the world of real estate," he continues, "so do horror stories—and not just the
stories of unwary investors purchasing swampland from a
fast-talking hustler."[1]

Land investing is a risky business in the best of times.

[1] Gary Klott, *Personal Investing* (New York: Times Books, 1987), p. 389.

People buy land in the hope that some new development
will occur near their parcel of property, which will then
zoom in value because a developer, city, or company will
want it badly enough to pay a pretty price. It has happened before. But for every success story, there are many,
many failures. Location is the main factor in the price of
land. But well-located land is already high-priced, and that
makes it risky. If the economy falters, the price can drop
quickly. Even when recovery begins, land prices do not
recover quickly. And land is the most illiquid of all investments. You can't even depreciate it, because it is not supposed to suffer wear and tear.

Land does not require a big down payment, as a large
portion of the cost of purchase can be financed by a mortgage. You may also be able to rent out your land for cultivation. Those who have the resources to wait patiently
and see their land appreciate over time are the best suited
for this investment. The long-term future for this type of
property is bright, because its scarcity increases with surg-
ing population. But in depressed times, land values can
drop by heartbreaking amounts. Moreover, the rentals, if
any, from land are much smaller than its maintenance
costs. Apart from the monthly mortgage payment, there
are property taxes, normal maintenance, liability insurance, etc. And when you sell your parcel of land, you have
to pay a commission to the sales agent of 3 to 10 percent.

As I advise about other types of real estate, I advise
against investing in land as well. There is no reason to get
into it now. If you already own some land and don't farm
it actively, you should sell it as quickly as possible. If you
are a farmer, you should consider selling a part of your
property. Farmers usually suffer a lot from falling commodity prices during a depression. Any money that you
now make from a land sale could come in handy in the
near future. It will be very difficult for you to sell land in
the early 1990s.

Some people think that buying land at this time would

be a good investment, so that as a last resort they could turn to farming in the future depression. In the meantime, they will learn how to farm. The idea does have some merit, but a better strategy would be to lease a parcel of land now and practice cultivation on it. You could buy the property later when land values plunge.

Real Estate Investment Trusts

Real estate investment trusts (REITs) are one of the easiest and cheapest ways to invest in real estate. They are like mutual funds, gathering money from thousands of investors to purchase income-producing properties or to make mortgage loans. They are what has been called the stock market's answer to real estate investments.[2] In other words, REITs can be bought and sold like stocks on various exchanges. This makes them unique among real estate investments, which are usually very illiquid. Apart from their high liquidity, REITs also enjoy some special tax benefits. Unlike other corporations, they don't pay any federal taxes, provided at least 95 percent of the profits are passed along to shareholders.

REITs first became popular in the 1960s, but suffered greatly during the 1973–75 recession, when real estate values plummeted. Several REITs went out of business at that time. Still, more than a hundred exist today, and at a time of rising property values and rents, they are a popular investment.

There are three types of REITs—equity trusts, mortgage trusts, and a hybrid called equity-mortgage trusts. Equity trusts buy income-producing properties, using funds from their shareholders as well as from their lenders to acquire office complexes, shopping malls, hotels,

[2]Ibid., p. 402.

apartments, duplexes, and similar rental properties. Their main sources of income are rents and capital gains from appreciation when the property is sold. Mortgage trusts, by contrast, are like lending institutions. They make money by making short-term construction loans and first mortgage loans on a long-term basis. Some trusts take an equity interest in the construction projects they finance in order to participate in possible capital gains upon sale of the property. Hybrid trusts, of course, perform the functions of both equity and mortgage trusts.

REITs are an inexpensive way for you to invest in real estate. You can buy some REIT stock for as little as $4 a share. But management fees tend to be high, running from 10 to 25 percent of your investment. This, apart from the high risk, is a major drawback. While REITs do offer the liquidity of stocks, they lack the tax advantages of other real estate investments. Even if your adjusted income is less than $100,000, you have no tax shelter losses from the purchase of REIT shares. Of course, if your shares fall in value, you can deduct up to $3,000 of losses from your other income.

With the decline in real estate values, rentals, new construction, and home buying that will inevitably accompany a depression, REITs are not a sound investment. The time to get into REITs, as into other real estate investments, will be the mid-1990s, when the depression will have seen its bottom. As for now, I suggest you sell your REIT shares.

Real Estate Limited Partnerships

Another way to participate in real estate is to buy interest in a real estate limited partnership (RELP). RELPs function in the same way as REITs, except that they are not traded on stock exchanges. In terms of tax consequences, the two concepts are more or less the same, but RELPs investing in low-income housing and historic rehabilitation projects can pass on their losses to their partners and other investors. These are the only categories of real estate investment that now offer tax shelter losses to investors, whether working individually or through a partnership.

Those who organize the RELP are called general partners. They set up a project, formulate its prospectus, acquire and manage the properties, and solicit investors, who are called "passive" investors, uninvolved in the day-to-day chores of property management. Like REITs, RELPs can invest in income-yielding properties, mortgage loans, or both. Investors get a share of rental income and any capital gains realized from the sale of properties. But they are also responsible for losses in proportion to their investment. Sometimes RELPs borrow money to buy properties. If the loans are nonrecourse loans, you are not personally liable for them; it they are recourse loans, you arc liablc. Make sure your RELP does not take recourse loans; otherwise you may end up with large losses if the project sours.

RELPs involved with low-income housing do offer tax shelter losses up to $25,000 to investors with adjusted incomes up to $200,000. For each dollar of income above that level, sheltered income falls by 50 cents, until the tax loss is reduced to zero at an income level of $250,000.

For historic rehabilitation projects, tax shelter loss depends on the type of building involved in renovation. The benefit is in the form of a tax credit that varies from 10 percent to 20 percent of eligible costs. There is no requirement with either shelter that you be active in the low-income or restoration project to qualify for the $25,000 deduction. All you need to do in these cases, unlike when you are a landlord, is to invest your money.

How sound are these investments? Even in good times, they carry huge risks. Mary Calhoun, quoted in *Money* magazine in December 1986, says that "in eight years as a Merrill Lynch broker, I never sold a limited partnership that made money."[3] RELPs may make general partners rich from their high fees and tax-sheltered losses. But for the investor, financial expert Andrew Tobias calls them "severely limited partnerships" or "paper castles."[4] I wouldn't recommend them to you even in a booming economy, much less under the looming threat of a depression.

Real estate values will be among the hardest hit in the 1990s. Generally speaking, if the cash cushion you are going to need for the years ahead is tied up in real estate, my advice is to sell while property values are still high. Otherwise, sit tight and ride out the storm.

The time for investing, or reinvesting, in real estate will come when the overall economy begins to recover. But don't buy a house or rental property that you cannot really afford, even if the sale price seems attractively low. The down payment could cut into your liquidity, and mortgage payments, even at moderate rates of interest, have to be paid every month regardless of your other expenses and obligations.

Moreover, if you invest in a rental property, you should be confident of a strong positive cash flow in which rental income exceeds taxes and utility, maintenance, and mortgage expenses (without even accounting for depreciation). You don't want to find yourself caught in a situation where a tenant's failure to pay the rent could push you to the edge of bankruptcy before you can evict him. Economic recovery in the real estate sector of our economy will be slow, so invest conservatively for value, safety, and future appreciation.

---

[3] Also quoted in Andrew Tobias, *The Only Investment Guide You'll Ever Need* (New York: Simon & Schuster, 1987), p. 163.
[4] Ibid., pp. 163, 170.

CHAPTER 12

Precious Metals and Gemstones

PRECIOUS METALS and gemstones have been a store of value for people for thousands of years. Until paper money was invented and stocks, bonds, and related assets came along, precious metals and gemstones were a popular way of saving for the future. Because of their glitter and long history, such investments have acquired a mystique of their own. Their prices are set not only by rational calculations related to their industrial use but also by psychological and emotional factors.

But how safe are precious metals and gemstones as investments for the troubled years ahead? Let's look at how great depressions have affected the prices of precious metals and gemstones in the past, and how the looming calamity is likely to affect them in the near future.

Diamonds

Most of the precious metals, like any commodity, have some industrial usage, but some are in demand much more than others. Diamonds come in the category of gemstones rarely in demand by industries. Their prices depend purely on their quality and the ability of the people to afford them. They are a good hedge against inflation, when nominal incomes generally soar. Super-rich people also buy them to hedge against political and economic risks. But they are not a popular hedge against calamity. That is why when inflation declines, diamond values sharply depreciate.

South Africa supplies about 80 percent of the world's new production of uncut diamonds. Political unrest in that country could quickly choke off new production, but since new supplies are limited anyway, a production cutoff is not likely to have much impact on diamond prices. Inflation is their main determining factor. And since the decade of the 1990s is likely to be a period of overall price stability, diamond prices are likely to drop in the future.

The 1970s were the peak decade for diamonds; they appreciated year after year. But then came the recession in the early 1980s and the diamond bubble burst. The price of this rare gemstone has still not fully recovered from that damper.

Still, if you want to invest in diamonds, you should be very careful about where you shop. Buy only from a reputable dealer, one who will buy the diamond back from you at the original price. Buy only one-to-three-carat diamonds, of high clarity grade ranging from D to H, and with finely cut proportions. If you are making a large investment, then have the gem appraised independently and ask the dealer for a certificate issued by the Gemological Institute of America to evaluate the quality of the gemstone. Gemstones of value should, of course, be insured and carefully safeguarded at home or in a bank.

Gold

Throughout the world, gold has been the most popular hedge against uncertainty and calamity for thousands of years. Our planet, after all, has not been a panorama of peace. As far back as records go, there have been wars, revolutions, pestilence, inflations, depressions, earthquakes, and other disturbances. At such times, gold is generally recognized and accepted as a valuable medium of exchange.

The price of everything is determined by supply and demand. But in the case of gold, supply is a minor player. This precious metal has been mined for thousands of years, but only a small fraction of its annual production is consumed by industry, the rest going into jewelry, coins, or bullion bars. As a result, a huge stock of gold has built up over time. Annual production is about 600 million ounces, which is minuscule in relation to its total stock spread over the world. Even if output were to jump suddenly in the future, it would hardly affect its supply.

Most of the volatility in gold's prices is caused by variations on the side of demand, which is sensitive mainly to inflation, interest rates, and uncertainty. Gold tends to move up with inflation or with fears of inflation, and to move down with the dissipation of such fears. That is why during recessions, when inflation generally declines, gold depreciates in value. This suggests that gold would take a beating during a depression, which is usually deflationary. There is some validity to this argument.

But depressions also create uncertainty and unrest, which nourish the value of the yellow metal. In depressions, therefore, two opposing forces interact on the price of gold: deflation tends to lower it and uncertainty to raise it. A falling dollar in foreign exchange markets, by contrast, spurs inflationary expectations and, therefore, also tends to raise the price of gold.

How is gold likely to behave in the coming depression?

In the 1990s, inflation would certainly fall and might even give way to moderate deflation. This, along with falling demand for gold jewelry, would tend to lower the price of gold. But the coming depression will most likely be the worst in history, and is bound to spawn social unrest and political unheavals, both of which are likely to boost the demand for and hence the price of gold.

I personally believe that initially, as stocks crash in 1989 or 1990 and a recession sets in, gold could depreciate in value. But as the downturn becomes a depression by the end of 1991, gold will gradually appreciate, peaking by 1994 or 1995, when the world economy will begin its slow recovery.

Gold has been used as a hedge against calamity for thousands of years. "The beauty of gold," as Rabbit Angstrom remarked in John Updike's novel, "is, it loves bad news."[1] But the news has to be really bad and long-lasting before people will shun their customary caution, abandon interest-bearing assets, and run after gold. The metal does not, after all, yield any return, is not as liquid as money, and costs something to store.

My advice is that you should gradually get into gold as soon as possible, but only as a hedge against calamity. If the coming depression turns out to be inflationary, as some people suggest, your gold holding will soar. If the downturn turns out to be moderately deflationary, gold will at least hold its value, while most other assets will sharply depreciate.

In the 1920s, the government fixed the price of gold at $20 per ounce; but as the depression set in, the price in the black market began to rise and people began to hoard the metal. In 1934, President Roosevelt barred Americans from holding gold but set its price realistically at $35 per ounce. Gold hoarders made a huge profit. The price rose even though production in America rose by 11 percent.

[1] John Updike, *Rabbit Is Rich* (New York: Knopf, 1981).

The gold market was deregulated, so to speak, in 1971, and its price rose quickly from $35 to $200 per ounce in 1974. It then dropped to a low of $103 in 1976. Thanks to roaring inflation, gold soared to a historic high of $875 in January 1980, but then dropped, as quickly as it had risen, to a low of $284 in 1984. At the time of this writing, it was selling in the $450 range. As the 1980s show, gold is a volatile metal and a speculative investment. Thus I don't recommend gold for speculation, but only as a hedge against future disaster.

There are a variety of ways in which you can buy gold. You can buy it outright as bullion and coins, or indirectly through the purchase of gold certificates, gold-mining stocks, and gold mutual funds. Gold coins are perhaps the most popular form of owning gold today. Their popularity has surged in the 1980s as America, Japan, and Australia have joined South Africa, Canada, Austria, Mexico, and Hungary in the minting venture. These coins have no collector value. Their price is strictly linked to their gold content and its "fineness." In general, I would stay away from rare or numismatic gold coins, which appreciate in value only during inflationary times.

For U.S. investors, the best gold coin may be the American Eagle, which is legal tender and might be exempt from sales tax in some states. National pride also makes it attractive to Americans. The Eagle comes in four sizes—one ounce, half ounce, quarter ounce, and one-tenth of an ounce. Like the South African Krugerrand, the coin with the largest global circulation, the American coin is 91.67 percent pure gold, which fades before the Canadian Maple Leaf with purity of 99.99 percent. Still, the two trade at the same price in the New York coin market, an indication of America's preference for its own version.

For a small quantity of gold, I suggest you go with the coin. For a larger quantity, you may look toward bullion, which comes in sizes varying from one ounce to four-hundred-ounce bars. But bars can be cumbersome to store and expensive to sell, because you have to have them assayed to assure the buyer of their fineness.

You can buy gold, in coins or bullion, from a variety of dealers, including banks, brokers, and jewelry stores. Look in the Yellow Pages for gold dealers. You may want to buy gold from out-of-state dealers to avoid the sales tax, which can sharply add to your cost. Use a "sight draft" through a bank, if you order by mail. Upon its shipment to the bank, the bank simultaneously hands you the gold and the dealer the money. If possible, you should rent a safe deposit box from the same bank to store your purchase. You should inquire of the bank if it will store and insure your purchase, and keep in mind that the fee may be high.

The most convenient way to get into the glitter of gold is to buy a gold certificate from a reputable dealer. Here the financial health of the dealer is very important. A gold certificate represents a certain amount of gold that the dealer stores for you in a vault. There are no assaying costs or local sales taxes. You simply cash your certificate with the same dealer whenever you are ready to sell. I suggest you choose a large bank from my list of safe banking institutions and ask if it will sell you a certificate. The seller, of course, charges a fee of about 3 percent and an annual storage charge of 1 percent of the purchase price.

Another way to own gold is to buy shares of the companies engaged in gold mining. Many such operations are located in South Africa, which is currently in social and political tumult. These companies, in spite of their higher dividends, should be avoided. Better choices are among non-African companies such as Newmont Mining, Cambell Red Lake, Homestake, and Dome Mining, traded on the New York Stock Exchange, or Echo Bay and Giant Yellowknife, traded on the American Exchange. Be careful here, because many gold stocks are overpriced with hefty price/earnings ratios. Gold shares move up or down with gold prices, but at a faster pace. This is because stock values normally anticipate company profits, which move faster than the product price, as costs, in the short run, are more or less stable.

Mutual funds are another way to invest in gold. A number of them specialize in gold shares. These funds offer the advantage of diversification in a number of gold issues and occasionally pay dividends.

One question that still remains is *when* to buy gold. As I stated earlier, I expect gold to lose its value in the earliest stages of the coming depression and to regain its value or even appreciate as the crisis endures and deepens. Even so, I recommend a gradual accumulation of gold as soon as possible. Don't wait until 1990, because the price could rise sooner than you expect; it could also fall, but it is very hard to time your purchase perfectly.

By the end of 1989, 20 percent of your investment portfolio should be in gold coins, bullions, or certificates. If the stock market crashes in 1989 or 1990, then a depression is sure to follow. That will be the time to buy gold shares and surviving gold mutual funds, because many such stocks could initially plummet.

Silver

Silver is often called poor man's gold, for two reasons. First, it's much more affordable than gold, and second, its price is said to fluctuate with the price of gold. Yet silver has sufficient qualities of its own to warrant separate treatment.

Like gold, silver is a good hedge against inflation; but unlike gold, it's not a good hedge against depression, because silver has many commercial applications. Its price, therefore, is determined not only by inflationary expectations, interest rates, and the foreign exchange value of the dollar, but also by industrial demand. Moreover, the price of silver has moved eratically since the early 1970s, and the gold-to-silver price ratio has swung wildly between

15:1 and 60:1 during the 1980s. So much for the silver-to-gold linkage.

Silver's main industrial use is in photography, which, being a luxury good, suffers during recessions and depressions. Social tensions, of course, spur the demand for silver; but this may not be enough to overcome the falling demand for the metal in industries. Paradoxically, then, during depressions gold appreciation may be coupled with silver depreciation. Between 1929 and 1933, while the value of gold production soared by 50 percent, that of silver production plunged by 33 percent. Something similar should happen again in the 1990s.

Silver is not likely to be a good hedge against the coming crisis. Still, if you want to invest in silver, you have the same options available as with gold, namely silver bars, coins, certificates, mining stocks, and mutual funds. With silver, bars are preferable to coins, because coins sell at a hefty premium above the market value of their silver content. The United States also mints the American Eagle silver coin. If there is a currency collapse within America —which is unlikely—then the new silver coins, as in the past, could become a means of exchange. Some people buy them just for this reason, but the scenario is very farfetched. At the end of 1987, silver was priced at about $7 per ounce, but the American coin was marked up 20 percent at $8.40—a sizable premium. However, for a thousand-ounce Comex silver bar, the premium is only 5 cents per ounce.

You can buy silver certificates from a safe bank or dealer in the same way you buy a gold certificate. As for silver-mining stocks or mutual funds, they are even worse performers during depressions, because silver is largely a by-product of the production of other metals, such as zinc, copper, and lead. The demand for these three metals and hence their prices sharply drop during severe economic contractions, and bring silver shares down with them.

Platinum

Platinum, because of the extreme volatility of its price, is a fit instrument only for experts, not for amateurs. South Africa supplies the bulk of the world's annual platinum production, which, at 3.3 million ounces, is minuscule relative to annual gold production, 620 million ounces. Like silver, platinum, also called white gold, has commercial applications, mostly in jewelry and catalytic converters in automobiles. But owing to the low level of annual output, platinum's price can swing wildly over rumors. With South Africa in turmoil, platinum can hardly be a safe haven. In 1987, prices initially soared, but later fell 30 percent before closing at $460 per ounce at year's end.

Platinum can also be purchased as a coin, although a rare one, and not as liquid as gold coins. The Isle of Man (a British colony) issues the Noble, which is the platinum coin. It usually sells at a 5 percent premium above the metal's spot price and is available from some U.S. coin dealers.

In general, platinum's disadvantages as an investment are the same as those of silver. Demand for autos and jewelry plunges during a depression. On top of that, it is not a cheap metal anymore. I do not recommend platinum as a hedge for the ensuing crisis.

Conventional wisdom holds that gold, silver, and platinum prices will rise when stock prices fall. But after the October 1987 crash, gold prices remained steady while silver dropped 20 percent and platinum dropped 23 percent. In other words, anything can happen in a climate of economic and emotional uncertainty. Of these three precious metals, gold is by far the best investment in such times. But the increase in its value will only come as the depression of the 1990s deepens.

CHAPTER 13

Retirement Plans

ONE OF OUR MOST CHERISHED lifetime goals is financial independence upon retirement. This is especially true today, when the extended family has all but disappeared and the elderly choose not to live with their children and maintain their own households. In fact, one reason why a person saves is to have a substantial nest egg in old age, which is usually associated with lower productivity and reduced potential for earnings. The older you get, the more concerned you become with your retirement income. For those in their fifties—and sixties —retirement plans can be crucial for a relaxed and worry-free life. How sound are these plans? Put another way, how vulnerable to a major economic collapse are the pension funds or insurance companies that offer various retirement options? This is a critical question for those who will be in or near retirement during the 1990s.

People save for retirement in a variety of ways—annuities, 401(k) plans, IRAs, Keogh plans, and life insurance, among others. Social Security, which we have already discussed in Chapter 7, is a source of retirement income, although the average payout is paltry. Let's look at these retirement plans and their advantages—and possible disadvantages—in the years ahead.

Annuities

Most people fear that after retirement they could outlive their savings. Since life expectancy has been slowly rising, this fear is not unfounded. One way to solve the problem is to buy from a life insurance company an annuity, which is so called because it guarantees an annual income to a retiree until his or her death. That is the main attraction of this form of retirement program. Another attraction is its tax-deferral feature, which permits the program to grow much faster than otherwise.

Basically, an annuity is a contract between you and an insurance company that provides you a guaranteed monthly payment after retirement. It is a lifetime contract, for which there is, of course, a price, which you can pay either before or upon retirement. If you wait until you retire, you buy what is called an immediate annuity; if you buy in advance of your retirement, you buy a deferred annuity.

In the case of an immediate annuity, you pay a single premium in a lump sum, and your periodic payment will begin within a year of your purchase. You can be paid either monthly, quarterly, or semiannually, and the amount will depend on the size of your initial payment, your life expectancy, and the return that the company expects to earn from your money. Women generally live longer than men; therefore, annuity payments for women fall short of those for males. When interest rates are high, insurance companies also offer large payouts to stay competitive with other forms of savings.

A deferred annuity, by contrast, is planned long before retirement. It has two phases, an accumulating phase and a payout period. In the first phase, you make payments to the insurance company, in fixed or variable installments, over a number of years during which your money accumulates and earns a tax-deferred return. Your account grows year after year at a certain rate, which, at least at the start, is guaranteed. Upon retirement, your account will shift into the payout mode, which works in the same way as the immediate annuity. In this second phase, you have various options. You may choose to take all your money out in one lump sum or in a few large sums or to accept a payment schedule extending over your lifetime. With lifetime arrangements, some more options are available at variable payment schedules. An individual-life annuity guarantees you payments as long as you live. A joint-and-survivor annuity ensures payments to you and your surviving spouse as long as a survivor lives, whereas with a guaranteed-minimum annuity, payment occurs to the beneficiary and his survivor for a minimum period even if the annuitant dies before the policy expires.

Flexibility is thus a major draw of annuities. Sometimes companies will even offer you the choice of how to invest your premiums. You are able to choose between fixed-rate and variable-rate annuities. If you choose a fixed-rate annuity, the company offers you a minimum guaranteed return, usually well below the long-term interest rate, plus a bonus return in case your money, invested in quality bonds, earns a higher yield. The bonus, of course, varies from year to year. If you choose a variable-rate annuity, the company will put your money into riskier assets, such as common stocks or real estate, and there is no guaranteed return. The actual return can be higher or lower than that of the fixed-rate annuity, depending on how riskier assets perform relative to bonds.

It seems to me that retirement savings are not something you should gamble with. In old age, few people have the will, stamina, and energy to make a new start if risky investments go sour. With the fixed-rate annuity, your payments are guaranteed; with the variable-rate annuity, you are gambling.

Many companies offer self-directed annuities in which you have a choice of investing your funds, tax-deferred until withdrawal, in stock, bond, and money market mutual funds. This way you can shift your funds into the investment that you feel is most appropriate to current economic conditions. You may also, in most annuities, withdraw up to 10 percent of your accumulated funds without penalty, other than any income tax that may be due.

In any case, an annuity's safety depends on the company that sells it. There is a real danger that the coming crisis could wipe out many insurance companies, especially those heavily involved in the stock market. My suggestion is that you postpone your retirement as long as you can. An annuity makes you illiquid in the short run, and there are heavy penalties, both from the company and from the IRS, if you cash in your policy early. If you draw funds from a deferred annuity before you turn fifty-nine and a half, you will have to pay a 10 percent tax penalty in addition to the income tax on interest earnings. This is not the time to buy annuities, especially those of the immediate variety.

If you must buy an annuity, it should be a fixed-rate annuity, invested in quality bonds. Many stocks will simply crash in the 1990s, whereas bonds could survive and continue to pay interest. Also, go with a reputable, highly rated company. Your insurance agent should be able to show you the firm's ratings as compiled by A. M. Best Company. I recommend that you invest in an annuity only after you have fully contributed to your IRA, Keogh plan, or other retirement plan related to your employment. All of the money you contribute to such plans is tax-deferred, while you will already have paid income tax on the money you invest in an annuity, and only the earnings are tax-deferred.

Keogh Plans and IRAs

Immediate or deferred annuities offer you an attractive way to plan for retirement, but you have to go through life insurance companies. A few years ago, Congress created two tax-deferred devices which you can set up on your own without any insurance agency acting as an intermediary and charging you substantial fees. The devices are the Keogh plan for the self-employed and the Individual Retirement Account (IRA) for others earning up to $50,000.

With the IRA, a qualified worker is eligible to tax-shelter up to $2,250 of his annual income, if married to a nonworking spouse, or up to $2,000 if unmarried. Individuals with incomes below $25,000 and couples with incomes below $40,000 are allowed to deduct their contributions fully from gross incomes. Partial deductions are allowed to individuals with incomes between $25,000 and $35,000 and to couples with incomes between $40,000 to $50,000. The money can be invested in any type of asset under the supervision of a trustee, which is usually a bank, thrift, brokerage, or other financial institution. The trustees usually charge a minimal fee for setting up an IRA account. However, precious metals and collectibles, except for gold and silver coins minted by the U.S. government, are barred as qualifying investments. There is another form of IRA, called a rollover IRA, which you may establish to deposit a lump-sum payment received from a profit-sharing plan or qualified pension program. The above limits are waived in the rollover version.

Keogh plans, by contrast, are available only to self-employed individuals. The amount permissible for tax sheltering in this case is far more generous than an IRA allows. You can shelter up to 20 percent of your self-employed income, up to a maximum of $30,000 per year. But the money, as with an IRA, cannot be invested in collectibles, including precious metals, rare coins, antiques, and art. The gold and silver coins minted by the U.S. government, as before, are exempt from this rule. Except for these, there are no restrictions on Keogh plan investments. Fees for setting up Keogh accounts vary. Most banks charge token amounts, while brokerages have an initial commission for stock or bond purchases. Insurance companies may impose somewhat higher charges.

In both IRAs and Keogh plans, income earned is tax-deferred until withdrawal. When you withdraw funds, they constitute income and are taxed. You have to start withdrawing money when you turn seventy and a half and you cannot withdraw any funds until you are fifty-nine and a half without paying a tax penalty. The penalty for early withdrawal is 10 percent of the funds withdrawn.

The safety of these retirement accounts also depends on the financial institution you select and the degree of risk associated with the investments you make with your account. Plans held with banks and thrifts are insured by the government for up to $100,000. My suggestion is that you keep your existing IRA or Keogh accounts with financial institutions included in my list of safe banks or thrifts, preferably in your area or in the vicinity, and even though the earnings from these accounts are tax-deferred, you should be as prudent in investing these funds as you are when investing your other savings.

Do you need to do anything now to your existing Keogh or IRA accounts in view of the coming depression? Yes—but it's just a minor action. Even if some fees are involved, you should transfer your retirement accounts to safer banks or thrifts which are unlikely to fold in the 1990s. And if you now hold high-risk investments in your account, switch to more conservative ones. The earnings on these accounts are tax-deferred, but that is no reason to gamble with the principal. In the troubled times ahead, your retirement accounts might include investments in bank CDs and other relatively risk-free instruments, as well as top-quality corporate bonds.

As for opening a new retirement account or continuing to fund your present account, I do not recommend it at this time unless you have an ample cash cushion for the years ahead. Because you cannot withdraw the money, which you might need in an emergency, before the age of fifty-nine and a half without paying a substantial penalty, you will lose some of your liquidity. In my opinion, it would make more sense to keep your funds in safe, liquid investments, even though you sacrifice the tax-deferred feature of a retirement account.

Company-Sponsored Plans

While Congress has encouraged individuals to act on their own to build a nest egg for retirement, it has also induced companies to nudge their employees toward the same goals. The incentive once again is in the form of tax savings. There is a wide variety of company-sponsored plans —thrift, profit-sharing, salary-reduction (401[k]), and defined-benefit plans, among others. In some, the employees make contributions, matched equally by their employer's contributions, to a fund, which grows and compounds over time, offering a limp sum or monthly payments upon retirement. Here the employer's contribution is part of the total compensation package and is also an inducement for keeping and attracting skilled employees. Whatever the nature of the company pension plan, both the contributions and their investment income are free from current taxes. These funds thus grow at a faster rate than otherwise would be the case. Most of the company-sponsored plans restrict their employees from prematurely withdrawing their funds, especially if there are no voluntary employee contributions. Others permit the withdrawal of voluntary contributions, but then there is the IRS tax penalty to discourage the practice.

Pension funds are invested in several different ways.

They can be used to buy the company's own stock, or handed over to an insurance company for expert management. Some businesses hire their own managers to administer the funds. Hence the performance of pension funds varies from company to company.

In the early 1980s many pension plans were found to be underfunded, as companies had failed to earmark enough funds for this purpose. The government has established an agency called the Pension Benefit Guaranty Corporation (PBGC) to insure pensions of workers employed in member firms. But like many other government agencies, this one is also in deficit at this time—to the tune of $4 billion. Many steel companies facing mounting losses have unloaded their pension plans on the doorstep of PBGC, which, like FSLIC, is now in need of a congressional bailout.

Most companies use a conservative strategy in managing their pension funds to ensure the safety of the principal. But the stock market bubble of the 1980s has created what can truly be described as a pension-fund time bomb which is ticking away toward the detonating year of 1990. Many companies, as mentioned earlier, had not fully funded their plans in the early 1980s, but as the stock market exploded, assets of pension programs also soared, giving the impression that the pension system is very healthy. Some of the companies that had deficits in their pension funds now boast remarkable surpluses. As a result, several companies have trimmed their annual pension contributions. But stock values can plunge rapidly, as Black Monday has already shown us, and pension plans can again be in trouble.

The pension system was unsound at the turn of the 1980s and is in even worse shape today, because underfunding has actually increased. In their rush to display immense earnings, companies are playing with the fate of those already retired and those about to retire. Most pension funds are heavily invested in common stock, up to 75 percent of their investment portfolios in some cases. Even some conservative funds allocate 60 percent of their assets to the purchase of stocks. A stock market collapse in the 1990s could ruin a vast majority of pension plans. Pension managers should beware of this danger, quickly sell much of their stock, and move at least 50 percent of their portfolios into government securities and high-rated corporate bonds, especially those of cash-rich corporations. The remaining 50 percent should be invested in the CDs of safer banks and thrifts.

For all these reasons, those who have the option of taking their pension money out in lump sums should exercise that option, and deposit their funds in an IRA "rollover" account with a sound bank or thrift. There is no hurry to buy "immediate annuities" at this time. It can be done after 1991, when the dust clears and we know how the depression is going to affect various sectors of the economy.

Single-Premium Life Insurance

Following the Tax Reform Act of 1986, the hottest-selling form of life insurance has been the so-called single-premium life insurance, or SPLI, policy. At many insurance companies, SPLI is outselling traditional best-sellers such as whole-life and term insurance policies. The product, in fact, has many attractive features.

You can buy the policy for as little as $5,000. It combines the virtues of tax saving, borrowing, and life insurance all in one package. You make one payment and obtain a life insurance policy. Earnings grow tax-free, and you can borrow up to 90 percent of the cash value of your policy without any tax liability. The borrowing cost may be only 1 percent above the tax-free return from the policy.

But SPLI is a life insurance policy only in name. The death benefits to your survivors are very small. Depending on your age, you may have to pay as much as $40,000 to get a death benefit of only $100,000. But the death benefit is not the chief attraction of SPLI; its flexibility is. While earnings grow rapidly, you have easy access to your money through low-cost borrowing. Not surprisingly, with most of the old tax shelters now gone, SPLI has already become very popular.

In spite of the coming depression, SPLI's flexibility continues to make it attractive. Of course, you still have to select a highly rated insurance company, one likely to survive the ravages of the coming crisis. Since you can borrow against your money at any time, you retain your liquidity, which you don't in the case of other insurance products. And liquidity is the key to surviving a depression.

A. M. Best Company rates insurance companies every year. Its top ten companies, according to asset size, are Prudential, Metropolitan Life, Equitable Life Assurance Company, Aetna, New York Life, TIAA, John Hancock, Travelers, Connecticut General Life, and Northwestern Mutual. These are solid insurance companies that are likely to weather the coming storms. Of course, you should do comparison shopping even among them—that is, compare the costs and benefits of various plans they offer.

Advice to Retirees for the 1990s

What is an average retiree likely to face during the coming depression? For some it perhaps will not make much difference. But for most, living standards will plunge. Those locked into fixed-rate annuities with healthy insurance companies will see no major change in their situation. But others will.

A retired person today has as many as three sources of income—Social Security, investments, and pensions. Of these, Social Security will be unscathed, but pension and investment income could plummet. As interest rates and dividends plunge, investment yields will drop substantially. Those retirees who currently depend largely on such income will suffer a major drop in their living standards, and they might have to eat into their savings to maintain their life-style.

With the fall in investment yields, pension payouts will also decline sharply. Some pension funds will go bankrupt, with the government unable to assume their liabilities. For pensioners, things could get really bad in the 1990s. However, for those relying mostly on Social Security, there will not be much change in the situation. They might even benefit somewhat, as the cost of living could drop slightly.

If you are nearing retirement, my advice is to continue working for as long as possible, meanwhile saving as much as possible and putting your savings in investments that are both relatively riskless and liquid. If you are already in retirement, do not dip into your capital for expenses that are either frivolous or unnecessary. And if your savings and investments are likely to be threatened in any way by the coming depression, I would advise that you shift your funds into safe banks and adopt a very conservative investment strategy.

CHAPTER 14

A Comprehensive Strategy for Financial Survival

IT IS TIME NOW to weave various strands together into a comprehensive strategy to prepare for and survive the depression that is only a few months away. Here is what I recommend:

1. *Individuals and families:* Save as much money as possible. You don't know how long you may be employed in the seven-year-long depression of the 1990s. Today a family of four living in a medium-sized city needs a minimum annual income of $11,000. That is where the official poverty line for a family of four begins at today's prices, which are not likely to be very different in the 1990s. Assuming that a family of four has to live mainly on its assets, it would need about $44,000 to survive the depression. Larger families will need more, small families and individuals less. If you live in a smaller town, you may need less; if you live in a large metropolitan area, you may need much more. According to your circumstances, figure your minimum annual income and multiply by four. That is the cash cushion you will need to survive the coming depression. If you already have that amount, make sure it is liquid, deposited in a safe bank, or put in riskless invest-

ments that can be sold immediately if necessary. If you do not already have a cash cushion, postpone major or unnecessary expenses and avoid buying on credit cards, which charge you interest rates of up to 18 percent. Pay such debts off as soon as possible and cut your other expenses so that you can save and build your cash cushion. If necessary, consider taking a second job or beginning a part-time business that will be recession-proof. Also make sure that your medical and disability insurance is adequate to your needs, either through your company-sponsored plan or, if you are unemployed or self-employed, through a private insurance company.

2. *Employees:* For new job seekers, I recommend service industries such as health care, education, nursing homes, repair services, and so on. The fields to avoid are heavy industry, construction, and durable goods. If you are already employed, do not change jobs at this time, participate as fully as possible in your company's investment and pension plans, work as hard as possible to please your superiors, and postpone retirement.

3. *The elderly and the retired:* You should not worry about Social Security, which has a large surplus at this time, but pensions and investment plans could be at risk. You should switch your IRA or Keogh to a safe financial institution and make only the most conservative investments.

4. *Businessmen:* In order to survive the coming catastrophe, a businessman should immediately eliminate or reduce his debt, diversify into repair-type services, prepare a contingency plan to reduce costs, and, if possible, start exporting his product.

5. *Investors:* First set aside a minimum of $44,000, your survival insurance, in safe banks and thrifts, while keeping some cash or traveler's checks at home to meet a month's expenses. Of your remaining assets, by the end of 1989, as much as 20 percent of the total should be in gold bullion, coins, or certificates and the rest in bonds, of which half should be in AAA bonds of cash-rich corporations

and the other half split between T-bills and municipals. As an example, suppose you have saved up $100,000. Out of this, you should set aside $50,000 as your survival money. Keep some of this at home, and deposit the rest in safe banking institutions in a NOW account or a CD. Of the remaining $50,000, you should invest $20,000 in gold-related assets. The remainder should be invested as follows: $15,000 in AAA corporate bonds, $10,000—the minimum—in a T-bill, and $5,000 in a municipal bond. This investment strategy is safe even if the depression turns out to be inflationary and interest rates continually rise. With half of your savings in interest-bearing bank accounts—as suggested by my example, which applies even if your assets exceed $100,000—and another 20 percent in gold, you will benefit from rising interest rates and the inflation-induced rise in the price of gold. Long-term bonds, especially of lower grades, could then depreciate, but T-bills, being short-term instruments, will not. With the strategy I have designed for you, 85 percent of your investments will be insulated from inflation. Note that real estate will still fall. My investment strategy is sound for both inflationary and deflationary depressions.

6. *Bankers:* Banks and other lending institutions have an especially great responsibility at this time to their depositors as well as to society to engage in prudent banking practices. The world is now on the precipice of an economic calamity, and sound bank management could blunt its blows. A bank manager should (a) diversify his portfolio of assets and invest a larger portion than is customary now in the AAA bonds of cash-rich companies, (b) refrain from lending surplus funds to large but troubled banks which could unexpectedly fail, (c) sharply raise his credit standards for energy and real estate loans, and (d) refuse to lend money for business mergers that only fuel speculation.

7. *City financial planners:* Cities usually live on balanced budgets. It's time now to maintain surpluses to be used in

the future crisis. A city financial planner should postpone all capital expenditures at this time. Funds should be allocated to repairs of city facilities, but not to the construction of new facilities such as roads, highways, bridges, college buildings, transit systems, and so on. All the funds so saved should be put in an escrow account to draw interest from deposits in safe banks and thrifts. During the 1930s many cities went bankrupt, and raised property taxes on residences owned by the jobless or people with part-time employment. This was the height of callousness. Many homeowners lost their homes because they could not pay their property taxes. In order to avoid such tyranny and turmoil, city planners should behave like prudent households and produce surplus budgets while there is time.

My advice may perhaps run counter to the grain of our materialistic society, but fiscal imprudence and irresponsibility are largely responsible for our economic plight. Only if we—as individuals and families, emplcyees and businessmen, local, state, and federal governments—begin to act with prudence and responsibility will we be able to survive.

PART IV

Diagnosis and Cure

CHAPTER 15

What Ails America?

SOME EXPERTS ARGUE that the American economy is very prosperous today and is still growing. Why then are people so concerned about their future? Between 1980 and 1982 the country suffered the worst recession since the Second World War, as unemployment jumped to 10.8 percent of the labor force, the highest rate of unemployment since 1940. We are now in the last years of the 1980s, and the economy is operating at near full employment. Inflation has also sharply declined from the double-digit levels prevailing during 1979 to 1981. In other words, the economic stagnation of the early 1980s has by now given way to a low-inflation, high-employment economy. Reflecting this prosperity, most stock prices have more than doubled since 1982. The Dow Jones Industrial Index hit an all-time high of 2722 in August 1987.

The stock market did plunge in October 1987, but not much else in our economy has changed. With such prosperity reigning today, the nation should be joyous and full of excitement. The popularity of President Reagan should be at its peak. Instead, there is an undercurrent of worry and anxiety about the future among the general public.

The national mood is somber, not exuberant, today, and the president gets only mixed reviews for his handling of the economy. Why? Why should there be persistent despair in a country that has just experienced the longest peacetime economic expansion since 1796? The reason is simple common sense.

You see this great prosperity right in front of you, but something keeps nagging at you anyway because you know that nobody can live on borrowed money forever. Despite assurances from politicians and pundits, you wish the economy were free from its various debts. Many economists tell you that deficits don't make any difference, that debts don't matter. You feel reassured, but only for a moment. The impressive credentials of the experts may calm you down for a few seconds, but your heart longs to hear something rational, something logical that doesn't so blatantly contradict common sense.

A commonsense view of our economy provides ample cause for worry. What are the major economic ills afflicting America today? Have a look at the following comprehensive list:

• The federal debt and deficit
• The foreign trade debt and deficit
• Consumer and corporate debt
• The Third World debt owed to American banks
• The stock market bubble
• The shrinking middle class and rising homelessness and poverty
• The growing concentration of wealth

These are the major economic problems in the United States as the 1980s come to an end. Note that inflation and unemployment are not in this list, because they are both now much lower than they were at the turn of the 1980s. But so fragile is our economy today that one or both of them can erupt at any moment. Let me tell you how these ills came about.

The Federal Debt and Deficit

You have already learned in Chapter 1 that the gargantuan federal debt and deficit are mainly the handiwork of one president out of a total of forty. Table 15 shows the comparative figures.

Table 15
Cumulative Deficits Under Successive Presidents
Since World War II

President	Total Deficit (billions)	Total GNP (billions)	Deficit as Percentage of GNP
Truman	−17.9	1,730.5	−1.0
Eisenhower	18.7	3,497.1	0.5
Kennedy	15.2	1,715.3	0.9
Johnson	44.8	3,836.0	1.2
Nixon-Ford	208.1	9,035.4	2.3
Carter	226.8	9,480.4	2.3
Reagan	1,183.3	26,078.1	4.5

Source: *Economic Report of the President, 1987.*

To be sure, government extravagance didn't begin with Reagan. The federal budget has been in arrears in virtually every year since 1949. Between 1939 and 1946, the United States was directly or indirectly involved in the Second World War and accumulated a deficit of $197 billion over seven years. This was unavoidable, because America was then caught in a worldwide struggle for survival.

At the end of that struggle, Truman was president for six years, and his administration managed a peacetime surplus of about $18 billion, or an average of $3 billion per year. The administration of the next president, Eisenhower, generated a deficit of around $19 billion, enough to wipe out Truman's surplus. Eisenhower's annual deficit averaged $2.4 billion, which more than doubled to $5 billion during Kennedy's term. In fact, the average annual deficit has jumped during every successive administration. It was $9 billion during Johnson's term, $26 billion during the Nixon-Ford era, $57 billion during Carter's tenure, and a hefty $169 billion in the first seven years of the Reagan administration.

History is full of surprises. In American politics, Republicans are known to favor balanced budgets, while Democrats advocate high government spending and budget deficits. Through some chance of history, the first deficit following the Second World War occurred during the term of a Republican president, Eisenhower, and also reached its zenith during another Republican administration—that of Reagan. It is the Republicans who gave birth to the pattern of peacetime deficits, and then lifted it to towering heights, while always managing to denounce it in principle. The postwar Democratic presidents, Kennedy, Johnson, and Carter, never pretended that deficits were morally or philosophically wrong, and yet could not match the Republican genius to produce red ink.

It's perhaps unfair to compare the average value of the deficit generated by each presidential administration. After all, the GNP, population, and prices have all soared over the years. A fairer evaluation emerges from the ratio of cumulative deficit to the GNP, which is displayed in Chart 3. Reagan's deficit ratio, at 4.5 percent, is as much as twice the ratio of any other president.

At less than 5 percent, the Reagan deficit ratio, though the highest in history, still appears to be small. But since the deficiency has occurred annually, it has led to a pyramid of government debt, which is the sum total of deficits occurring year after year. Table 16 reveals the enormity of this situation.

Table 16
Growth of Federal Debt in the 1970s and 1980s

Year	Debt Held by the Public (billions)	GNP in Each Fiscal Year (billions)	Debt as Percentage of GNP
1970	284.9	990.2	29
1971	304.3	1,055.9	29
1972	323.8	1,153.1	28
1973	343.0	1,281.4	28
1974	346.1	1,416.5	24
1975	396.9	1,522.5	26
1976	480.3	1,698.2	28
1977	551.8	1,933.0	28
1978	610.9	2,171.8	28
1979	644.6	2,447.8	26
1980	715.1	2,670.6	27
1981	794.4	2,986.4	27
1982	929.4	2,986.4	31
1983	1,141.8	3,321.9	34
1984	1,312.6	3,686.8	36
1985	1,509.9	3,937.2	38
1986	1,746.1	4,163.3	42

Source: *Economic Report of the President, 1987.*

Following the Second World War, the country inherited a huge debt, so that the debt-to-GNP ratio was abnormally high. It did not represent the normal peacetime pattern. In fact, until 1969, GNP grew faster than federal debt, so that the debt ratio continued to fall. Table 16, therefore, excludes the postwar years until 1969; it starts with 1970, and shows that the debt ratio was more or less constant during the 1970s. The decade started with a figure of 29 percent and ended with a slightly lower figure of 26 percent. But the 1980s have witnessed a steady and substantial rise in the debt ratio, to 42 percent in 1986. During each postwar decade, GNP grew faster than the federal debt, but in the 1980s something went awry: debt grew faster than GNP.

Chart 3

Deficit/GNP Ratio Under Successive Administrations Since the War

Deficit/GNP ratio
  (percentages)

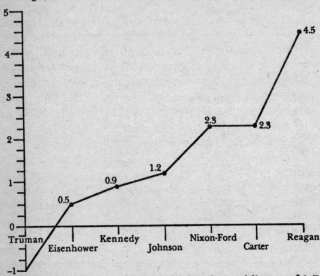

In 1986, the federal debt held by the public was $1.7 trillion, whereas the gross federal debt (not shown in the table) crossed the $2 trillion mark. In fact, that year the debt increased by $236 billion while GNP rose only by $226 billion. Thus, in 1986, for the first time in the postwar years, the absolute size of the debt jumped more than GNP. In other words, 1986 was a watershed year in Reagan's America, scoring many firsts of dubious distinction. And it is noteworthy that this occurred against the backdrop of steadily falling oil prices, which shrivel inflation as well as unemployment. Without this fortunate development the economy would have stagnated even more.

It is clear that the federal debt and deficits are already beginning to become a big drag on the economy. The immediate burden of the debt is the interest the government has to pay to individuals. This burden has sharply risen in the past ten years, so much so that almost 18 percent of the government's income, or $136 billion, was needed to meet its interest obligation in 1986. As recently as 1980, the interest burden was only 10 percent of the federal revenue. The weight of the debt on the current generation is at least $136 billion. Suppose the debt had not existed in 1986. Then $136 billion would have been available for education and other much-needed social programs, instead of going into the pockets of those who own government securities. The burden of the federal debt is therefore borne by those in our society who can least afford it.

How did all this begin? The sources of today's dilemmas go as far back as the 1930s, when the nation was trapped in a vicious circle of unemployment and poverty caused by the Great Depression. The government's answer to the mass misery was the New Deal, which introduced many new programs and institutions to restore public confidence and stabilize the economy. The Federal Deposit Insurance Corporation, the Securities and Exchange Commission, the National Labor Relations Board, and other agencies were established to arrest the spiraling fall in the economy. By itself the New Deal did little to expand government spending at the time. President Franklin Roosevelt, a Democrat, was averse to federal overspending and handouts. But a principle had been established. Henceforth the government would be constantly called upon to repair a faltering economy. Until then, federal interference with economic affairs was a taboo with experts and politicians. Economists believed that capitalism could cure all its ills by itself, and in fact outside intervention only made matters worse.

The New Deal was the antithesis to this philosophy. It established the tradition of transfer payments from the government to the needy, although at the time Roosevelt's programs were not very costly. As late as 1940, the transfer payment, at $3.1 billion, was only marginally higher than the $2.7 billion paid out in 1931, when Roosevelt had not yet taken office. Throughout the 1930s, however, new welfare programs were continually established under the New Deal. And the bill came due after the war; by 1946, transfer payments had moved to $11 billion. By 1950 they had risen to $15 billion; by 1960 to $28 billion; by 1970 to $80 billion; and by 1980 to nearly $300 billion. In 1986, they crossed the $500 billion mark. The growth from a paltry $1.5 billion in 1930 to half a trillion dollars in 1986 was phenomenal.[1]

If transfer payments are government handouts to the needy, their sharp rise since the war would suggest an economy caught in the throes of dire poverty. But the economy has actually grown enormously over this time. American living standards are still among the highest ever in history. Ours is a lavish life-style by any standard. Why then should we have a burden of debt that threatens to overwhelm the federal budget and the nation in a giant tide of red ink?

In 1981, Reagan persuaded Congress to cut taxes sharply for wealthy individuals and corporations. His argument was that this policy would generate so much economic growth that even with lower tax rates, total tax receipts would rise. This, along with reduced government spending, would balance the federal budget by 1984. We will examine the merits of this logic in Chapter 16. Suffice it here to say that because of sharp increases in the defense budget, government expenditures never went down and the budget deficit soared, settling in the range of $200 billion per year.

During the election campaign in 1980, Reagan promised the public he would cut taxes, raise defense spending, and balance the budget at the same time. No one dreamed Reagan's policies would raise the federal debt and deficits to unthinkable heights. Today we are so inured to massive deficit figures that politicians can claim progress when the deficiency is limited to a mere $150 billion.

Congress passed the Gramm-Rudman-Hollings Act in 1985, and modified it somewhat in 1987, to eliminate the deficit by 1993. The main deficit-reducing weapon of this law is that if the shortfall fails to decline by a certain amount during any year, then government spending will be trimmed automatically to that extent, with defense outlays and social spending sharing the cuts equally. Whether this law is successful in its objective remains to be seen. I have my doubts. The government debt and deficits are here to stay far into the future.

The Foreign Trade Debt and Deficit

In 1985, with President Reagan at the zenith of his popularity, something ominous happened in America. For the first time since the First World War, barely a year after the president won reelection in a landslide, the United States became a net debtor to other nations, and in this respect joined the ranks of the Third World nations. This development occurred at such a breathtaking pace that few were aware of it, and even fewer recognized what it portended. Just four years before, when Reagan was sworn in as president in 1981, the United States was the largest creditor to the world. The foreign debt flipflop of 1985 was the stuff of which legends are made. It marked the beginning of an end to nearly a century of American dominance over the world economy. An era came to a close. How did it all happen? Why did it happen so fast?

Obviously, for such a dramatic turnaround to occur, something must have happened during the Reagan years that had never taken place before. Something new must have emerged to produce such a swift transformation of America's position in the world. One moment the United

States was a lender to the world, and another moment, in a mere twinkling, it became a debtor.

The culprits clearly were the Reagan economic policies and the resulting budget deficit, unprecedented in its size and timing. Never before had federal overspending jumped so much during peacetime; never before had it crossed the $200 billion mark—in fact, not even the $100 billion mark. These were blows to the national psyche, which looked forward, expectantly, to a balanced budget by 1984.

The result was a sharp rise in American interest rates, so the argument goes, over those prevailing in other major economies such as those of Japan, West Germany, Britain, France, and so on. This, on the one hand, choked investment or kept it from rising in spite of massive incentives, in the form of tax cuts and credits, that the government provided to businessmen. On the other hand, it attracted funds from abroad, as capital usually moves to the place with the highest but relatively safe return. This inflow of capital created additional demand for U.S. currency in the foreign exchange market, leading to the appreciation of the dollar, which made exports dearer and imports cheaper than before. As a result, exports declined and imports surged, leading to a massive deficit in the balance of trade year after year. In order to finance the deficit, the United States borrowed huge sums from abroad. In the process, the country eventually moved from a creditor to a debtor nation.

This is the traditional argument for why the United States now owes so much to other countries, and continues to suffer massive trade deficits. In other words, the federal budget deficits, unprecedented as they are, also bear chief responsibility for the U.S. foreign debt and deficits. I have no quarrel with the essence of this argument. I agree that the high American interest rates relative to those in competing countries resulted in great appreciation of the dollar between 1981 and 1985, and in turn led to America's indebtedness to other nations. But I am not sure if the federal budget deficit was the only, or even the major, cause of relatively high interest rates.

Consumer and Corporate Debt

The third major problem facing the American economy is the massive consumer and corporate debt. Both consumers and corporations are in hock as never before since the late 1920s. This tends to create a shaky economy, but its effects remain hidden from view until the arrival of a recession, which, according to three centuries of historical record, has occurred at least once every decade. The bigger the consumer and corporate debt, the deeper the economic contraction, when it eventually comes, because in business downturns, many individuals and companies are unable to pay their bills and have to declare bankruptcy. Hence misery rises in proportion to the size of the debt.

Third World Debt

During the cataclysmic 1970s, when OPEC raised oil prices at will, many developing countries borrowed billions of dollars from international banks all over the world. But the biggest lenders were American banks, including Citicorp, Bank of America, and Manufacturers Hanover, among others. It has become clear in the 1980s that the poverty-stricken Third World countries are in no position to pay back their loans. They perhaps would have already defaulted in 1982, but the U.S. government, the International Monetary Fund (IMF), lending banks, and borrowers all coordinated their activities to prevent such a calamity.

Cooperation was in the interest of all parties concerned. The Third World foreign debt was nearly $1 trillion at the end of 1987; of that about half was owed to American banks. Two Latin American countries, Brazil and Mexico, are the largest debtors, owing over $100 billion each. The American banks' exposure to Latin America alone was on the order of $390 billion in 1987.

Most of the Third World borrowers have technically defaulted on their loans, because they have been able to pay back the interest only by borrowing more from the IMF and their lenders. If they were to default openly, the international financial system could collapse immediately, as the banks would have to charge these loans against their capital, generating a negative net worth in many cases. This, in turn, would undermine depositors' confidence, possibly creating a worldwide run on the involved banks. The Third World countries could then lose even short-term financing of their exports and imports that provide a sound collateral, leading to a wholesale disruption of their own economies.

The system of cooperation among involved parties has worked so far in the 1980s, because open default could unleash perils unimaginable at this time. This system has enabled the borrowers to service their debt only partially. Mostly their debt service involves the payment of interest, while payment on the principal amount is postponed. In some cases, such as Brazil, even interest has not been fully paid, because even that payment constitutes a severe drain on the meager foreign exchange earnings of the Third World. In the 1990s, however, all pretense of solvency will have to be abandoned, as American imports from the less developed countries plummet. The Third World borrowers will have to default openly, thereby adding one more nail to the coffin of the international financial system.

The Stock Market Bubble

Another major irritant for the American economy comes from an overheated stock market and the numerous avenues available to the public for speculation, which have the effect of turning investors into gamblers. Some go to the extent of calling these financial markets giant casinos or slot machines, where the odds are generally stacked against you. In spite of Black Monday on October 19, 1987, when the Dow plunged by 508 points in a matter of seven hours, stocks are still overpriced, which is reflected in the lowest average dividend rate since the 1920s.

Potentially, the economy faces enormous risks, of which some are unprecedented in history. But the stock market heeds no warning signs. In August 1982, the Dow stood at around 775, but soared to 2722 by August 1987. This was a 250 percent jump compared to only a 20 percent rise in GNP during that time. Some experts think that a swollen stock market is a sign of great prosperity. Nothing could be farther from the truth. True, it makes the super-rich richer. Since 60 percent of the total stock is in the hands of the top 1 percent of wealth owners in America, the ever-rising asset markets are, of course, very generous to the affluent. While other stockholders also benefit, they receive only a pittance compared to the opulent.

What is wrong with a super-high stock market? Plenty. Everything in this world rests on a foundation; if the foundation is weak, then the superstructure quickly collapses. For stock prices, the real cushion comes from the earnings of the companies that issue the stock. If the market rise reflects growth of earnings, there is no problem. The foundation underlying share prices is then strong, and there is no danger of a free fall in stock values. Thus if the market doubles or triples because company profits double or triple, leaving the average P/E ratio roughly unchanged, the stock market advance reflects general economic health.

But in the 1980s, as in the 1920s, stock prices have risen far more than corporate profits; they have risen because of speculation rather than because of economic expansion. Such a market is vulnerable to even slight shocks to the economy. It can plunge without notice, wiping out thousands of small investors, who generally enter the game at a late stage and buy stocks at high prices. This is one danger of an overheated stock market.

Another danger is that such a market holds the entire nation hostage to the whims of major shareholders. All economic and social policies have to be designed to appease Wall Street. The government and the nation are then at the mercy of the needs and behavior of the affluent. You can't adopt policies that might benefit the vast majority of the poor and the middle class, if they offend those massively engaged in the stock market, lest its shaky foundation collapse and bring about an economic disaster.

The economic policies followed by the Fed in the immediate aftermath of Black Monday are an obvious case in point. Just a month before, the Fed, after careful thinking, decided to raise interest rates to subdue fears of inflation. As soon as the Dow dropped by 23 percent in one day, the Fed made a 180-degree turn and reversed the well-thought-out policy by lowering the rate of interest. The threat of a market collapse was so great it smothered any other consideration.

I am not questioning the wisdom of either policy. What is disconcerting is the haste and thoughtlessness with which the Fed had to react to avert a continued market collapse. If the market had not been overheated to begin with, there would have been no crash and hence no need to act in a hurry. Hence, a stock market bubble, which is what a swollen market really is, may force policies on the nation that come back to haunt us later. As long as the market remains super-high, the policymakers have little flexibility to take bold initiatives that may be good for the nation.

The Shrinking Middle Class and Rising Homelessness and Poverty

Many scholars have pointed to the dangers of a vanishing middle class and rising homelessness in America, intertwined phenomena of the 1980s. Almost every major magazine and newspaper has publicized these dangers. The increasing numbers of the poor and homeless bring shame to the so-called recovery and the large peacetime economic expansion of the 1980s. Economic progress is not in the rich getting richer, but in the poor joining the middle class, and the middle class joining the ranks of the rich.

The middle class has never been officially defined, but in terms of economic conditions in the late 1980s, the group could be described as those households with incomes between $15,000 and $35,000. According to the Bureau of the Census, the middle class thus defined shrank from 46 percent of American families in 1970 to 39 percent in 1985. In the same period, families with incomes of $50,000 or more swelled from 13 percent of the population to 18.3 percent. Bob Rast of Newhouse News Service writes, "There is mounting evidence that the ranks of middle class are thinning . . . and that the rich are cornering a bigger slice of the income pie at the expense of the middle class and the poor."[2]

With rising poverty in the United States, it is not surprising that many of the poor and the unemployed can't afford any kind of housing and end up living in the streets and sleeping in shelters provided by churches and city welfare agencies. They are the true underclass, and their agony is a mighty blot on the nation's soul. What an irony! Today America has the largest GNP in history, and also the largest army of the destitute and the homeless. The

[2] Bob Rast, "Middle Class Bind," *Dallas Times Herald*, November 23, 1986, p. A-4.

existence of this army clearly points to and is directly related to yet another major economic ill of the 1980s.

The Growing Concentration of Wealth

Closely linked to the phenomenon of rising ranks of the
poor, the homeless, and the destitute is another social cancer, namely the soaring wealth disparity in America. Ever
since 1973, when OPEC imposed an embargo on oil and
then subsequently quadrupled its price, the concentration
of income and wealth has been rising in the United States.
With the sudden jump in oil prices, many energy produc-
ers became megamillionaires overnight, a trend which accelerated when oil prices rose again following the
revolution in Iran in 1979.

With soaring energy prices came soaring inflation,
which in turn caused a sharp rise in interest rates. High
interest rates hurt practically every segment of society except the lenders, who, with few exceptions, are very rich.
Rising interest rates, therefore, exacerbate the concentration trend. The man with a lot of cash is obviously the
biggest beneficiary of a rise in interest rates. During the
1960s the prime rate, the rate most banks charge their best
customers, averaged around 5 percent; during the 1970s
the average rate jumped to 8 percent and during the
1980s to about 13 percent. Thus rising oil prices were
generous to the opulent in many ways, while the poor and
the middle class suffered under the onerous burden.

When President Reagan cut income taxes sharply for
wealthy individuals and expanded the tax-dodging loopholes in 1981, the disparity in wealth got another lift. The
loopholes were so glaring and large that even some of the
multimillionaires could legally get away with paying no
taxes. Tax shelters became a growth industry, and people
poured money into them with wild abandon. With the
affluent managing to avoid their full share of taxes and

with interest rates soaring sky-high, the wealth inequality in the early 1980s rose even faster than in the 1970s.

In the so-called Tax Reform Act of 1986, tax shelters were virtually annihilated, but the top tax rate affecting the richest households came down from 50 percent to 28 percent—a 44 percent reduction in the marginal rate. Ostensibly, the law also dramatically benefited the poor, because several million penurious families were removed from the tax rolls. But this was and is a smokescreen without which the law itself would not have passed. Taxes rose sharply for corporations, which always pass them on to those who buy their products, and the vast majority of such buyers are lower-income individuals. Once again the rich came out ahead in the tax revision of 1986, while others were fooled by the seeming drop in their tax bill.

It should not, therefore, come as a surprise that the Congressional Budget Office, in a recent nonpartisan study, discovered that since 1977 the tax burden has jumped for the poor while sharply easing for the wealthiest. The poorest Americans experienced a tax rise of nearly 20 percent, whereas the richest enjoyed an equal decline. The report was prepared at the request of Democratic Senator George Mitchell, who commented that "the study shows the extent to which the most privileged in our society have reaped tremendous benefits from Reagan Administration tax policies."[3]

On top of all these developments favoring the wealthy —the oil-price rise, the interest-rate jump, the tax-rate drop—came the stock market bubble, with stock prices at least doubling between 1982 and 1987. Since 60 percent of the stock, according to a Joint Economic Committee study, is owned by just 1 percent of the population, wealth disparity rose at the fastest rate since the 1920s. A jump of nearly $1 trillion occurred in the stock portfolios of the

[3] Quoted in Associated Press, "U.S. Taxes Pinching Poor More," *Dallas Morning News*, November 11, 1987, p. 5A.

rich. Today the country suffers from the highest rate of wealth inequality since 1929.

It is true that oil prices have steadily fallen since 1982 and interest rates have also come down. These forces should have flattened the disparity somewhat, but their effect was outweighed by the stock market bubble. In any case, interest rates are still almost twice their level in the 1960s, and oil prices, at about $17 per barrel, are still about six times their level in 1973. Compare this with the Consumer Price Index (CPI), which has risen less than three times its 1973 level. In real terms, the oil prices are still very high.

Evidence for bulging wealth disparity is now everywhere. President Reagan's own economic report eminently displays this disturbing trend. Table 17 provides indirect but clear-cut support for this conclusion. I have argued earlier that wealth concentration began to rise from 1973, the fateful year of the oil embargo and the quadrupling of oil prices. Since concentrated wealth means an increase in poverty and a drop in workers' incomes, it is not surprising that both these consequences followed after 1973. Table 17 shows that the number of families below the official poverty line reached its low in 1973 and then began to rise. In fact, the number jumped by a staggering 33 percent during the 1970–86 period, rising from 5.3 million to 7 million. Still, during the 1970s, only 200,000 new households entered the ranks of the poor, but in the 1980s, a million more joined their company in barely half that time.

The figures on average weekly earnings paint the same picture. Earnings rose until 1972, but have steadily declined since—from $198.41 to $171.07 (in 1977 dollars). However, per capita income has by and large risen, reaching its highest level in 1986. Now, if the country as a whole prospers but workers and poor families suffer losses, there is only one conclusion you can draw: the upper-income

Table 17
Average Weekly Earnings, Family Income, and
Per Capita Income, 1970–86

Year	Average Weekly Earnings (1977 dollars)	Number of Families Below Poverty Level (millions)	Per Capita Income (1982 dollars)
1970	186.94	5.3	8,134
1971	190.58	5.3	8,322
1972	198.41	5.1	8,562
1973	198.35	4.8	9,042
1974	190.12	4.9	8,867
1975	184.16	5.5	8,944
1976	186.85	5.3	9,175
1977	189.00	5.3	9,381
1978	189.31	5.3	9,735
1979	183.41	5.5	9,829
1980	172.74	6.2	9,722
1981	170.13	6.9	9,769
1982	168.09	7.5	9,725
1983	171.26	7.6	9,930
1984	172.78	7.3	10,421
1985	170.42	7.2	10,583
1986	171.07	7.0	10,780

Source: *Economic Report of the President, 1987*, pp. 275–78, 293.

groups have gained at the expense of the poor and the middle class.

Meanwhile, CEOs (chief executive officers) earn more than ever. A recent study by Scott Burns reveals that during the ten years from 1976 to 1986, CEO compensation (including salary, bonus, and perks) at the top one hundred corporations rose by 181 percent, far exceeding the rise in workers' nominal income of 74 percent, which, not surprisingly, trailed the 94 percent hike in consumer prices.[4] In other words, CEOs gained at the expense of

[4] Scott Burns, "CEO Pay Is Not What It Used To Be: It Is Better," *Dallas Morning News*, March 3, 1987, p. 1–D.

workers. Shareholders were even bigger losers, because profits of these companies rose only by 65 percent, exploding the myth that American management works for its stockholders. It seems to be working only for itself. Above all, *Business Week* reported that executive compensation jumped by a whopping 48 percent in 1987 alone.[5]

Another confirmation for bulging wealth concentration comes from *Forbes* magazine's annual list of the four hundred richest Americans; 1987 was another banner year for billionaires, as their ranks swelled from twenty-six to forty-nine. In 1985 they numbered only fourteen, indicating a 250 percent jump in barely two years. In other words, in the more than two hundred years from 1776, the year of American independence from Britain, to 1985, the economy produced only fourteen billionaires, but then generated thirty-five more in just the next two years, while thousands of families slipped below the official poverty level. Something has gone awfully wrong in Reagan's America.

Finally, consider Table 18 for direct evidence of wealth concentration. I have taken this table from my book *The Great Depression of 1990,* and updated it to 1987. The table shows that in 1929 the share of wealth held by the richest 1 percent of families was 36.3 percent, an all-time high. The Great Depression followed that year, during which wealth disparity dropped, and the trend continued until 1949, when it reached its lowest level. In fact, the prime rate that year at 2 percent was the lowest in the postwar years. Then the prime began to rise, and so did wealth disparity, registering a huge jump from 24.9 percent in 1969 to 34.3 percent in 1983. My conservative estimates show that the share of the richest 1 percent rose to at least 36 percent by the end of 1987, largely because of a doubling of stock prices since 1983. We are essentially back to where we were in 1929. And that fact alone, quite apart

---

[5] *Business Week,* May 2, 1988, p. 50.

from the many other economic ills of the 1980s, is cause
for great concern.

Table 18
Concentration of Wealth in America

Year	Share of Wealth Held by 1 Percent of U.S. Adults or Families (percentages)
1810	21.0
1860	24.0
1870	27.0
1900	26.0–31.0
1922	31.6
1929	36.3
1933	28.3
1939	30.6
1945	23.3
1949	20.8
1953	27.5
1956	26.0
1958	26.9
1962	27.4
1963	31.6
1965	29.2
1969	24.9
1983	34.3
1987	36.0

Source: Ravi Batra, *The Great Depression of 1990*, p. 118.

CHAPTER 16

The Dire Consequences of Wealth Concentration

SOME PEOPLE ARGUE that wealth disparity has been unchanged in the 1970s and the 1980s. They are blind to the overwhelming evidence to the contrary. They shrug aside the testimony of rising poverty, the vanishing middle class, declining average earnings, the rocketing number of billionaires in the midst of climbing homelessness, historically high interest rates, and bloated stock speculation. There are others who admit the fact of rising economic inequality during the 1980s but, like ostriches, bury their heads in sand and fail to see any danger. To them, wealth disparity is good for everybody. "What is wrong with wealth disparity, anyway?" they ask.

My answer is that excessive wealth concentration is a social cancer that at the least reduces general living standards and at worst spawns depressions and ultimately revolutions. I believe that wealth concentration has the following deleterious effects on any economy:

1. It creates business takeovers and monopolies and hence destroys free enterprise.
2. It hurts incentive to work and increases speculation.
3. It increases domestic debt.
4. It raises interest rates.
5. It creates a trade deficit.
6. It creates a shaky banking system.
7. It eventually leads to depressions.
8. It is usually a prerequisite for violent upheavals.

I will discuss each of these effects in some detail.

Business Takeovers and Monopolies

Many economic variables in this century seem to be moving in a three-decade cycle. Industrial concentration caused by merger mania appears to be one of them. There was a great merger wave in the 1920s, which reappeared thirty years later during the 1950s. Today, again thirty years later, another giant merger wave has swept across our industrial heartland.

The term "monopoly" usually means the control of an industry by only one firm. But used more loosely, it also signifies regional centers of economic power, or a few firms that compete with one another in a sector but among them control that sector. Business mergers, or the takeover of one company by another, obviously generate monopolistic tendencies within the overall industry, as the number of competing firms declines. The control of an industry by one company or by a small group of companies obviously appeals to the top management. Businessmen usually hate competition, because it creates uncertainty and trims profits. But the real question is whether corporate concentration is in the public interest.

The advocates of industrial concentration argue that large combinations generate efficiency by concentrating production in the most efficient plants and shutting down the inefficient ones. Industrial concentration also promotes managerial efficiency as one group of top management ends up doing the job of two. A larger concern can also afford to allocate more resources to research and development, thereby stimulating the growth of the firm and eventually the economy. Thus, growth and efficiency are the main arguments traditionally offered in favor of corporate marriages.

However, mergers also create many side effects that can be fatal to the financial system. They restrain competition among firms and create monopolies, which usually charge higher prices for often inferior products. Without stiff competition there is no incentive for the company and its employees to work hard, manufacture quality goods, offer courteous service, and treat the customer as king.

Mergers might trim costs by more economical large-scale production, but they also promote inefficiency and lethargy among managers and workers. One reason why America has lost its longstanding edge in manufacturing products such as automobiles, televisions, and cameras, among countless others, is the rise of giant monopolies in these industries since the Second World War, whereas firms in Japan faced stiff competition from one another during the same years, forcing them to offer top-quality products at the lowest possible price. Having been tested in battles at home, the Japanese firms could easily outcompete U.S. companies.

Business combinations also reduce employment and wages, particularly among salesmen. Whenever one company takes over another, many employees and managers of the acquired firm invariably lose their jobs.

Merger activity frequently undermines the financial strength of merged firms. If a company acquires another by using its own funds, there is no such danger. But if the acquisition occurs through the creation of debt, acquired by banks or the public, the combined business is saddled with far higher indebtedness than before. This is especially true if the price paid to acquire the firm turns out to be much greater than anticipated. Often the management of the targeted company fights tooth and nail to resist the takeover. The top executives know that their exorbitant salaries spring from their control over a large fraction of the firm's stock. They know that if they had to compete with others in a free market, they wouldn't even come close to getting their current compensation. They are also aware that many would be willing to do their job at a fraction of their pay. So they do their best to obstruct the takeover.

When the management of the targeted firm resists, either by trying to find another buyer or by borrowing to acquire more of its own shares, then the acquiring company usually ends up paying much more than its initial offer. If the merger does occur, the combined business has a much larger debt; if it does not, then the targeted firm usually ends up with added debt it incurred to purchase its own stock.

Furious merger activity can be deleterious to the economy. Between 1984 and 1986, corporate debt rocketed by over $200 billion. What did the nation get in the bargain? Loss of thousands of jobs and a fragile corporate structure.

Companies normally raid other companies to acquire a new technology, to restrain competition, to diversify, or to pursue a corporate strategy. These mergers may serve some useful social purpose. The worst consequences, however, occur when raids are motivated purely by personal gain. Sometimes the raiding party merely wants to make a quick profit and targets a company whose management is likely to resist furiously. The strategy is simple. The raider —an individual, a group or firm—will first buy a big chunk of stock in the targeted company and then offer a very generous price for a portion of the remaining stock, enough to give the raider a majority interest in the acquisition. The raider has absolutely no interest in acquiring his target; all he hopes is that the management of the raided corporation will buy him out at a much higher price. Such raids happened frequently in the 1980s, giving birth to a number of new fortunes acquired through buyouts that are appropriately dubbed "greenmail."

Corporate raids purely for profit are pointless, wasteful, and destructive for society. They stimulate wealth disparity without generating any increase in goods and services that would be of public benefit. They promote insider trading and a general milieu for fraud and avarice. Worst of all, they foreshadow a great depression.

In 1975, merger deals that actually went through totaled $11.8 billion; in 1984, they soared to $122.2 billion; and in 1985 and in 1986 they were close to $180 billion. Compare this with the $140 billion that all manufacturing concerns invested in productive plants and equipment in 1986. By this and other measures, business takeovers are largely unproductive. They create no jobs; in fact, they trim jobs. The several hundred billion dollars that went into mergers during the 1980s could have gone into research, innovations, new technology, improved machines, and countless other productive activities. They went instead to increase the fortunes of already wealthy individuals. No wonder, then, that America can't compete with Japan and Germany, where merger activity has been subdued.

But the real question, ignored by scholars so far, is: What creates a merger mania? The answer lies in wealth disparity. The government's attitude is also important, but is not crucial to merger fever. Some amount of merger activity is normal, perhaps healthy, in a prosperous economy. When companies take over other companies with their own funds, they may stimulate growth and efficiency, provided competition remains. A company may also preserve jobs while acquiring another insolvent business. Not all mergers are bad.

But when wealthy individuals get involved purely for personal gain, the results are ultimately disastrous. That is exactly when merger mania develops. For individuals even to contemplate acquisition of huge corporations, they have to be wealthy themselves. They have to have the resources to line up the banks that back their proposed deals. The point is simple. You have to be a multimillionaire yourself before you can even dream of raiding a corporation worth billions and challenging its management. If you don't have the resources, no bank will lend you the huge amounts necessary for a successful takeover.

Normal merger activity heats up and turns into a fever when wealthy individuals get involved. Hence, high wealth disparity is a prerequisite for merger manias and all their ugly social consequences. Free markets are great for efficiency and economic growth. But how can you keep your markets free in the presence of excessive wealth disparity, which encourages merger manias, which, in turn, breed monopolies?

The Incentive to Work and Speculation

An argument commonly used by the rich is that if society controls wealth disparity, there is no incentive left to work hard, and productivity will suffer, leading to a general decline in the living standard. Let us examine this reasoning carefully. Everyone, with twenty-four hours available to him per day, faces a choice between work and leisure. Work brings monetary rewards, but can also cause fatigue and boredom. Leisure, on the other hand, brings entertainment and rest, but costs money in terms of lost compensation. Both work and leisure have merits and demerits. You have to choose between them in daily life; you can't have unlimited amounts of both.

A person normally chooses both work and leisure, simply because he must work to earn money. There are usually three reasons why people want money. They want it to fulfill their basic necessities of food, housing, clothing, education, and medical care; to save for the future; and to acquire the means to enjoy nonworking hours. For these reasons, a person is willing to work longer and harder, provided he earns more. Thus as salaries rise, the work effort also rises, but only up to a point. Once the three needs have been amply satisfied, the lure of higher income does not necessarily produce the same response in terms of work effort. In fact, a person may work less or with lower intensity as his income rises beyond that point, because he no longer needs to toil so hard to satisfy his three requirements. At that stage, he may even reduce his working hours and enjoy more leisure.

An already extremely wealthy person does not need more money as an incentive to work harder or longer. In fact, the opposite may happen. To a person who has made millions, or inherited them, money does not have the same attraction as it does to a poor man. The affluent have no reason to work hard. Thus, in theory at least, affluence tends to undermine the work ethic. But in the real world, we find that the rich run after money as hard as, if not harder than, the poor. Why do some people take undue risks, and even commit crimes, to earn more? Why did Ivan Boesky, a millionaire, indulge in illegal insider trading, which cost him millions in fines and a term in jail? For money, of course! But why?

Some people's answer to that question is that greed is an addictive disease: the richer a person is, the greedier he becomes. There perhaps is some truth to this. By one standard at least—an analysis of those who give money to charities in America—it would certainly seem to be confirmed in a resounding way. Scott Burns draws this surprising conclusion by analyzing the data published by the Internal Revenue Service. "Who does the giving in America?" he asks rhetorically, and concludes that "the affluent are conspicuous only by their absence."[1] I have reproduced the IRS table that Burns uses as my Table 19.

Table 19
The Distribution of Giving in America, 1985

Adjusted Gross Income (dollars)	Number of Returns (thousands)	Number Giving (thousands)	Percent Giving
Under $5,000	16,017	2,730	17.0
5,000–10,000	15,346	5,530	36.0
10,000–15,000	13,212	5,354	40.5
15,000–20,000	10,890	4,196	38.5
20,000–30,000	15,677	4,576	29.2
30,000–50,000	16,892	2,363	14.0
50,000–100,000	6,276	265	4.2
Over 100,000	997	15	1.5
Total	95,307	25,029	26.3

Source: Scott Burns, *Dallas Morning News*, November 25, 1986, p. 1D; or *Statistics of Income Bulletin*, Summer 1986.

Of some 95 million returns filed in 1986, merely 25 million or 26 percent claimed deductions for donations. The percentage of donors, 40.5, was the highest among those earning from $10,000 to $15,000, and the lowest, at 1.5, for those earning over $100,000. This is nothing short of amazing. Less than 2 percent of the really rich did any charitable giving, and among the really poor, 17 percent were donors. Among the upper-middle-class people, those earning between $50,000 and $100,000, only 4.2 percent were donors.

What about the total giving? You might think there may be fewer donors among the affluent, but perhaps they give a lot more. Well, think again. The IRS study also reveals

[1] Scott Burns, "A Surprising Portrait of Charity in America," *Dallas Morning News*, November 25, 1986, p. 1D.

that those in the $10,000–$15,000 income bracket donate more than twice as much as those in the $30,000–$50,000 bracket. And in 1985, those earning less than $50,000 could be classified as the poor or the middle class. The conclusion, though surprising, abhorrent, and paradoxical, is clear. Those with the most money are the least inclined to give it away.

What then do the extremely wealthy do with their money? If affluence tends to destroy the work ethic and generates avarice, I believe that it also destroys the willingness to invest and creates a penchant for speculation.

Economists usually define investment as expenditures in plant, equipment, and machines. Buying a new house is also considered investment. This kind of spending creates jobs and enhances labor productivity. Purchases of stocks, bonds, and other assets are not regarded as investment; they are termed portfolio management. And when portfolio management involves borrowing, economists call it speculation. In other words, if a person borrows money to acquire financial instruments, he is merely speculating. He is also said to speculate when he uses his own money to buy extremely risky stocks, bonds, and other instruments which offer relatively high returns, but also have a great potential to default.

Thus there is a crucial difference between speculation and true investment. Speculation is for quick personal gain; it fails to create employment or enhance productivity, and eventually destabilizes the economy. Investing is also for personal gain, but it works through opening or expanding a business. Investment requires hard work and patience for it to be profitable; the return is relatively low, but the risk of failure is also low.

A person, when poor, usually is averse to risk and more inclined to invest his money; but when rich, he starts speculating, largely because as a man grows richer, his aversion to risk declines. Furthermore, to a wealthy individual, a small return means nothing. To a multimillionaire, a return of only a few more thousands has little appeal. He wants a high and quick return. Such returns are available not from investment, but from speculation. Quick and big bucks can and have been made, for instance, from business takeovers, which are highly speculative in nature and which usually lead to layoffs. In other words, the rich normally don't invest; they speculate, and in the process, they play with the lives of others. They don't create jobs, they eliminate them. They are speculators, not entrepreneurs who start or expand their own businesses.

You may counter by saying that some billionaires own parts of giant firms. Doesn't that make them entrepreneurs? No, not really, because they didn't start those firms; they merely inherited or acquired stock in them. Of course, in a multitude of the opulent, you may discover one or two who started small and eventually, through effort, luck, or an inflationary environment, earned millions. They are, of course, exceptions. But in formulating a theory or public policy, one always disregards exceptions and focuses on generality.

In general, therefore, whenever wealth disparity rises, speculation rises with it. In 1929, barely 1 percent of Americans owned 36.3 percent of the nation's wealth, the highest concentration of wealth in the country's history. Hence the stock speculation was also the worst in history. During the 1970s, wealth inequality began to rise again, as did speculation in real estate, farmland, and gold. During the 1980s, the trend toward disparity sharply increased, as did the trend toward speculation, this time in the stock market as well as the markets for commodities, options, and stock-index futures. Such speculation, whether by wealthy individuals or by the managers of multimillion-dollar portfolios, inevitably drives up asset prices, creating an overinflated bubble that will keep bursting until the collapse of the economy.

Domestic Debt

Study after study tells us that the huge ocean of debt in which the American economy is now floating is unprecedented in our history. Total debt includes the indebtedness of corporations, consumers, and the government. In normal times, the debt/GNP ratio has been around 1.25; that is, total debt slightly exceeds the gross national product. At the end of 1987, this ratio was close to 2, the highest in the U.S. history. Total debt at the end of 1987 stood at around $8 trillion. This was domestic debt, which Americans owed to Americans, not foreigners. Much of the foreign debt of $400 billion was extra. Of the domestic debt, the government owed $2.3 trillion, consumers $3.2 trillion, and corporations $1.3 trillion. The rest was owed by miscellaneous agencies, such as state and local governments.

What has created such a vast ocean of debt? The answer, once again, is wealth disparity. Directly or indirectly, wealth inequality is the culprit behind the huge ocean of red ink.

There are three main players in the borrowing game today: the federal government, consumers, and corporations. Let's first consider why the government is so much in debt. Whenever government spending exceeds tax receipts, the government has to borrow money from the private sector, including individuals and institutions, to finance the shortfall. Government spending has been soaring since the 1960s, first on social programs and then on defense. Social spending had to be raised because the government accepted the noble challenge of alleviating poverty, which was widespread in the 1960s among both the young and the elderly. But poverty usually coexists with wealth disparity. If a small group has an overwhelming amount of assets, then a large multitude will, in most cases, be deprived.

If wealth inequality creates poverty, then it also generates the need for high social spending and the resultant big government and bureaucracy. In others words, high wealth disparity forced the government to raise social spending to help the needy. A better way to ease poverty would have been a direct assault on wealth inequality, rather than a wasteful expansion of government services. In any case, wealth concentration, not poverty, should be indicted for the massive growth of social spending since the 1960s.

In the 1980s, the growth of social programs was curbed somewhat, but defense spending climbed. So federal spending continued to follow its exponential growth of the two preceding decades. Still, if taxes had kept pace with rising spending, the federal debt would have been unchanged. In fact, because of soaring inflation that gradually put people into higher tax brackets in the 1970s, tax receipts also rose sharply, but not enough to match the increased spending. The result was a continuous rise in the federal debt since the 1960s.

Then in 1981, taxes were cut sharply, but federal spending continued to climb. This policy, on the one hand, gave a big boost to wealth inequality, and on the other, generated massive deficits, and eventually the debt. Here wealth inequality and debt climbed together. Thus, directly or indirectly, wealth disparity has been responsible for the growth of the federal debt. Until 1980 the government for the most part taxed the upper middle class and the rich to pay for social programs and to reduce poverty. Since 1981, however, the government has sharply increased its borrowing from the rich to maintain the living standards of others. Somehow the government decided that deficit financing was better accomplished by borrowing from the rich rather than taxing them, thus increasing federal debt.

High wealth inequality also generates high consumer debt. With higher wealth concentration, the number of persons with few or no assets rises. If an average person then buys a house, for example, he can afford only a small downpayment. This means he has to borrow more, increasing his debt burden. Others, whose living standard falls because of increased wealth inequality, are forced to borrow more to maintain their living styles. In other words, high wealth disparity is also the culprit behind the high consumer debt of the 1980s.

With corporate debt, the link with wealth inequality is not so evident. But a big chunk of the rise in this sector has come from business mergers. Between 1984 and 1986 alone, takeovers and mergers generated additional corporate debt of $200 billion. Merger mania cannot occur without wealth concentration. Hence wealth inequality is the scoundrel here as well. There are, of course, other social and economic reasons for the nation's huge ocean of debt. But wealth inequality is something that has been totally ignored in this regard.

Wealth Disparity and High Interest Rates

The rate of interest is one of the most important variables determining the state of the economy. Low interest rates generally stimulate spending and hence economic activity, while high rates do the opposite and eventually lead to recessions. What does wealth inequality do to the rate of interest? The answer is simple. High wealth concentration generates high interest rates.

What determines the rate of interest? The answer again is simple. The rate of interest is determined in the market for loanable funds. In every economy, there are some borrowers and some lenders. The lenders demand compensation to give anyone the right to utilize their money. Stated another way, the interest rate is influenced by the supply and demand for loans. Anything that raises this supply generates a fall in the interest rate. By contrast, anything that raises this demand produces a rise in the rate.

You have already seen that high wealth inequality forces the government, consumers, and corporations to increase their borrowing for a variety of reasons. Clearly, then, other factors remaining the same, wealth disparity creates a greater demand for loans and thus causes a rise in the interest rate. Even if the federal and corporate borrowing is unaffected, high wealth inequality forces the consumer to borrow, thus increasing the demand for loans.

What about the supply of loanable funds? It is true that the wealthy are generally the lenders and others generally the borrowers. As the rich get richer, there should be some rise in the supply of loans. But this rise falls short of the rise in loan demand, because not all of the wealth increase among the affluent ends up in the pool of loanable funds. Part of it goes into increased consumption and another part into speculation. Therefore, wealth inequality raises the demand for loanable funds faster than their supply, thereby raising the interest rates. There is thus a vicious circle, with high wealth inequality raising interest rates, and high interest rates further raising wealth inequality.

There is another reason why wealth disparity causes an interest-rate surge. Since wealth inequality raises poverty, the poor and the middle class, who are net borrowers, become less creditworthy than before. Therefore, lenders demand higher loan premiums and raise their interest rates.

Other factors that affect interest rates are inflation, the monetary policy of the Fed, and the state of the economy. Inflation tends to curtail the supply of loanable funds, because the lender, knowing that he will be paid back in depreciated currency, expects extra compensation. The interest-rate rise from this factor is called the inflation premium. Thus, interest rates always rise with inflation.

The Fed can also critically influence the interest rate through its monetary policy, which involves the management of the nation's money supply. The Fed usually does this by trading government bonds with the public. The Fed, by law, cannot deal directly with the government. When the Fed buys government bonds, it pays for them by pouring funds into the private sector; these funds, in turn, end up with banks or other lending institutions, raising the money or loan supply in the process. Consequently, the interest rate falls. On the other hand, if the Fed sells government bonds, money moves from the private sector to the Fed; the loan or money supply drops and interest rates rise. Hence an expansionary monetary policy lowers interest rates, and monetary restraint by the Fed raises them.

Another factor affecting interest rates is the state of the economy. An expanding economy generates increased loan demand, as people and businesses borrow more to finance increased transactions, thereby raising the rate of interest. A contracting economy leads to the reverse process and lowers the interest rate.

Statistics bear out my analysis of our economic situation. You may recall from personal experience that some of the highest interest rates in this century occurred between 1980 and 1982. The rate of inflation was also exorbitant at that time, which demonstrates that high inflation always results in high interest rates.

In order to adjust for the inflation factor, economists have developed the concept of the real interest rate, which is defined as the interest rate that you pay minus the rate of inflation. The real rate measures the purchasing power of interest income or the true cost of borrowing. The rate that you actually pay is called the nominal interest rate. Since the early 1980s, the nominal rates have come down sharply, because of declining inflation, but the real rates reveal a different trend.

Table 20 furnishes data on long-term nominal and real rates for various years in this century. I have omitted the 1930s and the 1940s from this table because these are usually regarded by economists as abnormal decades, one

Table 20
Nominal and Real Rates of Interest in Selected Decades

Year	Bond Rate (Moody's Aaa)	Rate of Inflation	Real Rate	Average Rate Per Decade
1920	6.12	15.8	−9.68	
1921	5.97	−10.6	16.57	
1922	5.10	−6.3	11.10	
1923	5.12	1.8	3.32	
1924	5.00	0	5.00	
1925	4.88	2.5	2.38	
1926	4.73	0.9	2.83	
1927	4.57	1.8	2.77	
1928	4.55	−1.3	5.85	
1929	4.73	0	4.73	4.50
1950	2.62	1.0	1.62	
1951	2.86	7.9	−5.04	
1952	2.96	2.2	0.76	
1953	3.20	0.8	2.40	
1954	2.90	0.5	2.40	
1955	3.06	−0.4	3.46	
1956	3.36	1.5	1.86	
1957	3.89	3.6	0.29	
1958	3.79	2.7	1.09	
1959	4.38	0.8	3.58	1.24
1960	4.41	1.6	2.81	
1961	4.35	1.0	3.35	
1962	4.33	1.1	3.23	
1963	4.26	1.2	3.06	
1964	4.40	1.3	3.10	
1965	4.49	1.7	2.79	
1966	5.13	2.9	2.23	
1967	5.51	2.9	2.61	
1968	6.18	4.2	1.98	
1969	7.03	5.4	1.63	2.68
1970	8.04	5.9	2.14	
1971	7.39	4.3	3.09	
1972	7.21	3.3	3.91	
1973	7.44	6.2	1.24	
1974	8.57	11.0	−2.43	

Table 20 (cont.)

Year	Bond Rate (Moody's Aaa)	Rate of Inflation	Real Rate	Average Rate Per Decade
1975	8.83	9.1	−0.27	
1976	8.43	5.8	2.63	
1977	8.02	6.5	1.52	
1978	8.73	7.7	1.03	
1979	9.63	11.3	−1.67	1.32
1980	11.94	13.5	−1.56	
1981	14.17	10.4	3.77	
1982	13.79	6.1	7.69	
1983	12.04	3.2	8.84	
1984	12.71	4.3	8.41	
1985	11.37	3.6	7.77	
1986	9.02	1.9	7.12	
1987	9.50	4.0	5.50	6.00

Sources: *Historical Statistics of the United States; Economic Report of the President, 1987.*

distorted by the Great Depression and the other by the Second World War. I have also omitted the 1910s, because they resemble the 1970s.

The Aaa bond rate is the long-term rate of interest relevant to business decisions concerning investment. Table 20 shows that the highest real interest rates occurred in the 1920s and again in the 1980s. My analysis implies that the real rates rise with wealth concentration, GNP growth (which is a measure of economic activity), and the Fed's restrictive monetary policy. GNP growth in the 1980s has been somewhat below that of the 1950s, 1960s, and 1970s, suggesting that the real rates in the 1980s should have been below their levels in the three preceding decades. Yet that is not the case. Note that inflation doesn't matter in the analysis now, because it has already been taken into account in the definition of the real rate.

As regards monetary policy, comparisons by decade are difficult to make. However, between 1980 and 1982, the

Fed followed a tight money policy, but it has eased up considerably since then. Nevertheless, real rates since 1981 have been stubbornly high, certainly higher than their levels since the Second World War. The conclusion is unmistakable: real rates in the 1980s have been exorbitant because of an extremely high level of wealth disparity. Another way of stating this conclusion is that even though inflation has fallen in the 1980s, nominal interest rates have not fallen fast enough because of rising wealth concentration.

What is the role of the federal deficit in this regard? No more than moderate—because the last time the real rates were stubbornly high was in the 1920s, another high-wealth-inequality decade, even though the government at the time had a consistent budget surplus.

The last column in Table 20 presents the average real interest rate for the decade. The average was exceptionally low for the 1950s and the 1970s, and moderate for the 1960s. For the 1980s, however, it has been at its highest in this century, even higher than in the 1920s—6 percent versus 4.5 percent. The higher average in the current decade may reflect the effect of budget deficits, which, in any case, are caused by wealth inequality. In the 1980s, therefore, wealth inequality has had a two-pronged impact on the real rate, through its effect on public as well as private borrowing. In the 1920s, wealth inequality produced only a private-borrowing effect, as the tradition of providing government assistance to the poor was not yet born and there were no federal deficits.

Wealth Inequality and the Trade Deficit

One of the most puzzling phenomena of the 1980s has been the persistence of huge trade deficits in the United States. The conventional explanation for this puzzle goes something like this. Because of high budget deficits, both the nominal and real interest rates in the United States have been higher than those prevailing among its major trading partners, such as Japan and Western Europe. As a result, starting from 1981, capital from abroad began to flow in large quantities toward the United States, leading to a sharp appreciation of the dollar. This made exports dearer and imports cheaper than before. As a result, exports declined and imports surged year after year. The balance of payments, which was in surplus in 1980 and 1981, turned into a deficit after 1982. In 1984, the deficit crossed the $100 billion mark for the first time in history—another dubious first during the 1980s.

This deficit itself should have sent the dollar reeling, but the dollar kept rising instead. Never before in history has a currency appreciated in the wake of deficits mounting with such rate and speed. Those who pointed to the peril of this phenomenon were overruled by the Reagan administration and its economists. Walter Mondale, the Democratic presidential candidate in the 1984 election, was ridiculed by the media and Reagan for his efforts to focus on the vast danger of the climbing dollar. But eventually, the foreign exchange market had to heed the threat of the mounting U.S. trade deficit. From February 1985, the dollar began to depreciate against major world currencies belonging to Japan and Western Europe. Immediately forecasts came pouring out from economists that within eighteen months the U.S. balance of trade would turn around and the deficit would at least begin to fall. They were wrong—once again.

Why eighteen months? The economists have invented a J curve, which suggests that currency depreciation takes as long as eighteen months to improve a nation's trade account, because as the currency falls, the import prices go up immediately, but import volume falls only later. Hence the lagged effect. But despite the depreciation of the dollar, the trade deficit kept rising. It was $125 billion in 1985, $150 billion in 1986, and more than $170 billion in 1987. What happened to the theory?

The culprit, as usual, was and is wealth disparity. First, the economists erred when they argued that high U.S. interest rates relative to those in other countries were caused by high U.S. budget deficits. Between 1981 and 1983, when this interest-rate differential began to cause the appreciation of the dollar, the budget deficits in Canada, Germany, Japan, and Britain as a percentage of GNP were at least as high as in America, if not higher. The main difference was that the U.S. deficit sprang from pro-affluent tax cuts that raised wealth disparity, whereas in other countries deficits occurred because of rising social spending, which generally helps the needy and thus tends to reduce wealth inequality. In other words, the dollar rose not because of high U.S. deficits relative to those among our trading partners, but because of the sharply rising wealth inequality caused by the Reagan tax cuts. This, in turn, generated high trade deficits.

Why didn't the trade deficit fall when the dollar began to depreciate after February 1985? One reason again is wealth disparity. Because of rising wealth inequality, stock speculation began to soar after August 1982, the first full year of the tax cut, helping the rich grow richer, enabling them to consume luxury goods without much regard to price. The import of luxury goods kept rising even though their prices also rose sharply because of the depreciating dollar. Writes Kathleen Hughes, a staff reporter of the *Wall Street Journal,* "Mercedes-Benz prices have climbed a whopping 21 percent in the past two years, yet unit sales have risen 25 percent. BMW prices have climbed about 15 percent in the same period, with unit sales up 30 percent."[2] Similarly, imports of other luxury goods, such as

[2] Kathleen A. Hughes, "Despite Rising Prices, Americans Remain Wedded to Imported Products," *Wall Street Journal,* September 9, 1987, p. 33.

caviar, specialty cheeses, and French wines, kept rising in spite of big price hikes, because the rising stock market helped the wealthy grow wealthier, so price didn't matter much to them. Therefore, it was not surprising that soon after the stock market crash in October 1987, the trade deficit fell sharply from the pre-crash peak of $17.6 billion to an average of $13 billion per month in the first quarter of 1988.

Where price did matter—among the rest of Americans —savvy foreign exporters chose to trim profit margins and raised their prices much less than the appreciation of their currencies. Between 1985 and 1987, the Japanese yen appreciated by almost 100 percent, but prices of many Japanese exports rose only 15 percent to 25 percent. Thus, rising wealth disparity in the 1980s played a crucial role first in the dollar appreciation up to 1985, and then in the stubborn refusal of imports to decline as the dollar began to depreciate. The major cause of the unprecedented trade deficit and the mounting foreign debt is none other than the bulging concentration of wealth.

The Shaky Banking System

Throughout the 1920s, bank failures soared, despite an otherwise prosperous economy. The same phenomenon has occurred in the 1980s, even though the country has enjoyed one of the longest economic expansions on record. A popular explanation is that falling energy and farm prices have been responsible for the crescendo of bank failures in the energy and farm-belt states such as Texas, Louisiana, Idaho, Colorado, Wyoming, Montana, and Oklahoma. But then banks have also failed in the oil-poor states of Massachusetts, Maryland, New York, Illinois, and Ohio, to name a few, where unemployment is generally lower than the national average. Throughout the 1970s, which experienced the worst recession since the Second World War, there were only ten bank failures, but over five hundred banks have already failed in the 1980s.

Why are the 1920s and the 1980s alike in this respect? Once again, wealth inequality stands implicated. With bulging wealth inequality the number of the poor rises and the middle class shrinks. These people, in order to maintain their life-styles or even to subsist, have to increase their borrowing, and since they generally have few assets, they become less creditworthy than before. Their credit rating declines overall.

If a bank rejects risky borrowers, its balance sheet remains sound. But when credit ratings in general have deteriorated, banks cannot afford to be picky; after all, they have to find customers for their loans. Only a really conservative bank then refuses to make risky loans, because with more money in the hands of the affluent, the banks are also flush with money, which they are eager to lend in order to maximize their earnings.

The poor usually deal with cash, but the rich generally deposit their money in the banks. Therefore, whenever wealth transfers from the poor to the rich, say, because of rising interest rates or sharp income tax cuts, the banks are flooded with money. Banks generally feel compelled to find outlets for their cash; funds that sit idle beyond a certain legally required level earn no interest. Funds that are lent, particularly in the form of mortgages and consumer credit, earn high rates of interest.

It is well known that during the 1980s, consumer debt has grown dramatically, making such loans far more risky. You would think that financial institutions would turn conservative. But read what Betsy Morris, a reporter for the *Wall Street Journal,* has to say: "Gone are the days when the grim-faced banker peered across the desk at a quaking customer who had come in search of a loan—the days when bankers felt the only good loan was a repaid loan.

Now, at almost every turn, banks and thrifts eagerly hawk consumer credit."[3]

Why are they doing it? Because they are flush with rising cash deposits from the rich. Thus bulging wealth disparity encourages risky loans and shaky banking systems, so that bank failures rise even in a growing economy, as happened in the 1920s and is now happening in the 1980s.

Wealth Disparity and Depressions

I have already discussed at length how wealth inequality eventually brings about a disaster in my book The *Great Depression of 1990,* and in the second chapter of this book. Suffice it to say here that history shows that usually every sixth decade in America, high wealth concentration first generates huge private and/or public debt, high real interest rates, speculative fevers, merger manias, fragile financial institutions, and a general environment of graft and greed, all of which climax into a cataclysmic depression lasting no less than seven years.

Wealth Disparity and Revolutions

Finally, let me remind you of another dictum of history. Time and time again throughout history, enormous concentration of wealth among the few has driven the poverty-ridden masses to rise up and dethrone the affluent from the lofty pedestal of power and prestige in a massive revolution. The wealth and greed of the Bourbon kings of France and their courtiers led to the French Revolution; the czarist regime and the Russian aristocracy were over-

[3] Betsy Morris, "Eager to Lend," *Wall Street Journal,* September 9, 1987, p. 29.

thrown by the Bolshevik revolution; the shah of Iran was deposed in a bloody uprising. History tells us, in no uncertain terms, that great wealth disparity eventually breeds great upheavals. I write this not as a prediction, but as a warning in the spirit of Thomas Jefferson, who warned the French public, just four years before the revolution, that their extreme wealth concentration would have grave consequences for their society.

CHAPTER 17

Tricklism

YOU MAY RAISE a legitimate question at this point. If excess concentration of wealth has such horrendous consequences for an economy and society, why are its dangers almost universally ignored?

The simple answer is that we are living in the midst of what may properly be called the age of acquisitors. An acquisitor is someone whose mind runs mostly after money, who covets money for its own sake and forgets that there are finer things in life worthy of enjoyment. Acquisitiveness is a state of mind, not a state of one's possessions. An acquisitor is usually a wealthy person, but a wealthy person need not be an acquisitor. It all depends on what you do with your wealth. If a person spends most of his time amassing wealth even though he is already affluent, he certainly is an acquisitor; but if a well-to-do man merely enjoys his wealth, spending it on himself and on others, he is not an acquisitor.

During the age of acquisitors, wealth is the main source of political power and social prestige. The wealthy then control government, religion, social customs, and most other social institutions. They hire intellectuals to invent theories justifying the supremacy of acquisitors in society. Some heretics may talk about the evils of greed or materialism, but such ideas, despite their intrinsic appeal, fail to become popular, because they castigate the attitude of the dominant class. The intellectuals holding such ideas are usually social outcasts.

Throughout its short history, the United States has been in the age of acquisitors. This is not to say that industrial capitalism has prevailed ever since immigrants from Europe first set foot on American soil, only that the wealthy have been the predominant social force throughout this period. Before the Civil War in the 1860s, respect and authority gravitated toward those who owned vast estates and land. Since then, wealthy businessmen and bankers have been the dominant force. Thus one way or another, affluence has meant power and prestige in American society from its very beginning.

In every society, intellectuals play a unique role. They mold ideas; from them spring forth inventions, religion, science, philosophy, ideology, and economic theories. Wealth does not bring power in every nation. In some places, the military is the dominant voice; in others, the clergy holds the reins. But no matter who is supreme, most intellectuals offer ideas justifying the privileges of the ruling group. They do this in the interest of their own well-being.

When monarchy was the dominant institution in history, intellectuals concocted a theory called the divine right of kings, arguing that the monarch had a God-given right to rule. When the priesthood reigned supreme, intellectuals invented a dogma called the divine rights of priesthood, suggesting that the head priest was the representative of God on earth. When acquisitors are the dominant force in society, intellectuals offer theories justifying greed, economic individualism, and wealth concentration.

Avarice is then anointed with a moral gloss, without which the rule of acquisitors might not appeal to the general public.

Such is the view that prevails in present-day American society. Popular economic thought holds that while wealth disparity may be somewhat unfair, at least it is good for economic prosperity. Isn't the wealth in the hands of savvy entrepreneurs and risk-takers, who generate investments and create jobs? We should not hinder their pursuit of money, because they plow their riches back into the economy in the form of new investment and in the process lubricate the engine of growth. Such arguments have prevailed for the past two centuries, even though there have been numerous recessions and at least four major depressions in U.S. history. They prevailed in the 1920s, which culminated in the Great Depression of the 1930s. They have come to the fore again in the 1980s in the guise of Reaganomics, whose chief characteristic, as we have seen, is the trickle-down theory.

Trickle-Down Economics

Trickle-down theory simply means that society should give businessmen free rein to accumulate wealth, and from the wealthy, prosperity will gradually, drop by drop, seep into the rest of society. The theory maintains that the more wealth the rich have, the more they will invest and the more job opportunities they will create. Greed is therefore good for society. Avarice of the affluent is crucial to the nation's ecnomic health. This idea may be called tricklism, and its proponents trickle-down theorists, or simply tricklists.

Tricklism asserts that whenever the economy is in trouble, because of high inflation, high unemployment, trade deficits, or some other ill, the government is mostly to blame. Some tricklists denounce the government for interfering too much, others for not interfering enough. Whatever the case, they hold the government at fault in most circumstances. The private sector driven by greed is never the culprit.

One branch of tricklism, called monetarism, claims that the Great Depression was caused by the faulty monetary policy of the government, as nothing was done to rescue the foundering banks. In other words, the state failed to do anything. Another branch of tricklism, Keynesian theory, holds the faulty fiscal policy of the government responsible for the debacle. The government should not have raised taxes in the middle of a downturn. In this view, the state did too much. Yet another school of tricklism holds that trade protectionism, also a form of government interference, was the main culprit. But blaming the government for the Great Depression is like blaming a doctor for his patient's sickness. Why was the economy so sick in 1929 that it needed the state's rescue? The cause, in my opinion, was excessive wealth concentration. Most tricklists ignore this variable. Government does make mistakes, but only because it is a government of the rich, by the rich, for the rich. Ultimately, it is private greed that was to blame for the worst economic cataclysm in U.S. history.

Macroeconomics, which is the study of economic behavior of society as a whole, is currently suffering from a great deal of confusion. At last count, excluding the socialists and radicals, there were eight schools of thought and their adherents—the classicists, the neoclassicists, the Keynesians, the post-Keynesians, the neo-Keynesians, the monetarists, the rational expectationists, and the supply-siders. All these schools diverge from one another, some radically, some only a shade, offering a variety of policy prescriptions. A closer study, however, reveals that all these viewpoints fall in two categories. Broadly speaking, there are only *two* schools of economic thought, namely the interventionist school and the noninterventionist school, whose two generic ideas encompass all macroeconomic philosophies.

According to the interventionist school, government should periodically fine-tune the economy with the aid of its monetary and fiscal policies. The private sector on its own is unstable, but the state can stabilize it by intervening in its financial institutions, such as the bond and money markets. During a downturn in the economy, for example, the Treasury ought to use the bond market to borrow from the public in order to finance the budget deficit, and the Fed should buy government securities to help banks expand the supply of money. Such are the intervening weapons of the interventionist school, which includes the Keynesians, post-Keynesians, and neo-Keynesians. The three may differ on the emphasis to be given to the various policy tools, but on the question of state intervention, also called policy activism, they concur. They all favor a large government sector as a bulwark against a faltering economy.

The noninterventionist school, comprising the remaining viewpoints, detests the idea of economic fine-tuning by the state on logical as well as ideological grounds. Government, in its view, ought to keep its hands off the economy and adhere to rigid rules regarding money growth and balancing the federal budget. The private sector on its own is efficient and stable, but government interference destabilizes it and makes it inefficient. State aid may offer short-term palliatives, but it cannot offer a long-term cure. The rigid monetary rule of the noninterventionist school is that each year the Fed should expand money supply equal to the long-term growth rate of the GNP, which over two centuries has averaged around 3.7 percent a year. The rigid fiscal rule is that the government budget should be balanced over the course of the business cycle.

Although the two broadly defined schools of economic thought occasionally offer radically different prescriptions, their underlying philosophy is much the same. They both believe in tricklism. The noninterventionist school espouses overt tricklism, whereas the interventionist school espouses covert tricklism.

Overt Tricklism

Overt tricklism openly exalts selfishness and greed. It argues that when people are allowed to act in their self-interest, they want to attain the best possible result at least cost, which makes the economic system highly productive and generates sound economic growth. The government should, therefore, have as few regulations as possible to obstruct individual economic behavior. All markets, such as those for commodities, stocks, bonds, financial and labor services, and foreign trade, should be as free as possible from government regulation.

This is the theory of overt tricklism. But in practice it has called for government intervention in hard times. In times of prosperity, overt tricklists want to leave big business, bankers, and stockholding barons alone and not hinder their quest for maximizing profits, even if it leads to monopolies. In hard times, however, they want the state to intervene and stabilize the economy by increasing wealth inequality, which can be achieved by cutting taxes for the wealthy and by offering business incentives in the form of tax credits, liberal depreciation rules, depletion allowances, financial deregulation, and so on. In short, overt tricklists condemn all forms of state regulation when the economy is booming, but in a crisis look to the government for help.

There are two decades in this century during which overt tricklism was in its heyday—the 1920s and the 1980s. Both began with serious "stagflation," a state of high inflation, high unemployment, and high interest rates. In both cases, the presidency transferred into the hands of a Republican—Harding and Reagan. In response to the pleas of noninterventionists, both presidents persuaded Congress to enact pro-affluent, probusiness tax cuts. They also accelerated the process of deregulation already underway. These policies generated a sharp rise in wealth disparity, which eventually led to the debacle of 1929, and which will again lead to the debacle of the 1990s.

What is wrong with overt tricklism? Apart from the fact that its prescriptions have frequently bred great depressions in U.S. history, it is also riddled with rank hypocrisy. This dogma acquires a moral gloss by claiming that the wealthy constantly invest their money and create jobs. Nothing, however, is farther from the truth. The affluent are mostly speculators, not investors. Why else would the government need to give them incentives in the form of investment tax credit, liberalized depreciation rules, and the like? If investing is natural to the rich, as overt tricklism claims, why under crises do they plead for state help? The fact is that the wealthy are natural speculators, and in order to induce them to invest in productive activities, the government has to offer them tax incentives. For instance, until 1986 the maximum tax on long-term capital gains was only 20 percent, while on every other form of income it was more than double that figure. While the top tax rate for income obtained from hard physical or intellectual labor was 50 percent, income earned from the sale of assets such as stocks and bonds was taxed at most at the 20 percent rate.

Does big business really create jobs? This is another myth which has been prevalent for the past two hundred years. David Birch finally explodes it in his recent book.[1] He concludes that since 1981, firms employing fewer than twenty people have created almost all new jobs. Small businessmen, those belonging to the middle class, are the real entrepreneurs and investors. The wealthy merely specu-

[1] David Birch, *Job Creation in America* (New York: Free Press, 1987).

late on already existing businesses or seek to take over smaller businesses. They don't generate jobs but eliminate them through mergers. Birch confirms this by his finding that small companies offer better job security than larger firms.

Covert Tricklism

Covert tricklism, or Keynesian economics, is not so blatant in its support of big business and the wealthy. It does not openly rationalize monopolies or a greed-based economy. It professes compassion for the poor, the handicapped, and the downtrodden. It favors big government and myriad regulations controlling business behavior. On paper, it denounces the immorality of high wealth inequality, but it has seldom offered practical ways to control the disparity. Concentration of wealth, to covert tricklism, is an ethical issue, not an economic issue—not something that generates stagflations and eventually depressions. For this reason, like the overt tricklists, covert tricklists seldom worry about the depredations of excessive wealth inequality, preferring to leave the wealthy alone. Instead, they champion a highly regulated economy, naively believing that myriad government regulations, riddled with loopholes and costly to enforce, are a panacea to economic ills. This in spite of history's revelation that regulating the financial sector is sound economic policy because it generates low interest rates, while excessive regulation of the nonfinancial sector is counterproductive and inflationary, breeding inefficiency and stifling entrepreneurship and initiative.[2]

Covert tricklism doesn't worry about budget deficits and excessive money growth—at least it didn't until the end of

[2] See Ravi Batra, *The Great Depression of 1990* (New York: Simon & Schuster, 1987), Chapter 5.

the 1970s. The horrendous budget deficits of the 1980s should have chastened even the staunchest defenders of fiscal shortfall, but a few continue to disregard the government extravagance.

According to covert tricklism, whenever unemployment rises, the government should raise budget deficits, primarily by raising spending, and finance it by expanding money growth. It has a simple solution to joblessness—an easy-money policy to finance budget deficits. This itself should show you how bankrupt the idea is. If printing money is the answer to the problem of unemployment, there should be absolutely no poverty on earth. Every nation can print money. If prosperity can be achieved by simply opening the money pumps, then Brazil, Mexico, India, Egypt, and other Third World countries should have no unemployment at all.

You don't need to be an economist to figure out that money creation cannot solve the problem of unemployment. Eventually it can only breed high inflation, high interest rates, and hence high wealth inequality. Yet it took the double-digit inflation rates prevailing between 1979 and 1981 to influence the covert tricklists to abandon their twenty-year-long fascination with easy-money policies designed to finance budget deficiencies.

Covert tricklism, despite its avowed concern for the poor and the elderly, supports business incentives, especially the investment tax credit and a relatively low capital gains tax. Yet its biggest failure to date has been in spawning stagflation by the end of the 1970s, as governments, hooked on this idea, frequently unleashed the engine of money growth, beginning in the 1960s.

During the 1980s, tricklism has combined the worst of the overt and the covert versions. From the overt school, it has borrowed the policy of enriching the rich, and from the covert school, the policy of budget deficits. Reaganomics is hybrid tricklism, an especially virulent form. In less than a decade, it has done to the U.S. economy what

America's worst enemies couldn't do in this entire century. With every passing day, the nation sinks deeper into domestic and foreign debt, and the world inches toward economic disaster.

Just four decades ago, when many countries were devastated by war, America stood alone with a healthy economy and the most productive industrial machine in the world. Japan was in shambles, England in shock, France in disarray, Germany reduced to rubble. America had no competition, and its economy was unrivaled. But now, forty years later, Japan and West Germany are more prosperous than ever before in their history, while the United States has become the world's largest debtor nation and is beset by an awesome array of other economic and social ills.

Tricklism and Forecasting

In every age, popular ideology serves the interests of the dominant class. Like the divine right of kings and the priesthood, tricklism is a self-serving dogma. Perhaps the most clear-cut evidence of that is the accuracy of the economic forecasts of tricklists. I have stated earlier that tricklism ignores excessive wealth inequality, which to me is the most critical variable determining the direction of the economy. Therefore, the forecasting record of tricklists, not surprisingly, is dismal. The logic and soundness of any theory are tested by its forecasts. If the forecasts are right, the theory is valid; if they are wrong, especially repeatedly, then the theory is pure rubbish.

Despite their elaborate theories and vast computer models, America's leading economists have had an awful record of forecasting since the 1970s. In October 1987, *Money* magazine compiled a list of celebrity economists and concluded: "Yet even these dazzling dismal scientists have a problem. Nothing seems to be working quite right for the profession in general. In Washington two decades of bogus economic models of the national economy have soured the reputation of policy economists. . . . On Wall Street they are reviled for conflicting forecasts that seem to have only a nodding relationship with the course of the stock market. . . . Never before have economists been more sought after to inform the citizenry—and rarely have they had less to say."[3]

Some of the forecasting errors of tricklism have by now become legendary. Professor Irving Fisher of Yale proclaimed in October 1929, "Stock prices have reached what looks like a permanently high plateau."[4] Within days after these immortal words, the stock market crashed and a ten-year-long depression began. Fisher was the most celebrated economist of his time. But he had only one brain. The Harvard Economic Society was working with several exceptional brains from Harvard University. In November 1929, barely a month after the market collapsed, the society assured the public that " a severe depression like that of 1920–21 is outside the range of probability. We are not facing protracted liquidation."[5] These assurances came from confirmed tricklists, who remained blind to reality even after the depression was underway.

When forecasts are repeatedly wrong, a wise person abandons his theories and looks for new ideas even if it is painful to confess ignorance. But today's tricklists are like tricklists in the 1920s, loudly asserting that depression in a capitalist society is logically impossible. Their views have nothing to do with logic. They are dogma, with potentially deadly consequences for the economy. Nevertheless, the

[3] Augustin Hedberg, "'Lights, Camera, Economists," *Money*, October 1987, p. 149.

[4] Quoted in "All Those Investment Forecasts: Why Most Are Wrong," *Staton's Stock Market Advisory* (Charlotte, N.C.), 1986.

[5] Quoted in John K. Galbraith, *The Great Crash, 1929* (London: Hamish Hamilton, 1955), p. 132.

tricklists are among the most highly respected members of the economics profession. They control the flow of ideas in top-ranked economic journals, censoring any work that criticizes them or points out the vicious economic effects of wealth disparity. In an acquisitive society, there is no place for economic heresy. Unfortunately, it is also a dictum of history that the intellectual establishment is the last to accept new ideas.

CHAPTER 18

How Can We Cure Our Economy?

EVERY DISEASE HAS SYMPTOMS and a cause. Remove the cause, and the sickness quickly disappears. But if you treat only the symptoms, the disease simmers and ultimately turns fatal.

The American economy had a disease in the form of virulent stagflation in 1980, and its symptoms were soaring inflation, interest rates, and unemployment. The Reagan administration decided to treat the symptoms by using the medicine of hybrid tricklism, calling for higher budget deficits along with a soak-the-poor tax-cut program. The medicine has worked; it has indeed treated the symptoms, but the disease is still simmering, and when it erupts next time, it could be fatal to our system.

There are steps that we and our government can take to cure our economy, and perhaps block the coming depression. It is too late to completely avoid the pain that will come from the inevitable retrenchment. Under the relentless onslaught of concentrated wealth, the country has been on a borrowing spree for a decade. The bills are coming due, and soon. But we can choose between an orderly withdrawal and a pell-mell retreat. The choice is still ours and our leaders' to make.

A Defense Tax

It is an age-old commandment of taxation that a person who can afford to do it should pay taxes in proportion to the benefits he receives from the government. The state provides everyone a variety of services. It maintains law and order, protects us from foreign enemies, tries to maintain a viable economy, helps us earn a living, manages the postal service, and does countless other things. Without government, there would be chaos, and we would all suffer from it. But our government is not in the business of producing goods; it depends on us for its sources of income. We, of course, pay taxes on our purchases and our incomes. The government gets revenue from the sales tax, the Social Security tax, the income tax, the corporate tax, and a variety of other fees. Collectively, we have to pay enough taxes to match government spending—federal, state, and local; otherwise, there will surely be a day of reckoning.

It's only fair that those receiving larger amounts of services should pay more in taxes. Take, for instance, defense spending. It protects our life, liberty, and wealth from foreign enemies. Life and liberty are equally dear to everybody, but we differ in the extent of our assets. The rich receive more from the government in the form of wealth protection than the poor and the middle class do. Obviously, therefore, there should be a tax on wealth, which is one of the objects protected by defense. Suppose you ask a security company to protect your wealth. Will the company do it for free? Of course not. Why then should the government provide such service freely to affluent beneficiaries? Defense spending also protects our economic system and thus enables us to earn relatively high incomes. So incomes should be also taxed for the same purpose. But incomes are already being taxed, whereas wealth is not. A wealth tax ought to be introduced to pay for a part of defense spending.

Defense spending achieves three goals: the protection of life, liberty, and wealth. Although it would certainly be difficult to give these three goals relative values, simple logic suggests that the wealth tax should pay for a third of our defense outlay. In 1988, the government spending for defense, including veterans' benefits, is expected to top $300 billion. So a third of this, equal to $100 billion, should come from a wealth tax.

But this is not all. The defense tax on wealth should be retroactive. After all, wealth has received defense protection for a long time without ever paying a penny for the service. In fact, a more careful look at the budget data over the period since the Second World War, decades spent largely in the defense of U.S. wealth at the expense of the poor and the middle class, reveals that if a wealth tax had existed in the past, we would have absolutely no federal debt today. If a third of the defense burden had been collected from a tax on wealth in the decades since the 1950s and used partly to retire the federal debt accumulated during the war and partly for continuing defense, the federal debt today would be zero.

Hence the defense tax on wealth, in all fairness, should be retroactive, and at least should pay for the current cost of the federal debt. This cost equals the interest the government pays on its debt, amounting to some $150 billion in 1988. To this, if we add the other $100 billion in defense spending, we obtain a figure of $250 billion to be collected annually from a defense tax on wealth.

This may look like an enormous sum, but compare it with the total wealth in the nation, amounting to over $15 trillion. The wealth tax should be imposed on an individual's net worth, including assets such as stocks, bonds, real

estate, precious metals, paintings, etc. For practicality and
fairness, certain types of assets should be exempted from
this tax. The necessities of daily life would fall into this
category. Thus a personal residence, car, clothing, furniture, applicances, etc. should be exempt.

House prices, however, differ sharply in different cities.
Suppose we took the average residence in the richest
neighborhood, and valued it at $1 million. The actual
value is much lower. But suppose the government gener-
ously exempts wealth up to $1 million and imposes a pro-
gressive wealth tax on anything higher than that. On the
second $1 million, for example, the tax could be 2 percent,
on the third $1 million, 4 percent, and so on up to 7
percent on the sixth $1 million or more. How much will
the government collect? I have constructed a defense tax
table in Table 21 and worked out how much a wealth-
owner will have to pay under the proposed tax.

According to revised estimates of the Joint Economic
Committee, 420,000 households or 0.5 percent of the population owned 27.3 percent of the nation's wealth in 1983.
In view of the massive climb of the stock market, this figure has now gone up to at least 28.5 percent. Suppose we
work with the figure 28 percent. With $15 trillion in total
wealth, the top wealth-owners owned $4.2 trillion, or an
average of $10 million per family. From the proposed de-

Table 21
Proposed Defense Tax Table

Total Wealth	Marginal Tax Rate	Tax Payable
$0–1 million	0	0
$1–2 million	2%	2% of excess over $1 million
$2–3 million	4%	20,000 + 4% of excess over $2 million
$3–4 million	5%	60,000 + 5% of excess over $3 million
$4–5 million	6%	110,000 + 6% of excess over $4 million
$5–6 million	7%	170,000 + 7% of excess over $5 million
over $6 million	7%	240,000 + 7% of excess over $6 million

fense tax table, the average tax on the richest families
would be $240,000 plus 7 percent of $4 million, or a total
of $520,000. With each of these 420,000 families paying
this amount on average, the tax receipt would be $218.4
billion.

The next group of 420,000 households, another 0.5
percent of the population, owns 8 percent of national
wealth, or $1.2 trillion. The average wealth there is $2.8
million. The average tax bill for each family in this group
would be $20,000 plus 4 percent of $0.8 million, or a total
of $52,000. The government's take from this group would
be $21.8 billion. Thus, 840,000 families, amounting to
1 percent of the population, would pay a total defense
tax of $240.2 billion.

Balancing the Budget

Revenue from the defense tax should be used to balance
the budget immediately, while freezing government
spending in real terms—that is, spending should not be
allowed to grow faster than the annual rate of inflation.
The federal shortfall in 1988 is expected to be around
$170 billion. The surplus revenue from the defense tax
should be used to retire the debt. In fact, it should be
written into law that real federal spending, having already
grown to dizzying heights, should be frozen.

What are the economic implications of this tax? It is
worth noting here that this tax will fall only on millionaires
and billionaires, who can easily afford to pay it. For instance, a man with $10 million in wealth, earning a 10
percent return net of current tax, would make $1 million
in investment income, out of which he could easily pay
$520,000 in defense tax. In fact, even a 6 percent net
return would be enough for him to pay the defense tax.
The wealthiest Americans would hardly miss their lost in-

come, while the economy would immediately move toward sanity.

The proposed defense tax would also slowly bring wealth disparity under check. At first the impact would be minor, almost imperceptible. As the deficit disappears and wealth inequality declines somewhat, interest rates would fall, which would induce the public to buy homes, cars, and appliances. It would also induce small businessmen, the real entrepreneurs and job creators, to borrow more for investment. The economy would boom. Wages would rise, and so would income tax receipts. This revenue should be used to retire the old debt further, so that within a few years, the entire federal debt would be gone, and we would be out of trouble for good. The government would then have a budget surplus, which could be used to trim the defense tax.

What would be the impact of the defense tax on the stock market? At first the market would fall somewhat, as some stockholders might have to sell their shares to pay the tax. But soon shareholders would realize the bonanaza of a balanced budget and low interest rates. On the whole, the market might be unaffected.

What are the potential dangers of the wealth tax? Only one. The wealthy would try to transfer their wealth abroad, leading to capital flight. This could, however, be stopped by doing what President Lyndon Johnson did in 1966, when he imposed capital controls, making it illegal to move money abroad.

Some people might suggest the defense tax would lower investment. This is not true, because the wealthy are speculators, not investors. Speculation would indeed cool, but investment would in fact rise because of a sharp decline in interest rates. Jobs would expand, not contract.

What about savings? President Reagan cut taxes for the rich in 1981 to increase savings and investment. While investment hasn't risen, the savings rate has plunged since then. This means the defense tax will have no adverse effect on savings and investment.

Is the proposed defense tax another scheme to redistribute wealth? No. It is a tax to eliminate the budget deficit and gradually retire the federal debt. It will go mainly for defense spending, which in the past has been financed mostly through deficit financing.

Re-regulation of the Financial System

Remember the good old 1950s and 1960s. Back then, banks and thrifts were regulated, interest rates were very low, the federal budget was more or less balanced, and inflation was minimal. Financial institutions paid no interest on checking accounts, which enabled them to offer long-term mortgages at fixed rates as low as 5 percent. This is exactly what our economy needs again. With low mortgages, people would be able to afford housing, and homelessness would decline; the American dream of owning your own home would once again be realized. Thus, there should be no payment of interest on checking accounts held by any institution, whether banks, thrifts, mortgages, or money market funds. This sounds like a small matter, but it has giant consequences.

The first time that banks began paying interest on checking accounts was in 1923. There was keen competition among New York banks to attract funds, and they responded by making checking deposits income-yielding assets. The rest of the country followed suit. This practice, however, raised the cost of funds to the banks, which, in turn, were forced to find borrowers to make a profit. The banks could no longer afford to let their funds sit idle; in the process, they relaxed credit standards and began to chase customers. The result was a drop in credit quality and further weakening of the financial system already ravaged by high inequality. In fact, bank failures began to soar right after 1923.

In 1933, after the Great Depression had shown the futility of this banking practice, Congress barred banks from paying interest on checking accounts. However, since 1983, sixty years later, banks and thrifts have been permitted to resume that mistaken practice and offer interest on checking accounts again. The result, not surprisingly, is the same as before—bank failures have risen sharply since 1983.

The mistake should be corrected immediately. All the financial institutions that were deregulated in the early 1980s should be brought under the umbrella of re-regulation. There should be only three types of deposits—checking, savings, and time. No interest should be permitted on checking accounts. Savings accounts should pay no more than 5 percent, and withdrawals from them should be permitted only once a month. Time deposits, where money is held for a year or longer, can pay the market-determined interest rate.

A healthy economy needs low interest rates. In order to ensure this, credit should be completely denied to speculative activities and allocated only for productive purposes, such as the purchase of real estate, cars, furniture, plant, equipment, etc. Stocks, bonds, commodities, futures, and all other types of speculative ventures should not be financed by loans from financial institutions. In this way, lendable funds would be available only to productive activities. Such re-regulation of the financial sector would further lower interest rates, cool the speculative fever, and restore the strength of tottering banks and thrifts.

Restraining the Growth of Money

In order to attain price stability, money growth should, over the course of the business cycle, be limited to the

GNP growth in the economy. This would keep prices more or less constant, and with inflation under control, interest rates would also stay low.

Money growth should be allowed to move only within a small range, depending on where the economy is on the path of the business cycle. The rule should be to permit slightly higher money growth during a recession, and a slightly lower growth as full employment draws near. For instance, suppose the average GNP growth over the business cycle is 4 percent. In that case, let the most basic measure of money, called M1, grow by 5 percent during high unemployment, and as unemployment nears its floor of, say, 4 percent, let money grow at a 3 percent annual rate. Overall, then, M1 would grow approximately at the level of GNP growth of 4 percent.

Defense Taxes in Allied Countries

The U.S. defense spending protects the life, liberty, and wealth not only of Americans, but also of citizens of countries allied with America. The United States has 510,000 troops stationed on foreign soil, from South Korea to West Germany. The high U.S. defense budget—6.7 percent of GNP in 1986—enables America's allies to keep their own defense outlays low. Table 22 shows that German defense spending is about half of the U.S. percentage, whereas Japan's is one-sixth. According to a report in *Business Week,* "as much as two-thirds of the Pentagon's $290 billion annual budget is spent on defense abroad."[1]

Following the Second World War, America's allies were crippled. They were in no shape to provide for their own defense. America offered them aid and a defense umbrella which at that time it could well afford. The United

[1] *Business Week,* November 6, 1987, p. 172.

Table 22
How the Allies Split Up the Burden of Defense

Country	Defense Spending as Percentage of Gross Domestic Product				
	1982	1983	1984	1985	1986
United States	6.2	6.5	6.4	6.7	6.7
Britain	5.4	5.3	5.5	5.3	5.2
France	4.1	4.2	4.1	4.1	4.0
West Germany	3.4	3.4	3.2	3.2	3.1
Italy	2.6	2.7	2.7	2.7	2.7
Canada	2.1	2.2	2.2	2.2	2.3
Japan	1.0	1.0	1.0	1.0	1.0

Source: *Business Week*, November 16, 1987, p. 172; NATO.

States generally had balance-of-payments surpluses and was the world's largest banker. Those surpluses, however, have given way to a sea of red ink in the 1980s, turning the country into the world's largest debtor.

America can no longer compete with its allies in world trade, and one reason is high defense spending, which prevents the nation from devoting as high a portion of its GNP to research and innovation as its allies. Some of the money for the Pentagon must come from investable funds. As a result, U.S. productivity growth has lagged behind that of allied nations, hurting American competitiveness abroad.

America is no longer a creditor nation, and can ill afford to offer its defense services free to its allies. However, if they were to develop their own armed system, they would have to spend billions of dollars per year to achieve a moderate capability. If would be far cheaper for them to pay America for defense services rather than improve their own military forces.

Suppose, for example, U.S. allies annually paid between 1 percent and 2 percent of their GNP to America to maintain defense of the capitalist world. Countries like Britain and France, whose military outlays are already high, though lower than those in America, should pay 1 percent of their GNP, whereas West Germany, Italy, Japan, Canada, Australia, and South Korea should pay 2 percent of their GNP. All this could bring about $100 billion to America, which would still be only half of what America spends on defense abroad. About 75 percent of this amount would come from the two wealthiest nations outside the United States—Japan and Germany. In fact, the Japanese share of the allied contribution would be about $50 billion, with its GNP of $2.5 trillion in 1987. This is only appropriate, because Japan's defense burden is the lowest among advanced economies.

American allies have large trade surpluses with the United States. They are also benefiting from free access to American markets. If the American trade account were to be balanced in some way, the allies would face heavy losses in production and employment. Thus it is also in their interest to keep the American economy going and to shore up the Pentagon budget. A defense subsidy of $100 billion to the United States is not a big price for the allies to pay, if it would maintain prosperity for the whole world. This would be one way to stave off a global depression. The subsidy would simply come out of our allies' trade surpluses.

Allied governments, however, would have to collect this much money from increased taxes on their own citizens. Since American defense spending is also protecting the wealth of their wealthiest citizens, the allies should also impose a defense levy on their millionaires. Using my defense tax schedule in Table 21, they would collect much more than the total defense subsidy. They should use the surplus revenue to eliminate their budget deficits and to retire their debts gradually, or cut income taxes for the poor and the middle class. Trimming income taxes would raise their domestic demand, which would not be adversely affected by the defense tax. This is because a small tax on millionaires would not crimp their consumption, only their speculation. As domestic demand rose, the allies would experience greater growth and not be so dependent on American markets. They would be less vulnerable to the vicissitudes of the U.S. economy. Needless to say, those U.S. allies that lack a surplus in their trade with America or have low per capita incomes should be exempt from the defense payment.

Finally, the defense subsidy I have proposed would go a long way toward solving the problem of the American trade deficit. It would stave off a worldwide depression and enable the allies to continue to enjoy their current prosperity. U.S. defenses would also remain strong. There would, of course, be a vehement reaction against my proposal among the allies, but the alternative is the military decline of the capitalist world along with a global depression. Nobody likes to pay for something he has been getting free all along. At least my proposal offers a way out of the mess in which the international financial system is now trapped.

A Grass-Roots Movement

I have offered the following measures to cure the world economy and possibly avert the coming global depression:

- A defense tax on American millionaires to balance the budget
- Re-regulation of the American financial system
- Restraint over money growth
- Defense taxes on allied countries to pay the United States for defense services

These are the short-term measures that need to be adopted immediately to cure the world economy, and to keep us from going over the brink. The capitalist world is controlled by the wealthy, and my proposals would keep their world intact. They will still retain their millions. Of course, there is a price, but the price is minuscule compared to the alternatives they and others face in the 1990s.

Even though my proposals are strictly in their best interests, I am under no illusion that the wealthy would accept them. Never in history have the rich offered to pay taxes to save themselves and their communities. Nor do my proposals have any chance of endorsement from conventional economists who mostly believe in tricklism. Even during the ten-year-long depression of the 1930s, economists refused to blame excessive wealth disparity for the disaster. To some extent, wealth concentration is good for the economy. But you can also have too much of a good thing. When 36 percent of the nation's wealth is in the hands of just 1 percent of the population, that is certainly excessive.

I am under no illusion that my proposals will be acceptable to established economists or politicians beholden to the wealthy. But how long can you believe them? Whatever they predicted, the opposite occurred. In the early 1980s, the economists said inflation would continue to rise; it fell. They said the nominal interest rate would soar; it dropped. They said the price of oil would go through the ceiling; it collapsed. They said stock and bond markets would be stagnant; both went through the roof. They said the federal budget would be gone by 1984; it rocketed. They said the trade deficit would decline after the depreciation of the dollar; it continued to climb. They said the economy would recede following Black Monday; it remained steady. No wonder the public mistrusts the economists. They have failed to see the handwriting on the wall. They won't do anything. Only you can do something.

The greatest opposition to my proposals will, of course, come from the wealthy 1 percent of our population, along with the conventional economists and the politicians beholden to them—ironically, the very same group that is responsible for our current dilemma and will have the most to lose when our economy goes into a tailspin, necessitating even more drastic measures to prevent total economic collapse and social upheaval. But even though this wealthy 1 percent has a disproportionate share of economic and political power in its hands, the rest of us have 99 percent of the votes, and we must do everything in our power, if not to avert the coming crisis, which may now be impossible, at least to shorten and soften its devastating impact. The challenge is formidable, but not impossible. I have provided you with sound and practical measures that will help you safeguard your own individual economic survival in the years ahead, and I strongly urge you to put these measures into action as soon as possible. That accomplished, we must all work together to persuade those in political power to enact the economic reforms I have proposed. They are equally sound and practical measures offering the only hope to cure the potentially fatal disease that infects our global economy.

POSTSCRIPT:
A GRASS-ROOTS MOVEMENT

———————

IN ORDER to stop the coming depression, blunt its deadly blows, or shorten it, I have personally started an organization of concerned citizens called SAD, for Stop Another Depression. Some might say it is too late to achieve SAD's goals. Perhaps. But it is well worth the effort to try.

I launched this grass-roots movement on August 21, 1987, from a radio talk show hosted by Ed Busch. Since then I have received letters from thousands of people from all over America and other countries. I have mailed out a free brochure to everyone who sent me a self-addressed envelope. There is no membership fee. I am not asking for money or donations; I only ask for your interest and time in the noblest cause of our generation, a cause you cannot afford to ignore.

I first talked about the coming depression in 1978, and, because of the numerous obstructions placed in my way, it took me nine years to get my message out to you. Thanks to my publisher, Simon & Schuster, the message has now gone to every corner of the world. Now I want your help in stemming economic disaster. It's true the challenge is formidable, and the 1 percent of the American population which could really help, because it has all the economic and political power in its hands, will fight the SAD movement tooth and nail. But we have 99 percent of the votes. Once united, we can persuade the politicians to enact the measures I have suggested to cure the global economy.

For more information, write to:

SAD
c/o Ravi Batra
P.O. Box 741806
Dallas, TX 75374
Phone: (214) 699-3838

Many grass-roots movements have eventually achieved sweeping social change. With your help, SAD can and will achieve its goals.

APPENDIX TO CHAPTER 4:
INDUSTRIAL PERFORMANCE,
1929–33

THIS APPENDIX TABULATES the performance of various segments of the economy during the 1930s (from 1929 to 1933) in terms of sales and output. If output fell more than 30 percent or sales (output value) fell more than 46 percent, then that industry did poorly relative to the rest of the nation, and conversely. In some cases, where output or sales actually rose, the percentage drop was negative—that is, it was a gain, not a drop. An asterisk indicates that the figure is for 1930–34 because the 1929 figure is not available. Price behavior conveys the same message. In the worst-hit industries, prices fell more than the national average, and conversely. Finally, crime statistics indicate how the crime prevention industry fared during the depression.

The figures in this appendix were compiled from *Historical Statistics of the United States, Colonial Times to 1970* (Washington, D.C., U.S. Department of Commerce, Bureau of the Census, 1975).

Go through this list carefully, see which industry applies to you, and prepare accordingly. For further explanation of this appendix, see text in Chapter 4.

---

[1] Negative figures throughout the appendix indicate a gain.

Output of Selected Commodities

	Percentage Drop, 1929–33[1]
Wheat flour	21
Refined sugar	10
Canned corn	42
Canned tomatoes	15
Shortening and cooking oils	22
Manufactured tobacco and snuff	10
Cigars	34
Cigarettes	6
Men's and boy's suits and separate coats	36*
Women's, misses', and juniors' dresses	11*
Carpets and rugs	43
Sodium hydroxide or caustic soda	10
Ammonia anhydrous or 100% NH_3	14
Ammonia aqua or 100% NH_3	60
Sulfuric acid	28
Paints, varnishes, and lacquers	28*
Super phospates	42
Light products of distillation	8
Illuminating oils	12
Fuel oils	30
Paraffin wax	26
Pneumatic motor vehicle tires	36
Men's shoes	6
Women's shoes	0.5
Iron and steel shapes	77
Raw steel	58
Copper products	60
Wheel tractors	68*
Typewriters	57
Electrical generators	73
Domestic ranges	77
Electric lamps	13
Radio-phonograph combinations	80
Locomotives	94
Railroad passenger cars	100
Railroad freight cars	98
Bicycles	−3

Value of Output of Finished Goods

	Percentage Drop, 1929–33
Toys, games, and sporting goods	55
Tires and tubes	55
Household furniture	62
Heating and cooking appliances	58
Radios	73
House furnishings	52
China	45
Musical instruments	79
Jewelry, silverware, clocks, and watches	71
Printing and publishing books	52
Luggage	73
Passenger motor vehicles	71

Indexes of Transportation Output

	Percentage Drop, 1929–33
All traffic	36
Passenger traffic	36
Freight traffic	37

Motor Vehicle Sales and Registration

	Percentage Drop, 1929–33
Passenger cars	65
Wholesale value of cars	72
Trucks and buses	63
Value of trucks and buses	72
Auto registrations	11
Buses	−32
Trucks	3

Miles of Travel by Motor Vehicles

	Percentage Drop, 1929–33
Total travel	−1.5
Urban travel	1.5
Rural travel	−5

Railroad Traffic, Revenue, and Income

	Percentage Drop, 1929–33
No. of passengers	45
Passenger miles	47
Total revenue	62
Revenue per passenger	28
Net income	97
Dividends	72

Health and Medical Care

	Percentage Drop, 1929–33
Physicians	
Number	−6
Rate per 100,000 population	−2
Medical schools	
Number	−1
Students	−8
Graduates	−10
Dental schools	
Number	2
Students	8
Graduates	19
Professional nursing schools	
Number	5
Students	−7
Graduates	−6
Hospitals	
General	1
Beds	−8
Mental	−8
Beds	−20
Total beds per 1,000 population	−11

Price Indexes

	Percentage Drop, 1929–33
Wholesale Price Index	
All commodities	31
Industrial products	22

Price Indexes

	Percentage Drop, 1929–33
Wholesale Price Index	
Farm products	52
Leather and related products	26
Fuel and power	19
Rubber and plastics	32
Lumber and wood products	24
Metals	22
Furniture and household durables	20
Minerals	8
Motor vehicles and equipment	16
Consumer Price Index	
All items	24
Food	35
Rent	29
House furnishings	25
Apparel	23

Education

	Percentage Drop, 1929–33
School enrollment	
Public day schools	−3
Public/teacher ratio	−1
Nonpublic schools	−3
Other secondary schools	13
Public school expenditures	
Total	26
Per Pupil	28
Administration	19
Instruction	15
Instructional staff	1
Higher Education	
No. of institutions	−0.6
Junior colleges	−16
Public	−18
Private	−15
Four-year colleges	3
Medical schools	−1
Dental schools	2

Faculty	−32
Bachelor's degrees	−11
Number per 1,000 persons 23 years old	−7
Master's degrees	−22
Number per 1,000 bachelor's degrees 2 years earlier	0
Doctoral degrees	
Number	−23
Number per 1,000 bachelor's degrees 10 years earlier	17

Crime Statistics

	Percentage Drop, 1929–33
Homicides	
Number	−26
Rate per 100,000 population	−15
Male	−29
Female	−13
Suicides	
Number	−25
Rate per 100,000 population	−14
Male	−28
Female	−13

Farming and Agriculture

	Percentage Drop, 1929–33
Farm population	
Total	−6
Percent of population	−2
Value of farm property	37
Index of Farm Real Estate	40
Farm Wages Rate Index	50
Farm Employment	0
Farm income	
Net income of farm	58
Average per farm	60

Forestry and Fisheries

	Percentage Drop, 1929–33
Production of timber products	50
Value of fisheries production	51

Gold and Silver

	Percentage Drop, 1929–33
Gold	
Value of production	−41
Production	−11
Silver	
Value of production	76
Production	62
Average price, New York (cents per fine ounce)	34

Books Published

	Percentage Drop, 1929–33
New books	21
New editions	18

Newspapers

	Percentage Drop, 1929–33
Total number of newspapers	2
Circulation	11
Morning newspapers	0.3
Evening newspapers	2
Sunday newspapers	4
Sunday newspaper circulation	11

APPENDIX TO CHAPTER 5: PERFORMANCE OF JOBS AND PROFESSIONS, 1929–33

THIS APPENDIX TABULATES the performance of various jobs and professions during the 1930s (from 1929 to 1933) in terms of employment, wages, payroll, or earnings in a sector. The hardest-hit jobs were in those sectors or professions where employment fell more than 18 percent, earnings fell more than 26 percent, or payroll fell more than 44 percent. Since the nature of jobs and professions has not changed dramatically since the 1930s, the conclusions to be drawn from the Great Depression are likely to apply to the coming depression as well.

The figures in this appendix were compiled from *Historical Statistics of the United States, Colonial Times to 1970* (Washington, D.C.: U.S. Department of Commerce, Bureau of the Census, 1975).

Go through this appendix carefully, see which category applies to you, and make preparations accordingly. For further explanation of this appendix, see text in Chapter 5.

Persons Engaged in Distribution and Selected Services

	Percentage Drop, 1929–33[1]
Wholesale trade	20
Retail trade	17
Hotels and other lodging	22
Personal services	15
Business services	2
Repair services	−18
Motion pictures	19
Recreation services	39
Medical and health care	9
Legal services	−12
Educational services	0.3
Miscellaneous professional services	17
Nonprofit membership organizations	4

Wholesale Establishments

	Percentage Drop, 1929–33
Tobacco distributors	
Number	−1
Sales	39
Drugs and chemicals	
Number	−7
Sales	39
Dry goods, apparel	
Number	15
Sales	56
Furniture, home furnishings	
Number	−2
Sales	65
Paper and paper products	
Number	3
Sales	53
Farm products	
Number	25
Sales	67

[1] Negative figures throughout the appendix indicate a gain.

Automotive wholesalers
  Number   −52
  Sales   68
Electrical and electronic appliance distributors
  Number   3
  Sales   67
Hardware, plumbing and heating
  Number   11
  Sales   60
Lumber, construction materials
  Number   30
  Sales   78
Machinery, equipment supplies
  Number   11
  Sales   60
Metals, metalwork distributors
  Number   13
  Sales   76
Scrap, waste-material dealers
  Number   14
  Sales   43
Petroleum bulk stations, terminals
  Number   −34
  Sales   10
Agents and brokers
  Number   25
  Sales   55
Volume of advertising   62
Banking industry
  Bank suspensions   −508
  Number of national banks   30
  Earnings of national banks   43
  Dividends of national banks   68
Life insurance companies
  Number   14
  Sales   39
  Dividends to stockholders   59
Government
  Federal employees   −4
  State and local   −3
  Armed forces
  Number   4

Wholesale Establishments

	Percentage Drop, 1929–33
Food and kindred products	
Number of employees	12
Payroll	29
Tobacco products	
Number of employees	21
Payroll	50
Textile mill products	
Number of workers	13
Wages	38
Lumber products	
Number of employees	52
Payroll	72
Paper and allied products	
Number of employees	14
Payroll	41
Printing and publishing	
Number of employees	30
Payroll	49
Chemicals and allied products	
Number of employees	21
Payroll	44
Petroleum and coal products	
Number of workers	20
Wages	37
Rubber and plastic products	
Number of employees	14
Payroll	52
Leather products	
Number of employees	14
Payroll	43
Stone, clay, and glass products	
Number of employees	47
Wages	67
Electrical equipment	
Number of employees	52
Payroll	67
Instruments and related products	
Number of workers	39
Wages	57

Railroad employment and wages
  Number of employees   42
  Compensation   52

Communications: Telephones, Average Daily Conversations, Income, Employees and Wages

	Percentage Drop, 1929–33
Number	13
Residence	20
Business	10
Long-distance calls	34
Number of employees	32
Wages and salaries	32
Dividends—Bell Cos.	− 39

Postal Service

	Percentage Drop, 1929–33
Postal Service deficit	− 27
Employees	5

Average Annual Earnings per Full-Time Employee in Distribution and Selected Service Industries

	Percentage Drop, 1929–33
Wholesale trade	29
Retail trade	24
Hotels and other lodging	26
Personal services	27
Business services	27
Repair services	29
Motion pictures	13
Recreation services	7
Medical and health care	12
Legal services	15
Educational services	9
Miscellaneous services	30
Nonprofit membership organizations	16

Retail Establishments

	Percentage Drop, 1929–33
General merchandise	
Number	9
Sales	40
Persons engaged	34
Department stores	
Number	16
Sales	41
Persons engaged	33
Variety stores	
Number	0.5
Sales	25
Persons engaged	2
Apparel group	
Number	24
Sales	55
Persons engaged	31
Shoe stores	
Number	22
Sales	47
Persons engaged	24
Women's ready-to-wear	
Number	3
Sales	48
Persons engaged	24
Furniture stores	
Number	33
Sales	65
Persons engaged	42
Household appliances, radio	
Number	29
Sales	67
Persons engaged	39
Car dealers	
Number	27
Sales	66
Persons engaged	39
Tire, battery, accessory dealers	
Number	28
Sales	62
Persons engaged	41

Gasoline service stations
  Number   − 40
  Sales   14
  Persons engaged   − 34
Lumber, building materials dealers
  Number   20
  Sales   70
  Persons engaged   41
Hardware stores
  Number   10
  Sales   56
  Persons engaged   25
Farm equipment dealers
  Number   19
  Sales   66
  Persons engaged   33
Drug and proprietary stores
  Number   − 0.3
  Sales   37
  Persons engaged   12
Hay, grain, feed stores
  Number   48
  Sales   65
  Persons engaged   57
Jewelry stores
  Number   28
  Sales   67
  Persons engaged   39
Florists
  Number   17
  Sales   63
  Persons engaged   44
Secondhand stores
  Number   − 38
  Sales   29
  Persons engaged   − 35

Employment and Earnings

	Percentage Drop, 1929–33
Labor force	
Number employed	18
Number unemployed	−728
Rate of unemployment	−22
Employment by industry	
Mining	31
Construction	46
Manufacturing	31
Transportation and public utilities	32
Wholesale and retail trade	22
Finance, insurance, and real estate	14
Services	16
Federal government	−6
State and local government	−3
Employee earnings	
Full-time employees	25
After deduction for unemployment	50
Real earnings in 1914 dollars	3
After deduction for unemployment	34

Annual Employee Earnings for Full-Time Employment by Industry in Dollars

	Percentage Drop, 1929–33
Agriculture, forestry and fisheries	42
Manufacturing	30
Anthracite Coal	17
Bituminous coal	42
Metal	35
Construction	48
Railroads	18
Water transportation	17
Local transportation	24
Gas and electric	9
Telephone and telegraph	10
Wholesale and retail trade	26
Finance, insurance, and real estate	25
Personal services	27

Employee Earnings by Industry

	Percentage Drop, 1929–33
Medical and other health care services	12
Domestic services	37
Nonprofit services	16
Educational services	9
State and local government	11
Public education	10
Federal government	13

APPENDIX TO CHAPTER 6: TOP-RATED U.S. BANKS, SAVINGS AND LOAN ASSOCIATIONS, AND CREDIT UNIONS

THIS APPENDIX CONTAINS a list of the top-rated U.S. banks and savings and loan associations, followed by a list of top-rated credit unions.

The lists are a selection from lists compiled by IDC Financial Publishing, Inc., and published in IDC's February 1988 issues of *Bank Financial Quarterly*, *S&L Financial Quarterly*, and *Credit Union Financial Profile*. Within each state, banks or credit unions are listed in order of their CAMEL rating. (For an explanation of this rating, see the text in Chapter 6.) Assets are given in millions of dollars. The following abbreviations are used in names of institutions, as provided by the FDIC data.

B&TC	Bank and Trust Company
BK	Bank
C	County
CMRC	Commerce
CTY	City
FS&LA	Federal Savings and Loan Association
FSB	Federal Savings Bank
MSB	Mutual Savings Bank
NA	National Association
NAT	National
NAT ASSN	National Association

NB	National Bank
NB&TC	National Bank and Trust Company
S&LA	Savings and Loan Association
ST BK	State Bank
SVG	Savings
SVG BK	Savings Bank
SVG INST	Savings Institution
T&SB	Trust and Savings Bank
TC	Trust Company
TR	Trust

Other abbreviations used can be inferred from the ones described above. For instance, S&LC stands for Savings and Loan Company, B&LC for bank and loan company, FA for federal association, etc.

Go through this list carefully and see which high-rated banks are close to you. If you diversify your assets among top-rated banks—even if you must suffer the inconvenience of dealing with some of them by mail—you will give yourself a better chance of surviving the coming economic catastrophe.

ALABAMA

Name	City	Rank	Assets
FIRST NB OF TUSCALOOSA	TUSCALOOSA	243	441
FIRST NB	SCOTTSBORO	241	118
FIRST NB OF JASPER	JASPER	231	276
COLONIAL BK E CNTRL ALABAMA	PELL CITY	220	183
FIRST FEDERAL SAVINGS BANK	DECATUR	218	212
SOUTHTRUST BK OF CALH NA	ANNISTON	209	282
UNITED SECURITY BK	THOMASVILLE	209	108
SOUTHTRUST BK OF ETAWAN NA	GADSDEN	206	184
SOUTHTRUST BK OF DOTHAN	DOTHAN	205	326
FIRST ALABAMA BK	MONTGOMERY	202	4,112
UNION B&TC	MONTGOMERY	200	417
SOUTHTRUST BK CULLMAN NA	CULLMAN	192	105
FIRST NB OF FLORENCE	FLORENCE	191	282
AUBURN NB	AUBURN	190	104
BANK INDEPENDENT	SHEFFIELD	189	102
SOUTHTRUST BK OF MOBILE	MOBILE	187	238
PEOPLES B&TC	SELMA	184	194
COLONIAL BK	MONTGOMERY	182	204

ALABAMA

Name	City	Rank	Assets
COLONIAL BK NORTHWEST REGION	HUNTSVILLE	180	749
FIRST NB ALEXANDER CTY	ALEXANDER CITY	176	117
SOUTHTRUST BK OF HUNTS NA	HUNTSVILLE	175	208
NEW SOUTH FEDERAL SAVINGS BANK	IRONDALE	175	221
FIRST NB OF OPELIKA	OPELIKA	166	102

ALASKA

Name	City	Rank	Assets
FIRST NB OF ANCHORAGE	ANCHORAGE	267	810
NATIONAL BK OF ALASKA	ANCHORAGE	212	1,245
FIRST BK	KETCHIKAN	167	165

ARIZONA

Name	City	Rank	Assets
CITIBANK OF ARIZONA	PHOENIX	277	915
ARIZONA COMMERCE BANK	TUCSON	243	111
NAT BK OF TUCSON	TUCSON	187	101
FIRST INTERSTATE BK AZ NA	PHOENIX	172	6,492

ARKANSAS

Name	City	Rank	Assets
FIRST NB	SEARCY	229	131
FIRST SECURITY BK	SEARCY	223	113
PEOPLES B&TC	MOUNTAIN HOME	205	127
FIRST NB OF MAGNOLIA	MAGNOLIA	201	186
FARMERS B&TC	MAGNOLIA	197	107
FIRST NB&TC OF MT	MOUNTAIN HOME	196	124
FIRST NB&TC	ROGERS	191	175
FIRST NB OF RUSSELLVILLE	RUSSELLVILLE	190	134
BANK OF BENTONVILLE	BENTONVILLE	189	180
BENTON ST BK	BENTON	189	132
FIRST NB OF EL DORADO	EL DORADO	185	243
UNION NB OF LITTLE ROCK	LITTLE ROCK	183	476
MERCANTILE BK	JONESBORO	182	193
FIRST NB	PARAGOULD	181	137
STATE FIRST NB OF TEXARKANA	TEXARKANA	179	375
CITIZENS NB OF HOPE	HOPE	176	129
FIRST NB OF SPRINGDALE	SPRINGDALE	175	226
FIRST NB OF CAMDEN	CAMDEN	174	101

CALIFORNIA

Name	City	Rank	Assets
FARMERS & MERCHANTS BK OF LB	LONG BEACH	300	1,021
FIRST INTERSTATE BANCARD NA	SIMI VALLEY	280	316
SECURITY PACIFIC ST BK	IRVINE	279	103
VALLEY NB HOUSEHOLD BK	SALINAS	256	1,070
ONTARIO S&LA	ONTARIO	251	111
MECHANICS BK OF RICHMOND	RICHMOND	244	510
EXCHANGE BK	SANTA ROSA	243	437
VALLEY NB	GLENDALE	243	243
STANDARD SAVINGS BANK	LOS ANGELES	239	145
MUTUAL S&LA	PASADENA	236	354
RIVERSIDE NB	RIVERSIDE	233	142
NATIONAL BK OF LONG BEACH	LONG BEACH	232	203
CALIFORNIA OVERSEAS BK	LOS ANGELES	232	120
EL CAMINO BK	ANAHEIM	231	110
ELDORADO BK	TUSTIN	230	197
FIRST NB	DALY CITY	230	129
CANADIAN IMPL BK CMRC (CA)	LOS ANGELES	230	612
FIRST ST BK OF THE OAKS	THOUSAND OAKS	223	124
HOME BK	SIGNAL HILL	223	300
CALIFORNIA STATE BANK	COVINA	222	144
IMPERIAL BK	LOS ANGELES	221	1,603
WATSONVILLE FS&LA	WATSONVILLE	221	120
SUNWEST BK	TUSTIN	220	173
GROSSMONT BK	LA MESA	220	251
ALAMEDA FIRST NB	ALAMEDA	219	191
TRANS-WORLD BK	SHERMAN OAKS	218	166
CALIFORNIA S&LA, A FEDERAL ASSOCIAT	SAN FRANCISCO	218	414
REPUBLIC BK	GARDENA	217	108
WESTERN BK	LOS ANGELES	216	172
LANDMARK BK	LA HABRA	215	143
BANK OF REDLANDS	REDLANDS	214	142
SAVINGS BK OF MENDOCINO CTY	UKIAH	214	213
CITICORP SAVINGS, A FS&LA	SAN FRANCISCO	212	6,939
FIRST NORTHERN BK OF DIXON	DIXON	210	128
SANTA MONICA BK	SANTA MONICA	210	596
SOUTHERN CALIFORNIA BK	DOWNEY	208	255
FARMERS & MERCHANTS BK OF CENTRAL CA	LODI	207	416
SANTA CLARITA NB	VALENCIA	207	203
HEART FS&LA	AUBURN	207	673
HAWTHORNE S&LA	HAWTHORNE	205	825
ASSOCIATES NB	CONCORD	204	121
SOUTHERN CALIFORNIA S&LA, A FS&LA	BEVERLY HILLS	204	1,369
CITIZENS BK OF COSTA MESA	COSTA MESA	203	119
CHINO VALLEY BK	CHINO	203	297
STERLING S&LA	IRVINE	203	148

CALIFORNIA

Name	City	Rank	Assets
GUARDIAN BK	LOS ANGELES	202	176
FIRST ST BK OF SOUTHERN CA	SANTA FE SPRINGS	201	105
CALIFORNIA REPUBLIC BK	BAKERSFIELD	200	350
FOOTHILL INDEPENDENT BK	GLENDORA	200	162
FREMONT BK	FREMONT	200	160
HARBOR BK	LONG BEACH	200	135
ORANGE NB	ORANGE	200	122
FIRST NB	SAN DIEGO	199	351
NATIONAL BK OF SOUTHERN CA	SANTA ANA	199	132
FIRST AMERICAN BK	ROSEMEAD	198	111
MECHANICS NB	PARAMOUNT	198	119
NEW HORIZONS S&LA	SAN RAFAEL	198	119
FAR EAST NB	LOS ANGELES	195	183
BANK OF STOCKTON	STOCKTON	194	556
MERCANTILE NB	LOS ANGELES	194	235
SANTA BARBARA B&TC	SANTA BARBARA	194	478
BANK OF FRESNO	FRESNO	193	136
BANK OF PALM SPRINGS	PALM SPRINGS	193	101
CITIZENS COMMERCIAL T&SB	PASADENA	193	103
MARATHON NB	LOS ANGELES	193	102
FIRST PUBLIC SAVINGS BANK	LOS ANGELES	193	133
AMERICAN INTL BK	LOS ANGELES	192	114
MID-STATE BK	ARROYO GRANDE	192	464
QUAKER CITY FS&LA	WHITTIER	192	305
AMERICAN PACIFIC ST BK	LOS ANGELES	190	142
CAPITAL BK	DOWNEY	190	101
RIVER CITY BK	SACRAMENTO	190	234
SAN DIEGO NB	SAN DIEGO	190	126
BANK OF INDUSTRY	CITY OF INDUSTRY	189	137
CATHAY BK	LOS ANGELES	189	394
LA JOLLA B&TC	LA JOLLA	189	323
MODESTO BKG CO	MODESTO	189	104
BANK OF SAN PEDRO	LOS ANGELES	188	138
FIRST BUSINESS BK	LOS ANGELES	187	342
STERLING BK	LOS ANGELES	187	101
VENTURA COUNTY NB	OXNARD	187	112
GENERAL BK	LOS ANGELES	186	295
PIONEER BK	FULLERTON	186	109
PLAZA BK OF COMMERCE	SAN JOSE	186	342
SAN DIEGO T&SB	SAN DIEGO	186	1,295
UNION SAFE DEPOSIT BK	STOCKTON	184	341
BOREL B&TC	SAN MATEO	183	104
DAI-ICHI KANGYO BK OF CA	LOS ANGELES	183	248
FIRST COMMERCIAL BK	SACRAMENTO	182	187
FIRST TR BK	ONTARIO	181	294

Name	City	Rank	Assets
HANMI BK	LOS ANGELES	181	120
NAPA VALLEY BK	NAPA	180	269
PENINSULA BK OF SAN DIEGO	SAN DIEGO	180	137
FIRST FS BANK OF CALIFORNIA	SANTA MONICA	180	1,729
COMMUNITY BK	HUNTINGTON PARK	178	992
BARCLAYS BK OF CALIFORNIA	SAN FRANCISCO	178	1,271
LIBERTY NB	HUNTINGTON BEACH	176	101
HIGHLAND FS&LA OF LOS ANGELES	LOS ANGELES	176	261
CALIFORNIA KOREA BK	LOS ANGELES	175	261
LINCOLN NB	ENCINO	175	281
PACIFIC BK NA	SAN FRANCISCO	174	388
SILICON VALLEY BK	SANTA CLARA	174	192
POMONA FIRST FS&LA	POMONA	174	1,169
BANK OF LOLETA	EUREKA	173	142
BANK OF MONTECITO	MONTECITO	173	133
FIRST NETWORK SAVINGS BANK	LOS ANGELES	173	192
STOCKTON S&LA	STOCKTON	172	683
BAY VIEW FS&LA	SAN MATEO	172	1,889
COMMERCE BK	NEWPORT BEACH	171	201
FIRST FS&LA	RIDGECREST	171	130
CALIFORNIA COMMERCE BK	LOS ANGELES	170	226
HEMET FS&LA	HEMET	170	429
HOME FS&LA	SAN FRANCISCO	170	434
LUTHER BURBANK S&LA	SANTA ROSA	170	127
BANK OF NEWPORT	NEWPORT BEACH	168	166
INVESTORS THRIFT	ORANGE	168	118
BANK OF SAN FRANCISCO	SAN FRANCISCO	167	178
TORREY PINES BK	SOLANA BEACH	167	333
TRI COUNTIES BK	CHICO	167	244
OMNI BK NA	MONTEREY PARK	166	114
WORLD S&LA, A FS&LA	OAKLAND	166	12,941
UNIVERSITY NB&TC	PALO ALTO	165	190

COLORADO

Name	City	Rank	Assets
COLORADO ST BK	DENVER	269	115
MOUNTAIN STATES BK	DENVER	244	142
FIRST NB IN LOVELAND	LOVELAND	230	103
FIRST NB IN BOULDER	BOULDER	208	271
LAKESIDE NB	WHEAT RIDGE	208	127
CITICORP SVG & IND BK	AURORA	202	127
FIRST NB OF WESTMINSTER	WESTMINSTER	190	107
FIRST INTERSTATE BK NA	ENGLEWOOD	182	135
CENTURY B&TC	DENVER	182	101
FIRST NB OF LONGMONT	LONGMONT	182	120
INTRAWEST BK OF BOULDER NA	BOULDER	181	219

CONNECTICUT

Name	City	Rank	Assets
BANK OF STAMFORD	STAMFORD	269	138
DIME SVG BK	WALLINGFORD	255	460
NEW MILFORD SVG BK	NEW MILFORD	253	646
MIDCONN BK	KENSINGTON	246	177
BANK OF CT	NEW HAVEN	240	177
FIRST FEDERAL BANK OF CONNECTICUT FSB	NEW HAVEN	240	1,628
CENTRAL BK FOR SVG	MERIDEN	234	440
NORWICH SVG SOC	NORWICH	234	571
PEOPLES SVG BK	NEW BRITAIN	234	225
SOUTHINGTON SVG BK	SOUTHINGTON	234	204
NEW ENGLAND SVG BK	NEW LONDON	233	821
BANKING CENTER	WATERBURY	222	1,428
FIRST FS&LA	WATERBURY	221	570
NAUGATUCK SVG BK	NAUGATUCK	219	187
FIRST FS&LA	TORRINGTON	218	201
BRISTOL FEDERAL SAVINGS BANK	BRISTOL	215	183
CITY SVG BK	MERIDEN	214	144
SAVINGS BK OF DANBURY	DANBURY	214	148
SEYMOUR TC	SEYMOUR	212	103
NEW MILFORD B&TC	NEW MILFORD	208	186
LAFAYETTE B&TC	BRIDGEPORT	201	239
CHELSEA GROTON SVG BK	MYSTIC	201	345
SHELTON S&LA INC	SHELTON	200	123
BRANFORD SVG BK	BRANFORD	200	207
AMITY BK	WOODBRIDGE	199	123
AMERICAN BK OF CONN	WATERBURY	199	238
AMERICAN SVG BK	NEW BRITAIN	199	814
THOMASTON SVG BK	THOMASTON	199	162
GREAT COUNTRY BK	ANSONIA	197	431
GATEWAY BK	SOUTH NORWALK	196	1,142
UNION SVG BK OF DANBURY	DANBURY	196	313
SALISBURY B&TC	LAKEVILLE	195	133
FIRST FS&LA	EAST HARTFORD	194	341
SHAWMUT FIDELITY BK	STAMFORD	189	269
DERBY SVG BK	DERBY	188	494
GLASTONBURY B&TC	GLASTONBURY	187	200
ESSEX SVG BK	ESSEX	187	130
PUTNAM TC	GREENWICH	186	456
GUILFORD SVG BK	GUILFORD	186	127
NEWTOWN SVG BK	NEWTOWN	182	180
CHESTER BK	CHESTER	181	113
BROOKLYN SVG BK	DANIELSON	181	119
WILLIMANTIC SVG INST	WILLIMANTIC	181	123
LANDMARK BK	HARTFORD	179	164
TORRINGTON SVG BK	TORRINGTON	179	247

Name	City	Rank	Assets
NAB B&TC	STRATFORD	176	167
BAYBANK CT NA	FARMINGTON	175	134
WESTPORT B&TC	WESTPORT	175	303
UNITED B&TC	HARTFORD	174	1,733
GREENWICH FS&LA	GREENWICH	173	213
AMERICAN NB	HAMDEN	172	303
SOUTH WINDSOR B&TC	SOUTH WINDSOR	172	113
FARMERS & MECHANICS SVG BK	MIDDLETOWN	171	503
FAIRFIELD COUNTY SVG BK	NORWALK	170	138
SAVINGS BK OF MANCHESTER	MANCHESTER	169	545

DELAWARE

Name	City	Rank	Assets
GREENWOOD TC	NEW CASTLE	296	2,654
CITIBANK - DELAWARE	NEW CASTLE	271	956
INTERFIRST BK (DELAWARE)	NEWARK	261	164
SOVRAN BK/DELAWARE	DOVER	255	201
COLONIAL NB USA	WILMINGTON	251	1,171
FIRST ATLANTA BK NA	NEW CASTLE	251	109
MBANK USA	WILMINGTON	237	1,196
FCC NB	WILMINGTON	236	1,999
BALTIMORE TC	SELBYVILLE	231	159
CHEMICAL BK - DELAWARE	WILMINGTON	226	1,230
J C PENNEY NB	HARRINGTON	222	205
REPUBLICBANK DELAWARE	NEWARK	222	403
BANKERS TR (DELAWARE)	WILMINGTON	218	1,583
CHASE MANHATTAN BK (USA) NA	WILMINGTON	217	5,598
FIRST NB OF WILMINGTON	WILMINGTON	212	333
FIRST OMNI BK NA	MILSBORO	212	502
BARCLAYS BK OF DELAWARE NA	WILMINGTON	211	302
MARINE MIDLAND BK (DEL) NA	WILMINGTON	211	1,569
AMERICAN EXPRESS CENTRION BK	STANTON	208	1,133
MORGAN BK (DELAWARE)	WILMINGTON	203	2,643
UNITED MISSOURI USA BK	NEW CASTLE	200	133
CORESTATES BK OF DEL NA	WILMINGTON	197	927
DELAWARE TC	WILMINGTON	195	1,088
NBD DELAWARE BK	WILMINGTON	191	365
EQUITABLE BK OF DELAWARE	DOVER	190	370
EQUIBANK DELAWARE NA	WILMINGTON	187	336
PNC NB	WILMINGTON	184	577
MARYLAND BK NA	NEWARK	181	2,189
FIRST PENNSYLVANIA BK (DEL)	WILMINGTON	179	164
MELLON BK DELAWARE NA	WILMINGTON	177	961
BANK OF DELAWARE	WILMINGTON	175	1,643
WILMINGTON TC	WILMINGTON	171	2,722
BENEFICIAL NB	WILMINGTON	169	191

DISTRICT OF COLUMBIA

Name	City	Rank	Assets
INDUSTRIAL BK OF WASHINGTON	WASHINGTON	205	106
SIGNET BK NA	WASHINGTON	197	302
CRESTAR BK NA	WASHINGTON	190	889
UNITED NB OF WASHINGTON	WASHINGTON	185	111
MCLACHLEN NB	WASHINGTON	179	156
OBA FS&LA	WASHINGTON	176	106
MADISON NB	WASHINGTON	169	395

FLORIDA

Name	City	Rank	Assets
KEY BISCAYNE B&TC	KEY BISCAYNE	283	105
COMMERCIAL BK IN PANAMA CTY	PANAMA CITY	279	191
CITICORP SAVINGS OF FLORIDA, A FS&LA	MIAMI	274	2,718
COCONUT GROVE BK	MIAMI	256	202
CITIZENS & PEOPLES NB OF PENSACOLA	PENSACOLA	247	240
WAUCHULA ST BK	WAUCHULA	240	122
KISLAK NB	NORTH MIAMI	238	138
PEOPLES BK OF LAKELAND	LAKELAND	234	452
FIRST NB OF SOUTH MIAMI	SOUTH MIAMI	230	220
SAFRABANK	MIAMI	227	182
TIB BANK KEYS	KEY LARGO	219	101
UNITED NB OF MIAMI	MIAMI	217	335
BANK OF PALM BEACH & TC	PALM BEACH	209	210
OCEAN ST BK	NEPTUNE BEACH	209	103
HILLSBORO SUN BK	PLANT CITY	209	162
FIRST FS&LA	FORT MYERS	207	805
BARNETT BK OF ST JOHNS CITY	ST AUGUSTINE	206	220
CAPITAL CITY FIRST NB	TALLAHASSEE	204	248
AMERICAN BK OF HOLLYWOOD	HOLLYWOOD	203	126
BEACH BK OF VERO BEACH	VERO BEACH	203	127
BANK OF INVERNESS	INVERNESS	203	182
FIRST NB OF CLEARWATER	CLEARWATER	202	359
SUN BK SO CNTRL FLA NA	AVON PARK	201	135
FIRST HOME FS&LA	SEBRING	201	201
SUN BK/WEST FL NA	PENSACOLA	200	201
COMMUNITY BK OF HOMESTEAD	DADE COUNTY	198	135
SUN BK TALLAHASSEE NA	TALLAHASSEE	197	102
BARNETT BK OF THE KEYS	KEY WEST	195	169
MERCHANTS BK OF MIAMI	WEST MIAMI	195	166
FIRST FS&LA	BROOKSVILLE	195	211
CITIZENS NB OF LEESBURG	LEESBURG	190	190
COMMERCIAL B&TC	MIAMI	190	305
SUN BK TREASURE COAST NA	VERO BEACH	186	380

COMMERCIAL BK OF PLM BCH CTY	LANTANA	185	127
SUN BK OF VOLUSIA CTY	DAYTONA BEACH	185	437
SUN BK SOUTH FL NAT ASSN	FORT LAUDERDALE	185	1,731
SUN B&TC TR/CHARLOTTE CITY NA	PORT CHARLOTTE	185	225
SKYLAKE ST BK	NORTH MIAMI BCH	183	170
AMERICAN NB OF FLORIDA	JACKSONVILLE	182	405
SUN FIRST NB OF POLK COUNTY	WINTER HAVEN	182	350
CITIZENS & SOUTHERN NB OF FL	FORT LAUDERDALE	181	4,772
FIRST NB OF HOMESTEAD	HOMESTEAD	179	153
BARNETT BK OF ALACHUA C NA	GAINESVILLE	178	219
BARNETT BK OF W FLORIDA	PENSACOLA	178	244
PEOPLES FIRST FINANCIAL	PANAMA CITY	178	140
FIRST NB&TC	STUART	177	366
BARNETT BK OF LK OKEECHOBEE	OKEECHOBEE	176	116
SUN BK OF TAMPA BAY	TAMPA	176	1,222
BARNETT BK OF JCKSVILLE NA	JACKSONVILLE	175	1,552
FIRST FLORIDA BK NA	TAMPA	175	4,638
SUN BK LEE COUNTY NA	CAPE CORAL	175	363
BARNETT BK OF LEE CTY NA	FORT MYERS	174	488
NORTHERN TR BK OF FL NA	MIAMI	172	311
BARNETT BK OF MARTIN C NA	HOBE SOUND	171	189
BARNETT BK OF SOUTH FL NA	MIAMI	171	4,875
BARNETT BK OF ST LUCIE CTY	PORT ST LUCIE	170	143
CONTINENTAL NB OF MIAMI	MIAMI	170	134
COMMERCIAL BK OF KENDALL	MIAMI	170	152
JEFFERSON NB	MIAMI BEACH	170	192
SUN BK N FLORIDA NAT ASSN	JACKSONVILLE	170	316
AMERICAN BK SO	MERRITT ISLAND	169	146
BARNETT BK OF MARION C NA	OCALA	169	357
HOME SAVINGS ASSOCIATION OF FLORIDA	HOLLYWOOD	169	828
BARNETT BK OF NW FLORIDA	DE FUNIAK SPRNGS	168	154
FIRST NB OF LIVE OAK	LIVE OAK	168	122
SUN BK&TC	BROOKSVILLE	168	385
CORAL GABLES FS&LA	CORAL GABLES	168	2,288

GEORGIA

Name	City	Rank	Assets
BANK OF COVINGTON	COVINGTON	258	128
ROSWELL BK	ROSWELL	258	175
FARMERS & MERCHANTS BK	DUBLIN	252	103
BRAND BKG CO	LAWRENCEVILLE	240	139
TRUST CO BK OF NORTHEAST GA	ATHENS	229	247
BANK OF CANTON	CANTON	227	133
ETOWAH BK	CANTON	227	127
TRUST CO BK OF CLAYTON CTY	JONESBORO	222	109

GEORGIA

Name	City	Rank	Assets
TRUST CO BK OF NW GA NA	ROME	221	195
TRUST CO BK COLUMBUS NA	COLUMBUS	220	212
TRUST CO BK SAVANNAH NA	SAVANNAH	219	261
MOULTRIE NB	MOULTRIE	218	102
TRUST CO BK OF SE GA NA	BRUNSWICK	217	287
FIRST ST B&TC	ALBANY	211	249
TRUST CO BK OF MIDDLE GA NA	MACON	211	407
TRUST CO BK - AUGUSTA NA	AUGUSTA	210	278
TRUST CO BK OF DOUGLAS CTY	DOUGLASVILLE	210	101
CENTRAL & SOUTHERN BK OF GA	MILLEDGEVILLE	208	129
TRUST CO BK OF ROCKDALE	CONYERS	208	155
NCNB NAT BK	ATLANTA	207	203
TRUST CO BK OF COBB CTY NA	ATLANTA	206	280
COLUMBUS BK CO	COLUMBUS	204	729
BANK SOUTH OF WAYCROSS	WAYCROSS	200	133
AMERICAN NB OF BRU	BRUNSWICK	199	195
TRUST CO BK GWINNETT CTY	LAWRENCEVILLE	199	152
COMMERCIAL BK	THOMASVILLE	198	124
CITIZENS BK	GAINESVILLE	195	105
GRANITE CITY BK	ELBERTON	195	101
FIRST NB OF GRIFFIN	GRIFFIN	194	100
FIRST FS&LA	LA GRANGE	192	136
CITIZENS TR BK	ATLANTA	191	101
NEWNAN FS&LA	NEWNAN	191	113
BANK OF CLAYTON	CLAYTON	190	105
BANK SOUTH MACON	MACON	189	262
HARDWICK B&TC	DALTON	186	179
TRUST CO BK OF S GA NA	ALBANY	186	184
FIRST NB OF GAINESVILLE	GAINESVILLE	184	487
HABERSHAM BK	CLARKESVILLE	183	116
CARROLLTON FS&LA	CARROLLTON	183	255
BARNETT BK NA	MARIETTA	182	506
FIRST UNION BK DALTON	DALTON	182	298
HERITAGE BK GWINNETT CTY	ATLANTA	181	335
TRUST CO BK	ATLANTA	180	5,221
FIRST UNION NB VALDOSTA	VALDOSTA	180	115
HOME FS&LA	ATLANTA	178	241
FIRST UNION NB ROME	ROME	176	184
FIRST BK OF SAVANNAH	SAVANNAH	175	156
HOME FEDERAL SAVINGS BANK OF GEORGIA	GAINESVILLE	174	270
CALHOUN FIRST NB	CALHOUN	173	115
GWINNETT FS&LA	LAWRENCEVILLE	173	210
FIRST ST B&TC VALDO	VALDOSTA	172	102
COMMERCIAL BK	DOUGLASVILLE	171	109
CITIZENS & SOUTHERN NB	ATLANTA	169	10,644

FIRST UNION BK GRIFFIN	GRIFFIN	169	201
TUCKER FS&LA	TUCKER	169	244
FIRST UNION BK AUGUSTA	AUGUSTA	166	720
ATHENS FEDERAL SAVINGS BANK	ATHENS	166	442

HAWAII

Name	City	Rank	Assets
FINANCE FACTORS LTD	HONOLULU	252	160
GECC FINANCIAL CORP	HONOLULU	237	374
FIRST FS&LA OF AMERICA	HONOLULU	234	731
CITY BK	HONOLULU	195	378
FIRST HAWAIIAN CREDITCP INC	HONOLULU	186	170
HAWAII NB	HONOLULU	183	218
FIRST INTERSTATE BK HI	HONOLULU	178	621
CENTRAL PACIFIC BK	HONOLULU	174	631

IDAHO

Name	City	Rank	Assets
BANK OF COMMERCE	IDAHO FALLS	250	124
TWIN FALLS B&TC	TWIN FALLS	215	176
FIRST SECURITY BK IDAHO NA	BOISE	171	1,744

ILLINOIS

Name	City	Rank	Assets
SOUTH CHICAGO SVG BK	CHICAGO	284	227
CITICORP SAVINGS OF ILLINOIS, A FS&LA	CHICAGO	277	5,514
PEOPLES NB OF KEWANEE	KEWANEE	259	103
FIRST SECURITY TR & SVG	ELMWOOD PARK	254	187
CHICAGO CITY B&TC	CHICAGO	253	186
COSMOPOLITAN NB CHICAGO	CHICAGO	236	113
FIRST NB OF ILLINOIS	LANSING	234	143
FIRST ST B&TC	PARK RIDGE	234	128
MANUFACTURERS BK	CHICAGO	233	294
BANK OF COMMERCE & INDUSTRY	CHICAGO	228	104
DEERFIELD FS&LA	DEERFIELD	224	244
MID CITY NB OF CHICAGO	CHICAGO	223	320
PARKWAY B&TC	HARWOOD HEIGHTS	220	244
MARQUETTE NB	CHICAGO	220	368
BOATMENS NB CHARLESTON	CHARLESTON	220	114
AMERICAN NB	LANSING	216	124
NORTHWESTERN S&LA	CHICAGO	214	927
DIXON NB	DIXON	213	203

ILLINOIS

Name	City	Rank	Assets
SECURITY FS&LA OF CHICAGO	CHICAGO	210	136
LASALLE BK LSL	LISLE	209	116
FIRST NB OF EVERGREEN PK	EVERGREEN PARK	209	620
FIRST NB OF LA GRANGE	LA GRANGE	207	103
FIRST NB OF PEORIA	PEORIA	207	228
OAK LAWN T&SB	OAK LAWN	207	123
WEST SUBURBAN BK	LOMBARD	207	253
GARY WHEATON BK	WHEATON	206	542
NORTH SHORE S&LA	WAUKEGAN	206	149
EUREKA S&LA OF LA SALLE	LA SALLE	206	171
HOYNE S&LA	CHICAGO	206	254
FIRST ST BK OF CHICAGO	CHICAGO	204	148
BANK OF O'FALLON	O'FALLON	204	129
FIRST NB OF OTTAWA	OTTAWA	204	164
GARY WHEATON BK OF BATAVIA	BATAVIA	204	110
FIRST BK OF OAK PARK	OAK PARK	203	106
CLEARING BK	CHICAGO	202	119
YORK ST B&TC	ELMHURST	202	130
UNIBANCTRUST CO	CHICAGO	201	465
LIBERTY SAVINGS	CHICAGO	201	412
FIRST AMERICA BK-GOLF MILL	NILES	200	118
FIRST AMERICA BK-ZION	ZION	199	105
ALTON MERCANTILE BK NA	ALTON	199	117
HOME ST BK	CRYSTAL LAKE	198	135
WORTH B&TC	WORTH	198	114
STANDARD B&TC	EVERGREEN PARK	198	205
LAKE SHORE NB	CHICAGO	197	710
FIRST NB IN HARVEY	HARVEY	196	130
UPTOWN NB OF CHICAGO	CHICAGO	196	186
SECOND FS&LA OF CHICAGO	CHICAGO	196	137
FIRST NB OF CICERO	CICERO	195	197
PARK NB OF CHICAGO	CHICAGO	195	147
BANK OF WHEATON	WHEATON	194	162
COMMERCIAL NB PEORIA	PEORIA	194	433
NORTHERN TR BK OHARE NA	CHICAGO	194	338
COMMERCIAL NB	BERWYN	194	226
STERLING FS&LA	STERLING	194	118
MCHENRY ST BK	MC HENRY	193	239
AMERICAN NB&TC OF WAUKEGAN	WAUKEGAN	192	128
FIRST NB OF JOLIET	JOLIET	192	318
NAPES BK NA	NAPERVILLE	192	224
HYDE PARK B&TC	CHICAGO	191	131
ORLAND ST BK	ORLAND PARK	191	155
ROCK ISLAND BK	ROCK ISLAND	191	126
FIRST NB OF DES PLAINES	DES PLAINES	190	432

FIRST NB	LINCOLNWOOD	190	137
INDEPENDENCE BK OF CHICAGO	CHICAGO	190	108
ITASCA B&TC	ITASCA	190	130
OLD SECOND NB	AURORA	190	235
SOUTH SHORE BK OF CHICAGO	CHICAGO	190	141
LIBERTYVILLE NB	LIBERTYVILLE	190	115
HARRIS BK WINNETKA NA	WINNETKA	190	169
FIRST FS&LA OF DES PLAINES	DES PLAINES	190	296
BANK OF MARION	MARION	189	103
FIRST GALESBURG NB	GALESBURG	189	156
FIRST NB OF WOOD RIVER	WOOD RIVER	189	105
HERITAGE BREMEN B&TC	TINLEY PARK	189	173
MERCHANDISE NB OF CHICAGO	CHICAGO	189	140
BANK OF WAUKEGAN	WAUKEGAN	189	204
CITIZENS B&TC	PARK RIDGE	189	571
BANK OF HIGHLAND PARK	HIGHLAND PARK	188	104
COLE TAYLOR BK	CHICAGO	188	269
DES PLAINES NB	DES PLAINES	188	115
STATE BK OF WOODSTOCK	WOODSTOCK	188	113
ADDISON ST BK	ADDISON	187	101
FIRST NB	MATTOON	187	127
FIRST NB IN CHICAGO HGTS	CHICAGO HEIGHTS	187	112
LAKE VIEW T&SB	CHICAGO	187	576
FIRST NB OF NILES IL	NILES	187	152
FIRST AMERICAN BK	SKOKIE	186	135
AVENUE B&TC	OAK PARK	186	167
NATIONAL BK OF CANTON	CANTON	186	119
STATE BK OF ST CHARLES	ST CHARLES	186	125
COLUMBIA NB OF CHICAGO	CHICAGO	185	300
BANK OF RAVENSWOOD	CHICAGO	185	391
SOUTH SIDE T&SB	PEORIA	185	101
UNITED BK OF ILLINOIS NA	ROCKFORD	185	253
SEAWAY NB OF CHICAGO	CHICAGO	184	141
STATE BK OF ANTIOCH	ANTIOCH	184	143
LIBERTY FS&LA OF CHICAGO	CHICAGO	184	333
AMALGAMATED T&SB	CHICAGO	183	335
FIRST NB OF COLLINSVILLE	COLLINSVILLE	183	135
CRAGIN FS&LA	CHICAGO	183	2,037
AFFILIATED BK WESTERN NAT	CICERO	182	209
MATTESON-RICHTON BK	MATTESON	182	108
COLONIAL B&TC	CHICAGO	182	321
FIRST GRANITE CITY NB	GRANITE CITY	182	161
B&TC OF ARLINGTON	ARLINGTON HEIGHTS	182	219
FIRST SECURITY FEDERAL SVG BK	CHICAGO	182	121
MICHIGAN AVENUE NB OF CHICAGO	CHICAGO	181	207
FIRST NB OF WAUKEGAN	WAUKEGAN	181	104
ST PAUL FEDERAL BANK FOR SAVINGS	CHICAGO	181	2,612
CALUMET FS&LA	CHICAGO	181	379
ALBANY B&TC NA	CHICAGO	180	204

ILLINOIS (cont.)

Name	City	Rank	Assets
CITIZENS NB OF PARIS	PARIS	180	105
FIRST NB OF BLUE ISLAND	BLUE ISLAND	180	195
FIRST NB OF MOLINE	MOLINE	180	166
FIRST NB OF LAKE FOREST	LAKE FOREST	180	418
OLD NB OF CENTRALIA	CENTRALIA	180	106
HARRIS BK ROSELLE	ROSELLE	180	234
AFFILIATED BK	FRANKLIN PARK	179	158
FIRST NB&TC	CARBONDALE	179	132
FIRST NB OF NORTHBROOK	NORTHBROOK	179	109
ELLIOTT ST BK	JACKSONVILLE	179	157
FIRST T&SB	TAYLORVILLE	179	120
FIRST NB	MT PROSPECT	179	295
STATE BK OF LAKE ZURICH	LAKE ZURICH	179	112
BOATMENS BK OF MT VERNON	MT VERNON	179	138
BANK OF WESTMONT	WESTMONT	178	119
MELROSE PARK BK&TR	MELROSE PARK	178	150
FIRST FS&LA OF CHAMPAIGN	CHAMPAIGN	178	116
BANK OF HOMEWOOD	HOMEWOOD	177	119
OAK LAWN NB	OAK LAWN	177	203
CITIZENS FIRST NB OF	PRINCETON	177	169
AMERICAN NB OF BNSNVLLE	BENSENVILLE	176	171
FIRST ILLINOIS BK OF WILMETTE	WILMETTE	176	298
OAK BROOK BK	OAK BROOK	176	236
BLOOMINGDALE ST BK	BLOOMINGDALE	176	131
JEFFERSON TR&SVG	PEORIA	176	215
JEFFERSON ST BK	CHICAGO	176	161
MILLIKIN NB OF DECATUR	DECATUR	176	329
RIVER OAKS B&TC	CALUMET CITY	176	114
CITY NB OF KANKAKEE	KANKAKEE	176	173
DU PAGE B&TC	GLEN ELLYN	176	160
BOULEVARD BK NA	CHICAGO	175	745
COLE TAYLOR BK CHICAGO	CHICAGO	175	286
FIRST NB OF STERLING	STERLING	175	100
FIRST NB OF SPRINGFIELD	SPRINGFIELD	175	335
LAKESIDE BK	CHICAGO	175	150
FIRST NB IN CHAMPAIGN	CHAMPAIGN	175	154
NATIONAL SECURITY BK OF CHIC	CHICAGO	175	186
SOUTH HOLLAND T&SB	SOUTH HOLLAND	175	306
STATE BK OF COUNTRYSIDE	COUNTRYSIDE	175	103
BOATMENS BK OF QUINCY	QUINCY	175	152
FIRST FS&LA OF WESTCHESTER	WESTCHESTER	175	206
HERGET NB OF PEKIN	PEKIN	174	113
FIRST NB OF MORTON GROVE	MORTON GROVE	174	156
PETERSON BK	CHICAGO	174	108
HARRIS BK HINSDALE NA	HINSDALE	174	248
AFFILIATED BK N SHORE NAT	CHICAGO	173	240

FIRST NB OF ELGIN	ELGIN	173	353
NORTHWEST NB OF CHICAGO	CHICAGO	173	683
DAMEN S&LA	CHICAGO	173	105
NATIONAL B&TC OF SYC	SYCAMORE	172	139
NEW LENOX ST BK	NEW LENOX	172	115
PIONEER B&TC	CHICAGO	172	282
FIRST NB&TC OF BARRIN	BARRINGTON	172	388
HARRIS BK GLENCOE-NRTHBRK NA	GLENCOE	172	161
AETNA BK	CHICAGO	171	160
CONTINENTAL BK BUFFALO GROVE NA	BUFFALO GROVE	171	111
FIRST NB OF GENEVA	GENEVA	171	141
MARINE BK OF SPRINGFIELD	SPRINGFIELD	171	571
METROBANK	EAST MOLINE	171	116
DREXEL NB	CHICAGO	170	113
AMERICAN NB OF LIBERTY	LIBERTYVILLE	170	209
GLENVIEW ST BK	GLENVIEW	170	356
MERCANTILE T&SB	QUINCY	170	172
MERCHANTS NB OF AURORA	AURORA	170	217
STANDARD FS&LA OF CHICAGO	CHICAGO	170	899
BEVERLY BK	CHICAGO	169	201
MIDWEST B&TC	ELMWOOD PARK	169	225
BANK OF PONTIAC	PONTIAC	169	102
NBD HIGHLAND PK BK NA	HIGHLAND PARK	169	413
FIRST NB OF SKOKIE	SKOKIE	169	390
CHICAGO BK OF COMMERCE	CHICAGO	169	180
LA SALLE NB	CHICAGO	168	1,448
EFFINGHAM ST BK	EFFINGHAM	168	117
HERITAGE PULLMAN B&TC	CHICAGO	168	221
ILLINOIS REGIONAL BK NA	ELMHURST	168	381
ILLINOIS NB OF SPRINGFIELD	SPRINGFIELD	168	297
PEOPLES BK OF BLOOMINGTON	BLOOMINGTON	168	200
DEVON BK	CHICAGO	167	151
DOWNERS GROVE NB	DOWNERS GROVE	167	129
OAK PARK T&SB	OAK PARK	167	421
CITIZENS NB OF DECATUR	DECATUR	167	204
FIRST NB OF QUAD CITIES	ROCK ISLAND	167	304
STATE BK OF FREEPORT	FREEPORT	166	152
BUSEY BK	URBANA	165	325
FIRST NB&TC ROCKFRD	ROCKFORD	165	404
FIRST ILLINOIS BK	LA GRANGE	165	230
STATE NB	EVANSTON	165	450

INDIANA

Name	City	Rank	Assets
FARMERS CITIZENS BK	SALEM	269	111
PEOPLES B&TC	MT VERNON	266	101

INDIANA (cont.)

Name	City	Rank	Assets
AMERIANA SVG BK, FSB	NEWCASTLE	257	235
PEOPLES FSB OF DEKALB COUNTY	AUBURN	248	165
BANK ONE CRAWFORDSVILLE NA	CRAWFORDSVILLE	233	134
BANK ONE NA	BLOOMINGTON	229	295
LINCOLN FEDERAL SVG BK	PLAINFIELD	217	115
FIRST FEDERAL SVG BK OF MARION	MARION	217	148
AMERICAN NB&TC OF MUNCIE	MUNCIE	213	171
FARMERS B&TC	WADESVILLE	212	119
LOWELL NB	LOWELL	211	116
FIRST OF AMER BK-INDIANAPOLIS	SPEEDWAY	209	259
BANK ONE	PLAINFIELD	208	116
TOWER FS&LA	SOUTH BEND	207	338
REGIONAL FEDERAL SVG BK	NEW ALBANY	207	147
BANK OF HIGHLAND	HIGHLAND	205	142
INDIANA FS&LA	VALPARAISO	203	477
OLD NB IN EVANSVILLE	EVANSVILLE	202	787
BEDFORD NB	BEDFORD	201	127
FIRST NB OF HUNTINGTN	HUNTINGTON	200	120
FIRST ST BK OF DECATUR	DECATUR	200	114
CITIZENS NB OF WHITLEY C	COLUMBIA CITY	196	113
FIRST BK OF BERNE	BERNE	195	131
SUMMIT BK	MARION	195	134
ELSTON B&TC	CRAWFORDSVILLE	192	128
CITIZENS NB OF TELL CTY	TELL CITY	191	111
FIRST FS&LA OF RICHMOND	RICHMOND	190	136
COMMERCE AMERICA BKG CO	JEFFERSONVILLE	189	328
BANK ONE LAFAYETTE NA	LAFAYETTE	188	375
FIRST NB	KOKOMO	187	179
NATIONAL CTY BK OF EVANSVILE	EVANSVILLE	187	321
MERCHANTS NB OF MUNCIE	MUNCIE	186	412
ANDERSON BKG CO	ANDERSON	185	279
UNION ST BK	CARMEL	185	175
NATIONAL BK OF GREENWOOD	GREENWOOD	185	144
UNION B&TC	KOKOMO	185	320
BOONE COUNTY ST BK	LEBANON	185	133
SALEM B&TC	GOSHEN	185	266
MISHAWAKA FS&LA	MISHAWAKA	185	129
BARGERSVILLE ST BK	GREENWOOD	184	117
BANK ONE NA	MARION	184	111
GAINER BK NA	GARY	183	860
GREENFIELD BKG CO	GREENFIELD	183	136
PEOPLES FS&LA	MUNSTER	183	180
MADISON BK&TC	MADISON	182	152
CITIZENS FS&LA	HAMMOND	181	542
FARMERS BK	FRANKFORT	180	150
MERCANTILE NB OF INDIANA	HAMMOND	180	392

Name	City	Rank	Assets
PEOPLES B&TC	INDIANAPOLIS	179	223
SUMMIT BK CLINTON CTY	FRANKFORT	179	116
FIRST AMERICAN BK LA PORTE NA	LA PORTE	179	147
CITIZENS ST BK	NEW CASTLE	178	112
FIRST NB OF WARSAW	WARSAW	178	248
FIRST NB OF MADISON CITY	ANDERSON	178	118
FIRST INTERSTATE BK IN NA	SOUTH BEND	177	220
CITIZENS FDLTY BK&TC	SELLERSBURG	176	122
BANK ONE	NA	175	106
CITIZENS FDLTY BK&TC	NEW ALBANY	174	345
FIRST UNION B&TC	WINAMAC	174	106
MERCHANTS NB TERRE HAUTE	TERRE HAUTE	173	271
CITIZENS NB OF GRANT C	MARION	173	110
FIRST FEDERAL SVG BK OF KOKOMO	KOKOMO	173	150
HOME LOAN SAVINGS BANK	FORT WAYNE	173	159
FIRST CITIZENS BK NA	MICHIGAN CITY	172	316
MONROE COUNTY ST BK	BLOOMINGTON	172	165
SECOND NB OF RICHMOND	RICHMOND	172	327
CITIZENS NB OF EVANSVILLE	EVANSVILLE	171	712
SECURITY B&TC	VINCENNES	170	132
INDIANA FIRST NB	CHARLESTOWN	169	101
LAFAYETTE NB	LAFAYETTE	169	365
VALLEY AMERICAN B&TC	SOUTH BEND	168	394
MUTUAL TC	NEW ALBANY	168	127
SHELBY FEDERAL SVG BK	INDIANAPOLIS	168	182
CHESTERTON ST BK	CHESTERTON	167	113
BANK ONE MERRILLVILLE NA	GARY	167	388
BANK ONE OF RICHMOND NA	RICHMOND	167	233
IRWIN UNION B&TC	COLUMBUS	166	254
FARMERS NB SHELBYVILLE	SHELBYVILLE	166	148
SUMMIT BK	FORT WAYNE	166	1,396
WORKINGMENS FS&LA	BLOOMINGTON	166	121
OLD CAPITAL B&TC	CORYDON	165	163

IOWA

Name	*City*	*Rank*	*Assets*
IOWA ST BK	DES MOINES	250	103
MONTICELLO ST BK	MONTICELLO	225	183
PEOPLES B&TC	CEDAR RAPIDS	224	262
CENTRAL ST BK	MUSCATINE	219	187
WATERLOO SVG BK	WATERLOO	212	226
WEST DES MOINES ST BK	WEST DES MOINES	210	226
DAVENPORT B&TC	DAVENPORT	209	1,477
FIRST NB	AMES	203	174
COUNCIL BLUFFS SVG BK	COUNCIL BLUFFS	203	235
FIRST NB IOWA CITY IOW	IOWA CITY	200	260

IOWA (cont.)

Name	City	Rank	Assets
SECURITY BK	MARSHALLTOWN	197	215
SECURITY NB SIOUX CITY	SIOUX CITY	197	307
UNITED BK&TR	AMES	196	140
CITIZENS FIRST NB	STORM LAKE	195	129
HILLS B&TC	HILLS	194	244
NORTHWEST B&TC	DAVENPORT	191	156
NATIONAL BK OF WATERLOO	WATERLOO	186	357
DECORAH ST BK	DECORAH	184	121
UNION B&TC	OTTUMWA	182	158
JASPER COUNTY SVG BK	NEWTON	182	108
FIRST NB COUNCIL BLUFFS	COUNCIL BLUFFS	176	141
VALLEY NB	DES MOINES	172	376
FIRST NB OF DUBUQUE	DUBUQUE	171	219
CLINTON NB	CLINTON	170	148
PEOPLES T&SB	INDIANOLA	167	119
MAQUOKETA ST BK	MAQUOKETA	167	100
DUBUQUE B&TC	DUBUQUE	165	272

KANSAS

Name	City	Rank	Assets
HOME NB OF ARKANSAS CITY	ARKANSAS CITY	224	111
FIDELITY ST BK	GARDEN CITY	210	107
BROTHERHOOD B&TC	KANSAS CITY	208	123
FIRST NB IN WICHITA	WICHITA	204	660
SHAWNEE ST BK	SHAWNEE	202	134
AMERICAN ST B&TC	GREAT BEND	201	107
FIRST NB OF LAWRENCE	LAWRENCE	198	119
INDUSTRIAL ST BK	KANSAS CITY	194	164
VALLEY VIEW ST BK	OVERLAND PARK	184	415
CAPITOL FS&LA	TOPEKA	184	2,533
BANK IV OLATHE NA	OLATHE	182	153
OVERLAND PARK ST B&TC	OVERLAND PARK	181	152
CITIZENS B&TC	SHAWNEE	176	106
COMMERCE B&TC	TOPEKA	174	170
INTER-STATE FS&LA	KANSAS CITY	174	190
COMMERCIAL NB OF KANSAS CTY	KANSAS CITY	172	309
BANK IV SALINA NA	SALINA	171	114
FIRST NB&TC SALINA	SALINA	170	132
UNION NB&TC OF MANHATTAN	MANHATTAN	170	150
FIRST NB OF HUTCHINSON	HUTCHINSON	169	146
HUTCHINSON NB&TC	HUTCHINSON	169	168

KENTUCKY

Name	City	Rank	Assets
FIRST FSB OF ELIZABETHTOWN	ELIZABETHTOWN	273	173
MID AMERICAN B&TC OF LOUISVILLE	LOUISVILLE	257	682
FARMERS B&TC CAPITAL TC	FRANKFORT	224	298
SUNRISE FS&LA	NEWPORT	219	159
FIRST CITY B&TC	HOPKINSVILLE	218	142
PEOPLES BK OF MURRAY	MURRAY	216	131
LEXINGTON FEDERAL SAVINGS BANK	LEXINGTON	215	170
FARMERS B&TC OF M	MADISONVILLE	214	137
PLANTERS B&TC	HOPKINSVILLE	212	180
FIFTH THIRD BK OF CAMPBELL CTY NA	NEWPORT	209	121
BANK OF MARSHALL COUNTY	BENTON	207	110
KENTUCKY B&TC	MADISONVILLE	206	141
FIRST & PEOPLES BK	RUSSELL	204	140
BOURBON-AGRICULTURAL DEP B&TC	PARIS	202	108
CITIZENS B&TC	PADUCAH	200	353
CITIZENS FIDELITY B&TC	ELIZABETHTOWN	198	232
CENTRAL B&TC	OWENSBORO	195	174
BANK OF WHITESBURG	WHITESBURG	194	115
THIRD NB OF ASHLAND	ASHLAND	193	189
OWENSBORO NB	OWENSBORO	191	283
BANK OF BENTON	BENTON	191	100
BANK OF LEXINGTON & TC	LEXINGTON	191	169
KENTUCKY NAT BK OF KENTON CTY	COVINGTON	191	173
CITIZENS NB OF SOMERSET	SOMERSET	190	126
FIRST FS&LA	BOWLING GREEN	188	200
CITIZENS ST BK	OWENSBORO	187	208
BANK OF MURRAY	MURRAY	185	186
CITIZENS NB OF PAINTSVILLE	PAINTSVILLE	185	122
NEWPORT NB	NEWPORT	185	123
GREAT FINANCIAL FEDERAL	LOUISVILLE	184	950
FIRST ST BK GREENVILLE	GREENVILLE	181	119
FIFTH THIRD BK BOONE CTY	FLORENCE	181	115
STOCK YARDS B&TC	LOUISVILLE	180	132
FIRST FS&LA	LEXINGTON	180	132
CITIZENS FDLTY B&TC, OLDHAM	LA GRANGE	178	105
PEOPLES B&TC	MADISONVILLE	177	115
CARDINAL FEDERAL SAVINGS BANK	OWENSBORO	177	247
FORT THOMAS-BELLEVUE BK	FORT THOMAS	175	160
PEOPLES-LIBERTY B&TC	COVINGTON	175	214
PEOPLES FIRST NB&TC	PADUCAH	173	287
STATE B&TC	RICHMOND	172	149
CITIZENS BK OF PIKEVILLE	PIKEVILLE	169	160
FIRST NB&TC CORBIN	CORBIN	167	135
FIRST AMERICAN BK	ASHLAND	167	170
HUNTINGTON BK OF KNT CTY INC	COVINGTON	166	310

LOUISIANA

Name	City	Rank	Assets
METAIRIE B&TC	METAIRIE	285	163
FIRST NB OF LAKE CHARLES	LAKE CHARLES	240	173
GULF NB OF LAKE CHARLES	LAKE CHARLES	232	152
ST BERNARD B&TC	ARABI	229	119
CONCORDIA B&TC	VIDALIA	223	197
PEOPLES B&TC OF ST BERNARD	CHALMETTE	219	108
RAPIDES B&TC	ALEXANDRIA	214	379
FIRST AMERICAN B&T	VACHERIE	208	102
PEOPLES B&TC	MINDEN	208	101
AMERICAN B&TC	NEW ORLEANS	207	315
BOGALUSA	FRANKLINTON	206	122
MINDEN B&TC	MINDEN	199	102
CALCASIEU MARINE NB	LAKE CHARLES	196	722
ST LANDRY B&TC	OPELOUSAS	192	171
OUACHITA NB IN MONROE	MONROE	184	479
SECURITY FIRST NB	ALEXANDRIA	180	188
LAKE SIDE NB	LAKE CHARLES	180	158
RACELAND B&TC	RACELAND	179	227
WHITNEY NB	NEW ORLEANS	176	2,598
FIRST NB OF WEST MONROE	WEST MONROE	175	128
FIRST NB ST LANDRY PARISH	OPELOUSAS	166	137
FIDELITY HMSTD ASSN	NEW ORLEANS	166	409

MAINE

Name	City	Rank	Assets
MID MAINE SAVINGS BANK FSB	AUBURN	285	110
PEOPLES HERITAGE SVG BK	PORTLAND	237	1,623
SACO & BIDDEFORD SVG INST	SACO	231	125
GARDINER SAVINGS INSTITUTION, FSB	GARDINER	225	116
BAR HARBOR B&TC	BAR HARBOR	224	147
UNION TC OF ELLSWORTH	ELLSWORTH	220	113
ANDROSCOGGIN SVG BK	LEWISTON	216	139
NORSTAR BK OF MAINE	PORTLAND	204	817
SKOWHEGAN SVG BK	SKOWHEGAN	204	149
MAINE NB	PORTLAND	198	993
CAMDEN NB	CAMDEN	194	167
NORWAY SVG BK	NORWAY	194	148
KEY BK OF CENTRAL MAINE	AUGUSTA	192	624
CITIBANK (MAINE) NA	SOUTH PORTLAND	191	143
KEY BK NORTHERN MAINE	PRESQUE ISLE	190	129
BANGOR SVG BK	BANGOR	186	470
KEY BK EASTERN MAINE	BANGOR	180	131
MERRILL TC	BANGOR	180	890

Name	City	Rank	Assets
GORHAM SVG BK	GORHAM	179	131
CASCO NORTHERN BK NA	PORTLAND	177	1,333
FRANKLIN SVG BK	FARMINGTON	177	159
KEY BK SOUTHERN MAINE	PORTLAND	173	515
FIRST NE DAMARISCOTTA	DAMARISCOTTA	167	122

MARYLAND

Name	City	Rank	Assets
CITIBANK (MARYLAND) NA	TOWSON	300	1,053
CRESTAR BK MD	BETHESDA	252	184
REISTERSTOWN FEDERAL SVG BK	REISTERSTOWN	235	143
FIRST NB OF ST MARYS	LEONARDTOWN	233	144
CARROLLTON BK OF BALTIMORE	BALTIMORE	230	151
FAIRFAX SAVINGS, A FSB	BALTIMORE	227	374
CITIZENS NB	LAUREL	226	296
HOME FEDERAL SAVINGS BANK	HAGERSTOWN	224	182
CALVIN B TAYLOR BKG CO	BERLIN	223	166
CHESTERTOWN BK OF MD	CHESTERTOWN	218	125
UNITED B&TC OF MD	UPPER MARLBORO	218	157
PENINSULA BK	PRINCESS ANNE	213	158
HAMILTON FS&LA	BALTIMORE	213	106
COMMERCIAL BK	BEL AIR	212	150
ANNAPOLIS BKG&TC	ANNAPOLIS	208	166
CITIZENS B&TC OF MD	RIVERDALE	205	1,684
FARMERS NB OF MARYLAND	ANNAPOLIS	205	389
COUNTY BKG&TC	ELKTON	205	160
WESTMINSTER B&TC CRL C	WESTMINSTER	205	143
MERCANTILE SAFE DEP & TC	BALTIMORE	203	1,315
POTOMAC VALLEY BK	GAITHERSBURG	203	103
ROSEDALE FS&LA	BALTIMORE	203	222
SANDY SPRING NB MD	OLNEY	201	303
FARMERS & MECHANICS NAT BANK	FREDERICK	200	457
FREDERICK CTY NB OF FRDRICK	FREDERICK	200	172
FARMERS & MERCHANTS BK OF HAGERSTOWN	HAGERSTOWN	198	185
SPARKS ST BK	SPARKS	195	113
BANK OF GLEN BURNIE	GLEN BURNIE	194	113
FIRST UNITED NB&TC	OAKLAND	192	262
FREDERICKTOWN B&TC	FREDERICK	192	156
HAGERSTOWN TC	HAGERSTOWN	191	287
CHASE BK OF MD	BALTIMORE	191	770
DOMINION BK MARYLAND NA	ROCKVILLE	190	237
FOREST HILL ST BK	FOREST HILL	188	134
TALBOT BK	EASTON	188	137
EASTERN SAVINGS BANK, FSB	PIKESVILLE	187	222
GARRETT NB IN OAKLAND	OAKLAND	178	122
MELLON BANK	BETHESDA	178	193

MARYLAND (cont.)

Name	City	Rank	Assets
CARROLL COUNTY B&TC	WESTMINSTER	177	300
LIBERTY BK OF MARYLAND	CUMBERLAND	171	148
ARUNDEL FS&LA	BALTIMORE	170	130

MASSACHUSETTS

Name	City	Rank	Assets
NEEDHAM CO-OP BK	NEEDHAM	283	263
TAUNTON SVG BK	TAUNTON	278	205
MASSBANK FOR SVG	READING	274	325
FIRST AMERICAN BK FOR SVG	BOSTON	268	642
SOMERSET SVG BK	SOMERVILLE	265	484
SANDWICH CO-OP	SANDWICH	261	183
NEW BEDFORD INST FOR SVG	NEW BEDFORD	258	870
ANDOVER SVG BK	ANDOVER	256	617
WALTHAM SVG BK	WALTHAM	251	284
FRAMINGHAM CO-OP BK	FRAMINGHAM	246	148
NATIONAL GRAND BK OF MARBLEHEAD	MARBLEHEAD	245	114
CAMBRIDGEPORT SVG BK	CAMBRIDGE	245	350
MEDFORD SVG BK	MEDFORD	245	410
PEOPLES SVG BK	WORCESTER	245	525
LOWELL INST FOR SVG	LOWELL	244	362
ABINGTON SVG BK	ABINGTON	243	176
FAMILY MSB	HAVERHILL	243	373
LEXINGTON SVG BK	LEXINGTON	242	206
WORCESTER CITY INST FOR SVG	WORCESTER	236	886
CO-OP BK OF CONCORD	CONCORD	235	274
GROVEBANK FOR SVG	BOSTON	235	154
COMMUNITY SVG BK	HOLYOKE	234	543
LOWELL FIVE CENT SVG BK	LOWELL	230	332
WOBURN FIVE CENTS SVG BK	WOBURN	227	274
EAST CAMBRIDGE SVG BK	CAMBRIDGE	226	284
PEOPLES SVG BK OF BROCKTON	BROCKTON	223	175
SOUTHSTATE BK FOR SVG	BROCKTON	222	215
EVERETT SVG BK	EVERETT	221	196
WHITINSVILLE SVG BK	WHITINSVILLE	221	105
LAWRENCE SVG BK	LAWRENCE	217	452
WEBSTER FIVE CENTS SVG BK	WEBSTER	217	117
CAPE COD B&TC	HYANNIS	216	501
CENTRAL CO-OP BK	SOMERVILLE	216	227
HYDE PARK SVG BK	BOSTON	215	175
WARREN FIVE CENTS SVG BK	PEABODY	215	322
WINTER HILL FS&LA	SOMERVILLE	214	171
FIRST BRISTOL CTY NB	TAUNTON	213	403
BRAINTREE SVG BK	BRAINTREE	213	163

EAST BOSTON SVG BK	BOSTON	213	246
DEDHAM INST FOR SVG	DEDHAM	212	278
FRAMINGHAM SVG BK	FRAMINGHAM	212	515
HERITAGE-INS BK FOR SVGS	NORTHAMPTON	212	873
COUNTRY BK FOR SVG	WARE	211	323
MERCHANTSBANK CO-OP BK	BOSTON	210	504
WORKINGMENS CO-OP BK	BOSTON	210	209
BEVERLY SVG BK	BEVERLY	210	251
NORTH ADAMS-HOOSAC SVG BK	NORTH ADAMS	210	150
GUARANTY FIRST TC	WALTHAM	209	427
QUINCY CO-OP BK	QUINCY	208	266
QUINCY SVG BK	QUINCY	208	609
FAIRHAVEN SVG BK	FAIRHAVEN	207	261
EASTHAMPTON SVG BK	EASTHAMPTON	206	141
BROADWAY NB OF CHELSEA	CHELSEA	205	108
NEWBURYPORT FIVE CNT SVG BK	NEWBURYPORT	205	155
HAMPSHIRE NB S HADLEY	SOUTH HADLEY	203	113
UNIVERSITY B&TC	NEWTON	203	216
NEW ENGLAND FEDERAL SAVINGS BANK	WELLESLEY	203	107
USTRUST/MIDDLESEX	CAMBRIDGE	201	315
HUDSON NB	HUDSON	199	158
GREATER BOSTON BANK A CO-OP BANK	BOSTON	199	135
BANK FOR SVG	MALDEN	199	423
CAMBRIDGE SVG BK	CAMBRIDGE	199	460
VANGUARD SVG BK	HOLYOKE	198	346
HOME NB OF MILFORD	MILFORD	197	458
FIRST ESSEX SVG BK	LAWRENCE	197	464
WOBURN NB	WOBURN	195	112
CAMBRIDGE TC	CAMBRIDGE	194	215
CAPE ANN SVG BK	GLOUCESTER	194	185
EASTERN SVG BK	LYNN	194	822
MARBLEHEAD SVG BK	MARBLEHEAD	194	138
MASSACHUSETTS CO INC	BOSTON	193	126
WEST NEWTON SVG BK	WEST NEWTON	193	209
BAYBANK NORFOLK CTY TC	DEDHAM	192	1,388
SOUTH BOSTON SVG BK	BOSTON	191	1,333
PARK WEST B&TC	WEST SPRINGFIELD	189	195
MALDEN TC	MALDEN	188	332
WAKEFIELD SVG BK	WAKEFIELD	188	275
MIDDLESEX SVG BK	NATICK	187	438
THE FEDERAL SAVINGS BANK	WALTHAM	186	274
PLYMOUTH FIVE CENTS SVG BK	PLYMOUTH	186	247
BANK OF CAPE COD	FALMOUTH	185	168
SALEM FIVE CENTS SVG BK	SALEM	185	516
PENTUCKET FIVE CNTS SVG BANK	HAVERHILL	184	116
UNITED SVG BK	CONWAY	183	113
SHAWMUT FIRST COUNTY BK NA	BROCKTON	182	193
WALPOLE CO-OP BK	WALPOLE	182	136
FIRST BK	CHELMSFORD	181	375

MASSACHUSETTS (cont.)

Name	City	Rank	Assets
PLYMOUTH HOME NB	BROCKTON	181	556
SHAWMUT BK OF FRANKLIN CTY	GREENFIELD	181	140
WESTFIELD SVG BK	WESTFIELD	181	264
PIONEER FINANCIAL, A COOPERATIVE BANK	MALDEN	180	460
ELIOT SVG BK	BOSTON	180	323
HIBERNIA SVG BK	BOSTON	180	135
WINTHROP SVG BK	WINTHROP	180	115
UNION NB	LOWELL	179	580
LINCOLN TC	HINGHAM	179	191
SAUGUS B&TC	SAUGUS	179	160
FITCHBURG SAVINGS BANK, FSB	FITCHBURG	179	165
CENTURY B&TC	SOMERVILLE	178	275
US TRUST NORFOLK	MILTON	178	451
FALL RIVER FIVE CENT SVG BK	FALL RIVER	178	206
UNITED CO-OP BK	SPRINGFIELD	178	216
COOLIDGE B&TC	BOSTON	176	314
MARTHA'S VINEYARD NB	VINYARD HAVEN	176	125
BAY STATE FEDERAL SVG BK	BROOKLINE	176	164
BRISTOL COUNTY SVG BK	TAUNTON	176	190
BROOKLINE SVG BK	BROOKLINE	176	414
FRAMINGHAM TC	FRAMINGHAM	175	376
BERKSHIRE B&TC	PITTSFIELD	175	223
SHAWMUT BK OF HAMPSHIRE CTY NA	AMHERST	175	159
SHAWMUT MERCHANTS BK NA	SALEM	175	220
US TRUST ESSEX	GLOUCESTER	175	152
FIRST SERVICE BK FOR SVG	LEOMINSTER	175	657
ESSEXBANK	PEABODY	174	615
PLYMOUTH SVG BK	WAREHAM	174	343
ROCKLAND TC	ROCKLAND	173	707
HOME FEDERAL SVG BK	WORCESTER	173	296
GEORGE PEABODY CO-OP BK	PEABODY	173	115
PEOPLES SVG BK	HOLYOKE	173	264
WATERTOWN SVG BK	WATERTOWN	173	212
MERCHANTS NB	LEOMINSTER	172	144
MARLBOROUGH SVG BK	MARLBOROUGH	172	121
SHAWMUT WORCESTER CTY BK NA	WORCESTER	170	1,287
SPRINGFIELD INST FOR SVG	SPRINGFIELD	170	920
HAYMARKET CO-OP BK	BOSTON	169	180
FALMOUTH NB	FALMOUTH	169	173
PACIFIC NB OF NANTUCKET	NANTUCKET	169	109
UNITED STATES TC	BOSTON	169	1,064
NORTH EASTON SVG BK	NORTH EASTON	169	102
UNION WARREN SVG BK	BOSTON	169	698
DURFEE ATTLEBORO BK	FALL RIVER	167	382
SOUTH SHORE BK	QUINCY	167	1,015
SHAWMUT BK OF SE MA NA	NEW BEDFORD	167	278

FIRST SAFETY FUND NB OF FITCHBURG	FITCHBURG	167	189
BOSTON FIVE CENTS SAVINGS BANK FSB	BOSTON	167	1,972
LUDLOW SVG BK	LUDLOW	167	230
CHICOPEE SVG BK	CHICOPEE	166	134
SOUTH WEYMOUTH SVG BK	SOUTH WEYMOUTH	166	162
DANVERS SVG BK	DANVERS	165	195

MICHIGAN

Name	City	Rank	Assets
PEOPLES ST BK	HAMTRAMCK	286	120
CITY B&TC NA	JACKSON	225	356
MONROE B&TC	MONROE	225	368
FIDELITY BANK	BIRMINGHAM	209	106
WARREN BK	WARREN	208	296
FIRST FS & LA OF LENAWEE COUNTY	ADRIAN	204	196
CLINTON B&TC	ST JOHNS	199	142
STATE SVG BK OF FENTON	FENTON	199	132
STATE BK OF FRASER	FRASER	198	125
FIRST OF AMERICA BK-CENTRAL	LANSING	197	461
OXFORD BK	OXFORD	197	102
BANK ONE	STURGIS	194	157
PEOPLES SAVINGS BANK, FSB	MONROE	194	369
COMMERCIAL & SVG BK	ST CLAIR	192	168
LIBERTY ST B&TC	HAMTRAMCK	192	303
NATIONAL BK OF ROYAL OAK	ROYAL OAK	190	103
NBD GRAND HAVEN	GRAND HAVEN	190	152
CITIZENS T&SB	SOUTH HAVEN	189	142
NBD ANN ARBOR NA	ANN ARBOR	189	319
FIRST NB IN MT CLEMENS	MT CLEMENS	188	292
INTER-CITY BK	BENTON HARBOR	188	240
DEARBORN B&TC	DEARBORN	187	246
SECOND NB OF SAGINAW	SAGINAW	187	594
FMB-FIRST MICHIGAN BK	ZEELAND	187	460
FIRST OF AMERICA BK	TROY	187	733
NBD NORTHWEST BK NA	TRAVERSE CITY	187	137
CHEMICAL BK CLARE	CLARE	186	128
CITIZENS NB OF CHEBOYGAN	CHEBOYGAN	185	114
KEY ST BK	OWOSSO	185	101
YPSILANTI SVG BK	YPSILANTI	184	139
NATIONAL BK OF YPSILANTI	YPSILANTI	183	119
BRANCH COUNTY BK	COLDWATER	182	111
CHEMICAL B&TC	MIDLAND	182	452
CITIZENS COMMERCIAL & SVG B	FLINT	182	1,190
FIRST OF AMERICA BK NA	PONTIAC	182	607
BANK OF COMMERCE	HAMTRAMCK	182	442
COMMERCIAL SVG BK	ADRIAN	182	140
FIRST MACOMB BK	MT CLEMENS	181	334

MICHIGAN (cont.)

Name	City	Rank	Assets
ISABELLA B&TC	MT PLEASANT	181	149
UNION B&TC NA	GRAND RAPIDS	181	965
WYANDOTTE SVG BK	WYANDOTTE	181	377
CHARTER NB	TAYLOR	180	146
FIRST OF AMERICA BK - NA	KALAMAZOO	180	1,107
SECURITY BK	IONIA	180	114
MICHIGAN NB - FARMINGTON	FARMINGTON HILLS	180	7,961
STATE BK OF STANDISH	STANDISH	179	111
FIRST OF AMERICA BK NA	BAY CITY	178	362
TRENTON B&TC	TRENTON	178	124
UNITED SVG BK OF TECUMSEH	TECUMSEH	178	149
FIRST OF AMERICA BK - ANN ARBOR	ANN ARBOR	177	485
FIRST ST BK	EAST DETROIT	177	236
LAPEER COUNTY B&TC	LAPEER	177	124
OLD KENT BK SOUTHEAST	TRENTON	177	244
SECURITY B&TC	SOUTHGATE	177	1,206
CITIZENS TR	ANN ARBOR	177	332
COMERICA BK - TROY	TROY	176	223
NBD ROSCOMMON BK	ROSCOMMON	176	145
OLD KENT BK OF GRAND HAVEN	GRAND HAVEN	176	261
OTTAWA SAVINGS & LOAN, FA	HOLLAND	176	209
FIRST NB IN HOWELL	HOWELL	175	101
FIRST OF AMERICA BK	GLADWIN	175	102
OLD KENT BK OF MICHIGAN	KALAMAZOO	175	510
PEOPLES ST BK	ST JOSEPH	174	168
SECURITY BK OF MONROE	MONROE	174	262
FIRST OF AMERICA BK LIVINGSTON	HOWELL	173	107
NBD CADILLAC BK	CADILLAC	173	224
FIRST NB&TC	PETOSKEY	173	142
FIRST OF AMERICA BK	ALPENA	172	122
FIRST OF AMERICA BK - NA	HOLLAND	172	113
FIRST OF AMERICA BK - MUSKEGON	MUSKEGON	172	262
OLD KENT BK SOUTHWEST	NILES	171	301
FMB - LUMBERMANS BK	MUSKEGON	170	216
PEOPLES BK OF PORT HURON	PORT HURON	170	280
CITIZENS FS&LA OF PORT HURON	PORT HURON	170	340
OLD KENT BK OF BRIGHTON	BRIGHTON	169	177
COMERICA BK - BATTLE CREEK	BATTLE CREEK	168	149
EMPIRE NB OF TRAVERSE CY	TRAVERSE CITY	168	206
MANUFACTURERS BK	LANSING	168	291
NBD GENESEE BK	FLINT	168	1,019
MANISTEE B&TC	MANISTEE	167	110
PONTIAC ST BK	PONTIAC	167	684
CHEMICAL BK BAY AREA	BAY CITY	166	118

| OLD KENT BK OF GAYLORD | GAYLORD | 166 | 122 |
| COMERICA BK - ANN ARBOR NA | ANN ARBOR | 165 | 183 |

MINNESOTA

Name	City	Rank	Assets
WINONA NAT & SVG BK	WINONA	277	110
MIDWAY NB OF ST PAUL	ST PAUL	230	244
MARQUETTE BK ROCHESTER	ROCHESTER	222	134
FIRST NB IN ANOKA	ANOKA	222	188
PARK NB	ST LOUIS PARK	213	132
BANK NORTH	CRYSTAL	204	106
ROSEVILLE BK	ROSEVILLE	204	126
EASTERN HEIGHTS ST BK	ST PAUL	200	207
FIRST NB OF BEMIDJI	BEMIDJI	198	140
ZAPP NB	ST CLOUD	196	143
MARINE BANK	BLOOMINGTON	196	214
FIRST AMERICAN NB OF CROOKSTON	CROOKSTON	195	128
RICHFIELD B&TC	RICHFIELD	195	217
DROVERS FIRST AMERICAN BK OF SSP	SOUTH ST PAUL	194	132
NORWEST BK MOORHEAD NA	MOORHEAD	187	110
LIBERTY ST BK	ST PAUL	184	138
SHELARD NB	ST LOUIS PARK	184	117
FIRST NB OF BRAINERD	BRAINERD	179	103
COMMERCIAL ST BK	ST PAUL	178	191
NORTHERN NB OF BEMIDJI	BEMIDJI	177	105
FIRST NB	STILLWATER	176	113
MERCHANTS NB OF WINONA	WINONA	175	184
GOODHUE COUNTY NB OF RED WING	RED WING	174	121
BANK WAYZATA	WAYZATA	169	166
NORWEST BK MAPLE GROVE NA	MAPLE GROVE	166	127

MISSISSIPPI

Name	City	Rank	Assets
PEOPLES BK OF BILOXI	BILOXI	250	184
MERCHANTS & MARINE BK	PASCAGOULA	239	137
BANK OF NEW ALBANY	NEW ALBANY	215	108
FIRST COLUMBUS NB	COLUMBUS	211	157
UNISOUTH BANKING CORP	COLUMBUS	201	117
NATIONAL BK OF CMRC OF MS	STARKVILLE	199	311
EASTOVER BANK FOR SAVINGS	JACKSON	198	480
PEOPLES BK	RIPLEY	195	118
FIRST ST BK	WAYNESBORO	193	112
PEOPLES B&TC	TUPELO	191	467
FIRST NB OF VICKSBURG	VICKSBURG	184	203
SECURITY BK	CORINTH	183	112

MISSISSIPPI (cont.)

Name	City	Rank	Assets
MERCHANTS & FARMERS BK	KOSCIUSKO	178	229
BANK OF MISSISSIPPI	TUPELO	175	1,170
MERCHANTS B&TC	BAY ST LOUIS	175	116
COMMERCIAL NB&TC	LAUREL	172	157
TRUSTMARK NB	JACKSON	172	2,517
CITIZENS BK	PHILADELPHIA	171	130
CITIZENS NB OF MERIDIAN	MERIDIAN	171	273
SUNBURST BK	GRENADA	170	1,261
HANCOCK BK	GULFPORT	170	905
DEPOSIT GUARANTY NB	JACKSON	169	3,195
COMMUNITY FS&LA	TUPELO	169	103
FIRST NB	NEW ALBANY	167	134

MISSOURI

Name	City	Rank	Assets
CASS B&TC	ST LOUIS	243	131
INVESTORS FIDUCIARY TC	KANSAS CITY	235	330
BANK OF WASHINGTON	WASHINGTON	232	133
CITIZENS B&TC	CHILLICOTHE	220	156
BOATMENS RAYTOWN BK	RAYTOWN	201	144
CITIZENS NB OF GR ST LOUIS	MAPLEWOOD	201	107
ST JOHNS B&TC	ST JOHNS	201	168
JEFFERSON B&TC	ST LOUIS	200	136
UNITED S&LA	LEBANON	199	366
UNITED MISSOURI BK OF KANSAS CITY NA	KANSAS CITY	198	1,463
EXCHANGE NB OF JEFFERSON	JEFFERSON CITY	195	225
FIRST BK	GLADSTONE	193	189
SOUTHERN COMMERCIAL BK	ST LOUIS	193	152
UNITED MISSOURI CITY BK	KANSAS CITY	190	200
LEMAY B&TC	LEMAY	187	308
MERCANTILE BK SPRINGFIELD	SPRINGFIELD	186	151
THIRD NB OF SEDALIA	SEDALIA	186	161
MIDLAND BK	LEES SUMMIT	185	149
BLUE SPRINGS BK	BLUE SPRINGS	184	131
EMPIRE BK	SPRINGFIELD	182	161
UNITED MO BK OF ST LOUIS NA	ST LOUIS	182	369
BOATMENS BK OF CAPE GIRARDEAU	GAPE GIRARDEAU	181	153
LANDMARK BK ST CHARLES CTY	ST CHARLES	180	193
FIRST NB&TC	JOPLIN	178	229
GUARANTY FS&LA OF SPRINGFIELD	SPRINGFIELD	178	141
COMMERCE BK OF ST CHARLES NA	ST CHARLES	177	137
FIRST NB	CAMDENTON	177	100

JEFFERSON S&LA	BALLWIN	176	342
CENTERRE BK OF S KANSAS CITY	KANSAS CITY	175	114
BANK OF SIKESTON	SIKESTON	174	101
JEFFERSON BK OF MO	JEFFERSON CITY	173	124
UNITED MISSOURI BK SOUTH	KANSAS CITY	173	108
BOATMENS BK OF JEFFERSON C	FESTUS	172	109
THE CAMERON S&LA	CAMERON	172	110
FIRST S&LA OF MT VERNON, MISSOURI	MT VERNON	172	131
COMMERCE BK ST LOUIS NA	CLAYTON	171	1,661
COMMERCE BK OF KC NA	KANSAS CITY	169	1,281
AMERICAN BK	KANSAS CITY	168	325
COMMERCE BK OF SPRINGFIELD	SPRINGFIELD	168	460

MONTANA

Name	City	Rank	Assets
UNITED SAVINGS BANK, FA	GREAT FALLS	257	109
SECURITY FEDERAL SVG BK	BILLINGS	191	186
FIRST FEDERAL SVG BK OF MONTANA	KALISPEL	184	138
FIRST INTERSTATE BK NA	MISSOULA	174	133
FIRST NB&TC HELENA	HELENA	173	148
NORWEST BK ANACONDA - BUTTE NA	ANACONDA	172	125
FIRST INTERSTATE BK NA	KALISPELL	171	128
FIRST NB IN BOZEMAN	BOZEMAN	168	128
FIRST BK BUTTE NA	BUTTE	168	111

NEBRASKA

Name	City	Rank	Assets
CONSERVATIVE SAVINGS BANK	OMAHA	244	109
FIRST NB OF OMAHA	OMAHA	221	857
FREMONT NB&TC	FREMONT	203	110
SCOTTSBLUFF NB&TC	SCOTTSBLUFF	194	230
UNION B&TC	LINCOLN	190	155
SOUTHWEST B&TC OF OMAHA	OMAHA	190	111
FIRST WEST SIDE BK	OMAHA	186	121
FIRST NB&TC COLUMBUS	COLUMBUS	185	201
CITY NB&TC HASTINGS	HASTINGS	176	107
FIRSTIER BK NA	LINCOLN	176	947
DELAY FIRST NB&TC	NORFOLK	167	171

NEVADA

Name	City	Rank	Assets
CITIBANK (NEVADA) NA	LAS VEGAS	248	2,959
NEVADA ST BK	LAS VEGAS	205	230

NEVADA (cont.)

Name	City	Rank	Assets
NEVADA FIRST BK	LAS VEGAS	196	181
VALLEY BK OF NEVADA	LAS VEGAS	176	1,542
FIRST INTERSTATE BK NV NA	RENO	169	2,992

NEW HAMPSHIRE

Name	City	Rank	Assets
FIRST NB OF PORTSMOUTH	PORTSMOUTH	266	207
FIRST S&LA OF NEW HAMPSHIRE	EXETER	235	136
LAKE SUNAPEE SAVINGS BANK FSB	NEWPORT	226	159
NASHUA FS&LA	NASHUA	220	460
CHESHIRE COUNTY SVG BK	KEENE	211	313
DERRYBANK	DERRY	209	115
PELHAM B&TC	PELHAM	205	182
BANK MERIDAN NA	HAMPTON	201	118
HOME BANK, FSB	LACONIA	201	242
LACONIA SVG BK	LACONIA	201	198
NORTH CONWAY BK	NORTH CONWAY	194	153
SUNCOOK BK	SUNCOOK	193	100
SALEM CO-OP BK	SALEM	192	109
BERLIN CITY BK	BERLIN	189	142
SOUTHEAST BK FOR SVG	DOVER	189	268
SOUHEGAN NB OF MILFORD	MILFORD	187	125
SOMERSWORTH BK	SOMERSWORTH	187	110
INDIAN HEAD B&TC	PORTSMOUTH	185	360
KEENE SVG BK	KEENE	185	129
NASHUA TC	NASHUA	183	320
FIRST NEW HAMPSHIRE BK	LEBANON	183	123
WOLFEBORO NB	WOLFEBORO	181	124
MASCOMA SVG BK	LEBANON	181	150
EXETER BKG CO	EXETER	180	221
PORTSMOUTH SVG BK	PORTSMOUTH	179	235
FIRST DEPOSIT NB	TILTON	177	819
MERRIMACK COUNTY SVG BK	CONCORD	177	126
MONADNOCK BK	JAFFREY	176	107
LACONIA PEOPLES NB&TC	LACONIA	175	159
DARTMOUTH NB	HANOVER	174	155
INDIAN HEAD BK - NORTH	LITTLETON	174	191
INDIAN HEAD NB	NASHUA	174	839
CONCORD SVG BK	CONCORD	172	259
GRANITE ST NB	SOMERSWORTH	171	128
PLAISTOW CO-OP BK	PLAISTOW	168	115
BANK OF NEW HAMPSHIRE NA	MANCHESTER	166	554

NEW JERSEY

Name	City	Rank	Assets
LAKELAND S&LA	SUCCASUNNA	284	240
NEW JERSEY SVG BK	SOMERVILLE	261	236
PULAWSKI S&LA	SOUTH RIVER	257	282
AMERICAN S&LA OF BLOOMFIELD	BLOOMFIELD	242	130
SHREWSBURY ST BK	SHREWSBURY	240	110
MONTCLAIR SVG BK	MONTCLAIR	235	400
KEARNY FS&LA	KEARNY	233	467
MANASQUAN S&LA	WALL TWP	228	108
LAKELAND ST BK	WEST MILFORD TWP	227	136
PROSPECT PARK S&LA	WEST PATERSON	226	430
SPENCER S&LA	GARFIELD	222	609
MIDLANTIC NB/UNION TR	WILDWOOD	221	134
UNION COUNTY SVG BK	ELIZABETH	221	270
UNITED COUNTIES TC	CRANFORD	217	1,062
POLIFLY S&LA	HASBROUCK HEIGHTS	217	284
BANKERS SVG	PERTH AMBOY	215	643
PEAPACK GLADSTONE BK	GLADSTONE	213	121
UNITED NB	PLAINFIELD	212	509
VALLEY NB	PASSAIC	211	1,477
CENTURY FS&LA OF BRIDGETON	BRIDGETON	211	138
NEWTON TC	NEWTON	210	118
UNITED JERSEY BK WOOD RIDGE NA	WOOD RIDGE	210	100
MINOTOLA NB	VINELAND	207	133
MORSEMERE FEDERAL SVG BK	FORT LEE	207	343
STARPOINTE SVG BK	PLAINFIELD	207	395
COUNTY TC	LYNDHURST	206	121
INTERCHANGE ST BK	SADDLE BROOK	205	192
THE GUTTENBERG S&LA	GUTTENBERG	205	110
UNITED jERSEY BK FRST COLONIA	COLONIA	203	110
BOILING SPRINGS S&LA	RUTHERFORD	203	373
PHILLIPSBURG NB&TC	PHILLIPSBURG	202	158
FIRST S&LA OF PENNS GROVE	PENNS GROVE	202	105
UNION CENTER NB	UNION	201	175
HUDSON UNITED BK	UNION CITY	200	464
BROAD NB	NEWARK	199	315
FLEMINGTON NB&TC	FLEMINGTON	199	175
UNITED JERSEY BK EDGEWATER NA	ENGLEWOOD CLIFFS	199	156
RAHWAY SVG INST	RAHWAY	199	161
TRENTON SVG FUND SOC	TRENTON	199	217
WAYNE S&LA	WAYNE	198	138
CENTRAL JERSEY B&TC	FREEHOLD TWP	197	1,176
NORTH PLAINFIELD ST BK	NORTH PLAINFIELD	197	106
WEST ESSEX S&LA	CALDWELL	197	213
PENN FEDERAL SAVINGS BANK	NEWARK	196	383
SOUTH BERGEN S&LA	WOOD-RIDGE	196	151

NEW JERSEY (cont.)

Name	City	Rank	Assets
SOMERSET TC	BRIDGEWATER TWP	195	373
NATIONAL BK OF SUSSEX CITY	BRANCHVILLE	194	196
FIRST NB FORT LEE	FORT LEE	193	147
HORIZON BK NA	MORRISTOWN	193	1,660
PRINCETON BK	PRINCETON	193	1,376
VALLEY S&LA	CLOSTER	192	292
FIRST JERSEY NB WEST	DENVILLE TWP	191	312
GLENDALE NB OF NJ	VOORHEES TWP	191	136
FIRST NB OF CENTRAL JERSEY	BRIDGEWATER TWP	191	856
FIRST MORRIS BK	MORRIS TWP	190	117
MIDLAND B&TC	PARAMUS	190	310
GARDEN ST BK	JACKSON TWP	189	179
UNITED JERSEY BK/MID ST	HAZLET TWP	189	307
MIDLANTIC NB/NORTH	WEST PATERSON	188	2,861
ORITANI S&LA	HACKENSACK	188	313
INDEPENDENCE BK OF NJ	ALLENDALE	187	130
STURDY S&LA	STONE HARBOR	185	158
MAINSTAY FS&LA	RED BANK	185	144
HUDSON CITY SVG BK	PARAMUS	185	2,777
FARMERS & MERCHANTS NB	BRIDGETON	184	194
WOODSTOWN NB&TC	WOODSTOWN	184	116
NVE SAVINGS AND LOAN ASSOCIATION	ENGLEWOOD	184	290
FIRST STATE BK	HOWELL TWP	182	165
UNITED JERSEY BK NORTHWEST	DOVER	182	359
CENTRAL JERSEY S&LA	EAST BRUNSWICK	182	318
MIDLANTIC NB MERCHANTS	NEPTUNE TWP	181	1,293
FIRST FIDELITY BK NA/S JERSEY	BURLINGTON TWP	180	1,810
FIRST FIDELITY BK NA N JERSEY	TOTOWA	179	2,092
MIDLANTIC NB SUSSEX & ME	NEWTON	179	221
BANK OF MID-JERSEY	BORDENTOWN TWP	178	387
CHATHAM TC	CHATHAM TWP	178	297
CAPE S&LA	CAPE MAY COURT HOUSE	178	181
NEW BRUNSWICK SVG BK	NEW BRUNSWICK	178	709
FIRST JERSEY NB SOUTH	ATLANTIC CITY	177	1,103
MAPLEWOOD B&TC	MAPLEWOOD	177	221
OCEAN NB	POINT PLEASANT	176	431
GLOUCESTER COUNTY FS&LA	WASHINGTON TWP	176	140
RARITAN SVG BK	RARITAN	176	129
CITIZEN FIRST NB OF NJ	RIDGEWOOD	175	2,136
NATIONAL COMMUNITY BK OF NJ	RUTHERFORD	175	2,894
PEOPLES NB CTRL JERSEY	PISCATAWAY	174	242
WASHINGTON SVG BK	HOBOKEN	174	320
FIRST PEOPLES BK OF NJ	HADDON TOWNSHIP	173	829
SUMMIT TC	SUMMIT	173	1,176
THE FRANKLIN S&LA	SALEM	173	114

Name	City	Rank	Assets
OCEAN FS&LA	BRICK TOWN	172	532
ROMA S&LA	TRENTON	172	340
UNITED JERSEY BK NA	PRINCETON	171	713
COMMERCE BK NA	EVESHAM TWP	170	386
MARINE NB	WILDWOOD	170	563
TOWN &COUNTRY BK	RARITAN TWP	170	191
UNITED JERSEY BK FRANKLIN ST	FRANKLIN TWP	170	871
NATIONAL ST BK ELIZABETH	ELIZABETH	169	1,885
FIRST JERSEY NB CENTRAL	TRENTON	169	500
RAMAPO BK	WAYNE TWP	169	210
NEW JERSEY NB	EWING TWP	169	2,141
UNITED JERSEY BK	HACKENSACK	167	3,674
FIRST JERSEY NB	JERSEY CITY	166	2,366
MIDLANTIC NB SOUTH	MT LAUREL	166	2,050

NEW MEXICO

Name	City	Rank	Assets
FIRST NB OF FARMINGTON	FARMINGTON	220	206
CARLSBAD NB	CARLSBAD	203	121
FIRST NB IN ALAMOGORDO	ALAMOGORDO	202	106
WESTERN BK	ALBUQUERQUE	193	115
CITIZENS BK	CLOVIS	187	151
WESTERN BK	LAS CRUCES	185	109
FIRST FEDERAL SVG BK	ROSWELL	179	144
FIRST NB OF BELEN	BELEN	177	161
SUNWEST BK OF GALLUP	GALLUP	176	122
SUNWEST BK OF SANTA FE	SANTA FE	171	152
FIRST NB OF DONA ANA CTY	LAS CRUCES	166	261

NEW YORK

Name	City	Rank	Assets
JAMAICA SVG BK FSB	LYNBROOK	282	1,388
MITSUBISHI TR & BKNG CORP	NEW YORK	271	165
MASPETH FS&LA	MASPETH	264	459
SOUTHOLD SVG BK	SOUTHOLD	264	604
HOME SVG BK	BROOKLYN	259	1,628
CITY NB&TC OF GLOVERSVILLE	GLOVERSVILLE	257	106
BANK OF UTICA	UTICA	256	100
MID-HUDSON SAVINGS BANK FSB	FISHKILL	255	236
LTCB TC	NEW YORK	253	351
FIDUCIARY TC	NEW YORK	249	183
WILBER NB	ONEONTA	247	203
FIRST WOMENS BK	NEW YORK	246	225
NORTH SIDE SVG BK	NEW YORK	246	634
GATEWAY ST BK	DONGAN HILLS	243	205
ADIRONDACK TC	SARATOGA SPRINGS	239	183

NEW YORK (cont.)

Name	City	Rank	Assets
RICHMOND HILL SVG BK	RICHMOND HILL	235	1,124
FIRST NB LONG ISLAND	GLEN HEAD	232	237
KEY BK OF LONG ISLAND	SAYVILLE	227	202
ROYAL B&TC	NEW YORK	227	402
CANADIAN IMPRL BK OF CMRCE	NEW YORK	225	756
THE LONG ISLAND CITY S&LA	LONG ISLAND CITY	224	296
CENTRAL NB - CANAJOHARIE	CANAJOHARIE	221	201
SUFFOLK CITY NB OF RIVERHEAD	RIVERHEAD	220	361
STERLING NB&TC OF NY	NEW YORK	218	782
MERCHANTS BK OF NEW YORK	NEW YORK	217	538
NATIONAL B&TC NORWICH	NORWICH	217	458
ONEIDA VALLEY NB OF ONEIDA	ONEIDA	217	138
LOCKPORT SVG BK	LOCKPORT	217	428
GREENPOINT SVG BK	BROOKLYN	215	3,445
HERKIMER COUNTY TC	LITTLE FALLS	213	107
COMMUNITY NB&TC NY	NEW YORK	212	166
BANK OF THE HAMPTONS NA	EAST HAMPTON	211	123
HUDSON VALLEY NB	YONKERS	210	180
CHEMUNG CANAL TC	ELMIRA	208	279
FIRST NB OF HIGHLAND	HIGHLAND	207	219
UNION ST BK	NANUET	206	168
ROSLYN SVG BK	ROSLYN	206	917
RIDGEWOOD SVG BK	RIDGEWOOD	204	1,130
STATE BK OF LI	NEW HYDE PARK	203	164
BATH NB	BATH	201	155
PAWLING SVG BK	PAWLING	201	582
FIRST NB OF RHINEBECK	RHINEBECK	200	105
JEFFERSON NB	LAFARGEVILLE	200	158
BANK OF SMITHTOWN	SMITHTOWN	200	150
FIRST NB OF CORTLAND	CORTLAND	199	129
KEY BK OF SOUTHEASTERN NY NA	CHESTER	198	639
NORSTAR BK	HEMPSTEAD	196	2,037
NORTH FORK B&TC	MATTITUCK	196	678
TOMPKINS COUNTY TC	ITHACA	196	298
GLENS FALLS NB&TC	GLENS FALLS	195	337
FISHKILL NB	BEACON	195	186
NANUET NB	NANUET	195	330
FIRST FS&LA OF MIDDLETOWN	MIDDLETOWN	195	162
RICHMOND CTY SVG BK	WEST NEW BRIGHTON	195	490
SCHENECTADY TC	SCHENECTADY	194	629
FOURTH FS&LA OF NEW YORK	NEW YORK	193	193
NORSTAR BK OF UPSTATE NY	ALBANY	192	3,095
NORSTAR BK OF HUDSON VALLEY NA	NEWBURGH	192	793
ALBANY SAVINGS BANK FSB	ALBANY	192	1,816
GEDDES FS&LA	SYRACUSE	191	101

EASTCHESTER SVG BK	MT VERNON	191	437
ST LAWRENCE NB	CANTON	188	258
SCARSDALE NB&TC	SCARSDALE	188	441
INDEPENDENCE SVG BK	BROOKLYN	187	1,338
SAVINGS BK OF ROCKLAND CTY	MONSEY	187	148
EXTEBANK	STONY BROOK	186	460
FIRST FS&LA OF PEEKSKILL	PEEKSKILL	186	140
FULTON SVG BK	FULTON	186	130
FIRST NB OF GLENS FALLS	GLENS FALLS	184	501
DUTCHESS B&TC	POUGHKEEPSIE	184	257
ELLENVILLE NB	ELLENVILLE	182	113
THE LONG ISLAND SAVINGS BANK, FSB	SYOSSET	182	2,518
AMSTERDAM SAVINGS BANK, FSB	AMSTERDAM	182	266
BANK LONG ISLAND	BABYLON	181	268
SOUND FS&LA	MAMARONECK	181	133
ULSTER SVG BK	KINGSTON	181	269
SAVINGS BANK OF THE FINGER LAKES FSB	GENEVA	180	135
NORSTAR BANK NA	BUFFALO	178	3,432
CATSKILL SVG BK	CATSKILL	178	176
CORTLAND SVG BK	CORTLAND	178	177
QUEENS COUNTY SVG BK	FLUSHING	178	797
WYOMING COUNTY BK	WARSAW	177	148
KEY BK OF CENTRAL NY	SYRACUSE	177	1,432
ASTORIA FS&LA	LONG ISLAND CITY	177	2,521
ROCHESTER COMMUNITY SVG BK	ROCHESTER	177	3,182
FIRST NB OF ROCHESTER	ROCHESTER	176	168
STATEN ISLAND SVG BK	STAPLETON	176	813
EXCHANGE NB	OLEAN	175	106
ATLANTIC BK OF NEW YORK	NEW YORK	174	976
CANANDAIGUA NB&TC	CANANDAIGUA	174	218
RELIANCE FEDERAL SAVINGS BANK	GARDEN CITY	174	652
AMERICAN SAVINGS BANK, FSB	NEW YORK	174	3,894
BINGHAMTON SVG BK	BINGHAMTON	174	752
PEOPLES WESTCHESTER SVG BK	HAWTHORNE	174	1,474
CITIZENS SAVINGS BANK FSB	ITHACA	173	479
MANUFACTURERS & TRADERS TR C	BUFFALO	172	2,800
PIONEER S&LA	BROOKLYN	172	224
EAST NEW YORK SVG BK	BROOKLYN	171	1,788
KEY BK OF WESTERN NY NA	JAMESTOWN	170	955
HOME & CITY SVG BK	ALBANY	169	804
THE LONG ISLAND SVG BK OF CENTEREACH FSB	CENTEREACH	168	3,187
WARWICK SVG BK	WARWICK	168	178
YORKVILLE FS&LA	BRONX	167	321
PUTNAM COUNTY SVG BK	SOUTHEAST TWP	167	168
MERCHANTS NB&TC	SYRACUSE	166	623

NORTH CAROLINA

Name	City	Rank	Assets
MUTUAL FS&LA	ELKIN	275	109
FIRST NB OF SHELBY	SHELBY	268	155
FIRST CHARTER NB	CONCORD	251	183
PEOPLES BK	NEWTON	246	110
RALEIGH FEDERAL SAVINGS BANK	RALEIGH	245	478
SECURITY B&TC	SALISBURY	238	303
BANK OF GRANITE	GRANITE FALLS	228	224
REPUBLIC B&TC	CHARLOTTE	224	160
FIRST NB OF RANDOLPH CTY	ASHEBORO	218	130
HOME S&LA	DURHAM	216	231
FIDELITY BK	FUQUAY-VARINA	212	178
LEXINGTON ST BK	LEXINGTON	212	301
C-K FEDERAL SVG BK	CONCORD	211	209
PIEDMONT FS&LA	WINSTON-SALEM	205	453
FIRST BK	TROY	203	159
PEOPLES B&TC	ROCKY MOUNT	202	929
MID-SOUTH B&TC	SANFORD	200	116
FIRST NB OF REIDSVILLE	REIDSVILLE	195	102
HAYWOOD S&LA	WAYNESVILLE	195	117
FIRST FS&LA	SOUTHERN PINES	193	158
SOUTHERN B&TC	MT OLIVE	192	191
PLANTERS NB&TC	ROCKY MOUNT	191	892
FIRST-CITIZENS B&TC	RALEIGH	188	2,996
YADKIN VALLEY B&TC	ELKIN	187	100
GASTON FS&LA	GASTONIA	186	122
HOME FS&LA	SALISBURY	185	180
COMMUNITY FS&LA	BURLINGTON	183	122
CENTRAL CAROLINA B&TC NA	DURHAM	182	1,355
UNITED CAROLINA BK	WHITEVLLE	182	1,788
NORTH WILKESBORO FS&LA	NORTH WILKESBORO	182	107
GATE CITY S&LA	GREENSBORO	181	426
WORKMAN'S FEDERAL SAVINGS BANK	MOUNT AIRY	180	212
SOUTHERN NB OF NC	LUMBERTON	178	1,799
MACON S&LA	FRANKLIN	177	121
EAST CAROLINA BK	ENGELHARD	175	111
HOME FS&LA	CHARLOTTE	174	441
FIRST FS&LA	HENDERSONVILLE	174	453
WACHOVIA B&TC NA	WINSTON-SALEM	173	11,284
HOME FS&LA	FAYETTEVILLE	171	166
FIRST FS&LA	WINSTON-SALEM	171	334
BRANCH B&TC	WILSON	169	3,523
HIGH POINT B&TC	HIGH POINT	169	342
FIRST FEDERAL OF THE CAROLINAS, FA	HIGH POINT	167	236
CLYDE S&LA	CLYDE	165	227

NORTH DAKOTA

Name	City	Rank	Assets
VALLEY B&TC	GRAND FORKS	222	100
FIRST NB OF GRAND FORKS	GRAND FORKS	217	198
FIRST AMERICAN B&TC MINOT	MINOT	201	115
FIRST BK OF ND NA - GRAND FORKS	GRAND FORKS	170	102

OHIO

Name	City	Rank	Assets
CITY LOAN BK	LIMA	251	627
FIRST NB OF ZANESVILLE	ZANESVILLE	230	236
BANK ONE ALLIANCE NA	ALLIANCE	226	176
CITIZENS BKG CO	SANDUSKY	223	176
THIRD FS&LA	CLEVELAND	223	1,895
FIRST SECURITY BK	HILLSBORO	222	120
STATE B&TC	DEFIANCE	216	129
FIRST NB OF OHIO	AKRON	215	1,814
PARK NB	NEWARK	215	505
LIBERTY NB OF ADA	ADA	211	109
NORTH SIDE B&TC	CINCINNATI	211	201
HORIZON S&LC	BEACHWOOD	211	203
NATIONAL B&TC	WILMINGTON	206	141
ELYRIA SVG&TR NB	ELYRIA	205	383
METROPOLITAN BK	LIMA	204	197
BANK ONE DOVER NA	DOVER	203	255
COMMERCIAL BK	DELPHOS	202	102
FIFTH THIRD BK OF N. WESTERN OH NA	FINDLAY	201	234
SECURITY NB&TC	SPRINGFIELD	201	325
COTTAGE SA, FA	MADEIRA	201	176
CITIZENS FIDELITY OH NA	CINCINNATI	198	113
DELAWARE COUNTY BK	DELAWARE	198	173
BANK ONE MILFORD NA	MILFORD	197	315
THIRD S&L CO	PIQUA	197	110
CITIZENS COMMERCIAL B&TC	CELINA	196	156
FIRST NB OF TOLEDO	TOLEDO	196	795
LORAIN NB	LORAIN	196	275
SPRINGFIELD FS&LA	SPRINGFIELD	196	107
FIRST FINANCIAL SA, FA	CINCINNATI	196	135
BANK ONE PORTSMOUTH NA	PORTSMOUTH	195	242
FIRST FS&LA	YOUNGSTOWN	195	387
FIRST NB SOUTHWESTERN OH	MONROE	194	616
OLD PHOENIX NB OF MEDINA	MEDINA	193	277
DOLLAR SVG&TC	YOUNGSTOWN	193	890
BANK ONE AKRON NA	AKRON	192	1,099

OHIO (cont.)

Name	City	Rank	Assets
BANK ONE MANSFIELD	MANSFIELD	192	337
CITIZENS HERITAGE BK NA	PIQUA	192	250
OHIO CITIZENS BK	TOLEDO	192	1,035
CROGHAN COLONIAL BK	FREMONT	191	188
FIRST NB	DAYTON	190	801
PERPETUAL FS&LA	URBANA	189	113
FIRST FS&LA	LAKEWOOD	189	311
FIRST NB IN MASSILLON	MASSILLON	188	176
WAYNE COUNTY NB OF WOOSTER	WOOSTER	188	208
BANK ONE COSHOCTON NA	COSHOCTON	187	165
CITIZENS BKG CO	SALINEVILLE	187	227
COMMERCIAL NB OF TIFFIN	TIFFIN	187	187
LEBANON CITIZENS NB	LEBANON	187	154
FIRST NB SIDNEY OH	SIDNEY	186	174
FIDELITY FS&LA	NORWOOD	186	149
FIRST NB BARNESVILLE	BARNESVILLE	185	123
BANCOHIO NB	COLUMBUS	185	4,761
SECOND NB OF HAMILTON	HAMILTON	182	222
BANK ONE DAYTON NA	DAYTON	181	1,827
FIFTH THIRD BK	CINCINNATI	181	2,895
CHEVIOT B&L CO	CHEVIOT	181	102
METROPOLITAN SAVINGS BANK	YOUNGSTOWN	180	208
BANK ONE LIMA NA	LIMA	179	114
FIRST FS&LA	AKRON	179	268
MIAMI BK NA	FAIRBORN	178	168
FIRST NB OF SHELBY	SHELBY	178	100
UNIBANK	STEUBENVILLE	178	122
DOLLAR FEDERAL SAVINGS BANK	HAMILTON	178	147
SUBURBAN FS&LA	CINCINNATI	178	157
RICHLAND TC	MANSFIELD	177	181
UNITED NB&TC	CANTON	177	255
BANK ONE CLEVELAND NA	CLEVELAND	176	1,487
BANK ONE WAPAKONETA NA	WAPAKONETA	176	113
COMERICA - MIDWEST NA	TOLEDO	175	224
BANK ONE CAMBRIDGE NA	CAMBRIDGE	175	115
CENTRAL TC NE OHIO NA	CANTON	175	734
BANK ONE BELLAIRE NA	BELLAIRE	173	265
THE FRANKLIN S&LC	CINCINNATI	173	161
HUNTER SA	CINCINNATI	173	1,256
BANK ONE MARION	MARION	172	156
POTTERS S&L CO	EAST LIVERPOOL	172	130
FARMERS & MERCHANTS ST BK	ARCHBOLD	171	211
FIRST FS&LA	WARREN	170	308
MECHANICS B&LC	MANSFIELD	170	149
FIRST FS&LA	LORAIN	170	162

BANK ONE SIDNEY NA	SIDNEY	169	179
MID AMERICAN NB&TC	NORTHWOOD	169	420
SECOND NB	GREENVILLE	169	130
CUYAHOGA SAVINGS ASSN	CLEVELAND	169	260
FIRST NB OF IRONTON	IRONTON	168	157
NATIONAL CITY BK	AKRON	168	891
SOCIETY NB	CLEVELAND	168	5,178
THRIFT S&L CO	NORWOOD	168	124
TRUMBULL S&L CO	WARREN	168	282
COUNTY SVG BK	NEWARK	168	615
OHIO ST BK	COLUMBUS	167	322
CENTRAL TC	NEWARK	167	427
FIRST NB OF CINCINNATI	CINCINNATI	165	2,495
FIRST-KNOX NB IN MT VERNON	MT VERNON	165	231

OKLAHOMA

Name	City	Rank	Assets
FIRST NB OF MIDWEST CITY	MIDWEST CITY	226	129
AMERICAN NB&TC	SAPULPA	217	111
CENTRAL BK	OKLAHOMA CITY	187	165
F&M B&TC	TULSA	183	393
FIRST INTERSTATE BK OK NA	OKLAHOMA CITY	181	1,068
COMMUNITY BK	WARR ACRES	181	105
FIRST NB IN DURANT	DURANT	177	110
FIRST NB OF ALTUS	ALTUS	174	107
CITIZENS NB&TC OF MUSKOGEE	MUSKOGEE	172	107
FIRST NB BARTLESVILLE	BARTLESVILLE	171	243
FIRST NB&TC MC ALESTER	MC ALESTER	168	272

OREGON

Name	City	Rank	Assets
WASHINGTON FEDERAL SAVINGS BANK	HILLSBORO	211	200
KLAMATH FIRST FS&LA	KLAMATH FALLS	205	233
WESTERN SECURITY BK	SALEM	191	130
KEY BK OF OREGON	PORTLAND	186	1,037
WESTERN BK	COOS BAY	172	318
SOUTH UMPQUA ST BK	ROSEBURG	170	101
UNITED STATES NB	PORTLAND	166	7,602
UNITED SVG BK	SALEM	166	210

PENNSYLVANIA

Name	City	Rank	Assets
PEOPLES BK OF UNITY	PLUM BORO	291	120
ROYAL BK OF PENNSYLVANIA	KING OF PRUSSIA	284	213

PENNSYLVANIA (cont.)

Name	City	Rank	Assets
FIRST AMERICAN SAVING FA	JENKINTOWN	280	486
DENVER NB	DENVER	267	134
FIRST FINANCIAL SVG ASSN	DOWNINGTOWN	263	110
FIRST NB OF PALMERTON	PALMERTON	257	151
FARMERS B&TC	HUMMELSTOWN	243	121
HATBORO FS&LA	HATBORO	242	114
DEPOSIT BK	DU BOIS	237	239
JOHNSTOWN SVG BK, FSB	JOHNSTOWN	235	288
BLOOMSBURG BK COLUMBIA TR CO	BLOOMSBURG	234	113
HAZELTON NB	NUREMBERG	229	260
FARMERS FIRST BK	LITITZ	228	606
FARMERS TC	CARLISLE	227	256
BEAVER TC	BEAVER	226	176
FIRSTRUST SVG BK	FLOURTOWN	224	1,008
COMMERCIAL NB WESTMORELAND	LATROBE	223	150
SAVINGS & TC OF PA	INDIANA	223	694
ALLEGHENY VALLEY BK OF PITTSB	PITTSBURGH	221	115
UNITED FEDERAL SAVINGS BANK	STATE COLLEGE	219	428
COUNTY NB OF MONTROSE	MONTROSE	218	146
BELL S&LA	UPPER DARBY	217	511
BRANDYWINE S&LA	DOWNINGTOWN	217	167
FIRST B&TC	MECHANICSBURG	216	119
HAMLIN B&TC	SMETHPORT	216	113
PRUDENTIAL SA	PHILADELPHIA	216	141
BRYN MAWR TC	BRYN MAWR	214	244
CENWEST NB	DALE	214	234
ELMWOOD FEDERAL SVG BK	MEDIA	213	187
COUNTY NB	CLEARFIELD	212	214
MINERS NB	POTTSVILLE	212	177
FIRST NB&TC	WAYNESBORO	211	149
CITIZENS & NORTHERN BK	RALSTON	209	294
FIRST NB OF PIKE CITY	MILFORD	209	116
MID PENN BK	MILLERSBURG	209	128
EPHRATA NB	EPHRATA	207	189
MERCHANTS BK (NORTH)	WILKES-BARRE	206	668
CHAMBERSBURG TC	CHAMBERSBURG	206	120
FIRST NB OF BERWICK	BERWICK	206	102
FIRST NB OF WESTERN PA	NEW CASTLE	206	277
SECOND NB OF NAZARETH	NAZARETH	206	150
HANOVER BK OF PENNSYLVANIA	WILKES-BARRE	205	118
CHARLEROI FS&LA	CHARLEROI	205	147
FIRST NB OF WEST CHESTER	WEST CHESTER	204	190
HARLEYSVILLE NB&TC	HARLEYSVILLE	204	272
FIRST FS&LA OF GREENE CO	WAYNESBURG	204	256
JUNIATA VALLEY BK	MIFFLINTOWN	201	131
PEOPLES FIRST NB&TC	HAZLETON	201	279

VALLEY B&TC	CHAMBERSBURG	201	254
FIRST NB OF HERMINIE	HERMINIE	200	107
NATIONAL BK OF OLYPHANT	OLYPHANT	200	122
BLUE BALL NB	BLUE BALL	200	196
SOUTHWEST NB OF PA	GREENSBURG	200	488
B&TC OF OLD YORK	WILLOW GROVE	199	181
FIRST NAT TR BK	SUNBURY	198	209
WILLIAMSPORT NB	WILLIAMSPORT	198	173
CENTRAL PENNSYLVANIA SA	SHAMOKIN	198	296
DOWNINGTOWN NB	DOWNINGTOWN	197	128
FIRST NB&TC	NEWTOWN	197	167
PENN CENTRAL NB	HUNTINGDON	197	125
HERSHEY BK	HERSHEY	197	151
HOMESTEAD SA	MIDDLETOWN	197	153
SNYDER COUNTY TC	SELINSGROVE	196	146
RELIABLE S&LA	BRIDGEVILLE	196	100
IRWIN B&TC	IRWIN	195	141
WILLOW GROVE FS&LA	MAPLE GLEN	195	149
DROVERS & MECHANICS BK	YORK	194	210
PEOPLES BK OF GLEN ROCK	GLEN ROCK	194	115
SEWICKLEY S&LA	SEWICKLEY	194	117
PENNSYLVANIA NB&TC	POTTSVILLE	193	632
THREE RIVERS B&TC	JEFFERSON BORO	193	108
ELLWOOD FS&LA	ELLWOOD CITY	192	207
CENTURY NB&TC	ROCHESTER	191	201
FIRST NB OF BATH	BATH	191	101
THIRD NB&TC	SCRANTON	191	321
QUAKERTOWN NB	QUAKERTOWN	191	176
FIRST FS&LA	PERKASIE	191	206
FIDELITY DEPOSITS & DISCOUNT	DUNMORE	190	131
FIRST NB OF BRADFORD CTY	TOWANDA	190	103
WAYNE COUNTY B&TC	HONESDALE	189	136
PROGRESS FEDERAL SAVING BANK	BRIDGEPORT	188	250
DAUPHIN DEPOSIT B&TC	HARRISBURG	187	2,021
MERCHANTS BK NA	ALLENTOWN	187	1,690
CHELTENHAM BK	CHELTENHAM	187	502
MELLON BK NORTH NA	OIL CITY	187	807
KEYSTONE SA	BETHLEHEM	187	329
CITIZENS NB OF EVANS CTY	EVANS CITY	186	135
MID-STATE B&TC	ALTOONA	186	779
KEYSTONE NB	PUNXSUTAWNEY	186	255
HOLLIDAYSBURG TC	HOLLIDAYSBURG	185	132
FIRST FS&LA	HAZLETON	184	243
FULTON BK	LANCASTER	182	862
LEBANON VALLEY NB	LEBANON	182	354
BANK OF PENNSYLVANIA	READING	181	739
MELLON BK (CENTRAL) NA	MAPLETON	181	672
PEOPLES NB OF CENTRAL PA	STATE COLLEGE	181	242
SOMERSET TC	SOMERSET	181	126

PENNSYLVANIA (cont.)

Name	City	Rank	Assets
LAUREL BK	EBENSBURG	180	203
JOHNSTOWN B&TC	JOHNSTOWN	180	413
UPPER DAUPHIN NB	MILLERSBURG	180	112
UNION NB&TC	SOUDERTON	180	442
ECONOMY SA	ALIQUIPPA	180	114
FIRST FS&LA OF BUCKS CO	BRISTOL	180	192
FIRST SENECA BK	BUTLER	179	1,111
FIRST VALLEY BK	LANSFORD	178	928
BANK OF LANCASTER CTY NA	STRASBURG	178	307
ADAMS COUNTY NB	CUMBERLAND TWP	177	328
FIRST NB OF CARBONDALE	CARBONDALE	177	180
MERIDIAN BANK	READING	176	6,726
FRANKFORD TC	PHILADELPHIA	176	440
LINCOLN SAVINGS BK	CARNEGIE	175	191
GETTYSBURG NB	GETTYSBURG	174	197
CUMBERLAND COUNTY NB NA	NEW CUMBERLAND	174	688
RUSSELL NB OF LEWISTOWN	LEWISTOWN	174	156
GALLATIN NB	UNIONTOWN	174	1,069
PEOPLES NB OF LEBANON	LEBANON	174	115
HAMILTON BK	LANCASTER	173	2,665
PENN SECURITY B&TC	SCRANTON	173	275
UNION NB OF PITTSBURGH	PITTSBURGH	173	2,189
FARMERS B&TC	HANOVER	172	370
FARMERS & MERCHANTS TC CH	CHAMBERSBURG	172	189
CHELTENHAM FS&LA	PHILADELPHIA	172	135
GREATER DELAWARE VALLEY S&LA	BROOMALL	172	212
NATIONAL BK OF THE CMNWLTH	INDIANA	171	322
FIRST EASTERN BK NA	WILKES-BARRE	171	1,673
NATIONAL BK OF WESTERN PA	BERLIN	171	112
FRANKLIN FIRST FS&LA	WILKES-BARRE	171	698
MOXHAM NB OF JOHNSTOWN	JOHNSTOWN	170	113
PHOENIXVILLE FS&LA	PHOENIXVILLE	170	122
NAZARETH NB&TC	NAZARETH	169	184
UNITED PENN BK	WILKES-BARRE	168	1,203
COMMERCIAL CREDIT SVG BK	PITTSBURGH	168	176
BANK OF HANOVER & TC	HANOVER	168	182
JERSEY SHORE ST BK	JERSEY SHORE	168	110
MARS NB	MARS	168	109
FIRST NB OF MERCER CTY	GREENVILLE	166	431
YORK FS&LA	YORK	166	644
PENNBANK	WARREN	165	1,001

PUERTO RICO

Name	City	Rank	Assets
SCOTIABANK DE PUERTO RICO	SAN JUAN	217	441
ORIENTAL FEDERAL SVG BK	HUMACAO	193	188

RHODE ISLAND

Name	City	Rank	Assets
CENTREVILLE SVG BK	WEST WARWICK	260	206
CITIZENS SVG BK, FSB	PROVIDENCE	220	1,832
WASHINGTON TC	WESTERLY	203	337
EASTLAND BK	WOONSOCKET	186	116
BAY LOAN & INVESTMENT BK	EAST GREENWICH	174	129

SOUTH CAROLINA

Name	City	Rank	Assets
UNITED S&LA	GREENWOOD	290	222
OCONEE S&LA	SENECA	209	141
UNITED CAROLINA BK SC	GREER	205	184
CONWAY NB	CONWAY	204	169
HOME FEDERAL SVG BK	CHARLESTON	202	119
NCNB SOUTH CAROLINA	COLUMBIA	200	3,055
COMMUNITY BK	GREENVILLE	189	280
FIRST NB	ORANGEBURG	189	205
NATIONAL BK OF SC	SUMTER	185	384
ROCK HILL NB	ROCK HILL	183	244
SOUTHERN NB SC	COLUMBIA	182	269
PALMETTO BK	LAURENS	180	144
LEXINGTON ST BK	LEXINGTON	179	284
CITIZENS & SOUTHERN NB	CHARLESTON	178	3,170
FIRST FS&LA	CHARLESTON	176	769
FIRST-CITIZENS B&TC	COLUMBIA	174	807
FIRST UNION NB	GREENVILLE	171	1,096
FIRST FS&LA	SPARTANBURG	170	220
HERITAGE FS&LA	LAURENS	170	138
FIRST FS&LA	GEORGETOWN	168	101
SOUTH CAROLINA NB	CHARLESTON	166	4,518

SOUTH DAKOTA

Name	City	Rank	Assets
FIRST CITY BK SIOUX FALLS NA	SIOUX FALLS	228	621
FARMERS & MERCHANTS BK	HURON	220	109
CITIBANK SOUTH DAKOTA NA	SIOUX FALLS	205	10,775
FIRST FEDERAL SVG BK	WATERTOWN	173	147

TENNESSEE

Name	City	Rank	Assets
BARRETVILLE B&TC	BARRETVILLE	270	164
CITIZENS BK	CARTHAGE	269	127
HOME FS&LA OF UPPER EAST TENNESSEE	JOHNSON CITY	268	596
FIRST NB OF MCMINNVILLE	MCMINNVILLE	262	115
FIRST FS&LA	CHATTANOOGA	245	613
FIRST NB OF SPARTA	SPARTA	235	104
CITIZENS UNION BK	ROGERSVILLE	231	163
PIONEER BK	CHATTANOOGA	230	344
GREENE COUNTY BK	GREENEVILLE	226	183
COMMERCE UNION BK GRNVILLE	GREENEVILLE	223	110
VALLEY FIDELITY B&TC	KNOXVILLE	214	419
FIRST NB OF PULASKI	PULASKI	210	132
FIRST FARMERS & MERCHANTS NB	COLUMBIA	209	220
FIDELITY FS&LA OF TENNESSEE	NASHVILLE	205	923
CLEVELAND B&TC	CLEVELAND	204	148
FIRST NB OF LOUDON CTY	LENOIR CITY	203	117
FIRST NB OF LAWRENCEBURG	LAWRENCEBURG	201	104
COMMERCIAL B&TC	PARIS	201	124
THIRD NB IN SEVIER COUNTY	SEVIERVILLE	200	108
COMMERCE UNION BK EASTERN	OAK RIDGE	200	175
METROPOLITAN FS&LA	NASHVILLE	198	1,151
TIPTON COUNTY BK	COVINGTON	197	127
FIRST NB&TC ATHENS	ATHENS	196	101
UNITED AMERICAN BK	MEMPHIS	193	149
THIRD NB IN KNOXVILLE	KNOXVILLE	192	364
COMMERCE UNION BK CLARKSVILLE	CLARKSVILLE	192	116
JACKSON NB	JACKSON	192	224
MERCHANTS BK	CLEVELAND	190	110
BANK OF GOODLETTSVILLE	GOODLETTSVILLE	190	121
NORTHERN BK OF TENNESSEE	CLARKSVILLE	190	193
CITY B&TC	MCMINNVILLE	189	151
FIRST NB OF CLARKSVILLE	CLARKSVILLE	189	211
AMERICAN B&TC	COOKEVILLE	187	148
LEBANON BK	LEBANON	187	130
CITIZENS BK	ELIZABETHTON	185	110
WILLIAMSON COUNTY BK	FRANKLIN	185	331
UNION NB OF FAYETTEVILLE	FAYETTEVILLE	184	111
HAMILTON BK OF MORRISTOWN	MORRISTOWN	182	117
FIRST AMERICAN NB	CHATTANOOGA	181	180
MIDDLE TENNESSEE BK	COLUMBIA	181	148
SECURITY FS&LA	NASHVILLE	181	462
THIRD NB IN ANDERSON CITY	LAKE CITY	179	118
COMMERCE UNION BK OF MEMPHIS	MEMPHIS	179	255
MERCHANTS & PLANTERS BK	NEWPORT	179	116
HAMILTON BK OF UPPER E TN	JOHNSON CITY	178	224

TRI CITY B&TC	BLOUNTVILLE	177	182
FIRST NB OF CROSSVILLE	CROSSVILLE	176	109
BANK OF ROANE COUNTY	HARRIMAN	176	116
MID-SOUTH B&TC	MURFREESBORO	175	440
LIBERTY FSB	PARIS	175	164
ELIZABETHTON FS&LA	ELIZABETHTON	175	128
FIRST NB OF SHELBYVILLE	SHELBYVILLE	174	132
AMERICAN NB&TC	CHATTANOOGA	172	1,037
FIRST AMERICAN BK	MEMPHIS	171	605
BOATMENS BK OF TENN	MEMPHIS	169	481
COMMERCE UNION BK	NASHVILLE	169	2,598
NB OF COMMERCE	MEMPHIS	169	1,317
HOME FEDERAL SAVINGS BANK OF TENNESSEE	KNOXVILLE	169	818
FIRST AMERICAN BK KNOXVILLE NA	KNOXVILLE	168	1,132

TEXAS

Name	City	Rank	Assets
USAA FEDERAL SVG BK	SAN ANTONIO	300	458
FIRST ST B&TC	CARTHAGE	258	101
SNYDER NB	SNYDER	256	107
FIRST NB OF BAY CITY	BAY CITY	253	135
LIBERTY NB IN PARIS	PARIS	250	124
ALICE NB	ALICE	241	126
FIRST NB IN PAMPA	PAMPA	235	169
FIRST B&TC	GROVES	230	194
LOCKWOOD NB	HOUSTON	230	133
SEGUIN ST B&TC	SEGUIN	219	126
KELLY FIELD NB	SAN ANTONIO	218	116
NORTH DALLAS B&TC	DALLAS	218	271
FIRST ST BK	RIO VISTA	217	125
FIRST ST B&TC	MISSION	215	228
HARRISBURG BK	HOUSTON	213	127
SAN ANTONIO FEDERAL SAVINGS BANK	WESLACO	213	212
UNITED BK NA	MIDLAND	208	168
UNITED NB	DALLAS	207	123
WESTSIDE BK	SAN ANTONIO	203	126
SULPHUR SPRINGS ST BK	SULPHUR SPRINGS	201	126
WAGGONER NB OF VERNON	VERNON	201	129
FIRST NB IN BIG SPRING	BIG SPRING	200	179
AMERICAN ST BK	LUBBOCK	198	391
NORTH FT WORTH BK	FORT WORTH	198	163
CITIZENS NB OF HENDERSON	HENDERSON	195	199
FIRST ST B&TC	PORT LAVACA	195	116
JEFFERSON ST BK	SAN ANTONIO	193	106
FIRST NB OF ATHENS	ATHENS	189	117
KLEBERG FIRST NB	KINGSVILLE	189	133
BANK OF HOUSTON	HOUSTON	185	135

TEXAS (cont.)

Name	City	Rank	Assets
CENTRAL B&TC	FORT WORTH	185	220
CITIZENS FROST BK NA	SAN ANTONIO	184	116
FIRST NB OF TEMPLE	TEMPLE	183	154
FIRST NB OF BOWIE	BOWIE	183	100
FIRST NB RIO GRANDE CTY	RIO GRANDE CITY	181	101
SOUTHWEST BK	FORT WORTH	181	132
BENT TREE NB	ADDISON	180	106
HARLINGEN NB	HARLINGEN	178	122
FIRST ST BK	ATHENS	178	120
GRAND BK NA	DALLAS	176	155
FIRST NB OF ABILENE	ABILENE	175	360
CITIZENS B&TC	BAYTOWN	174	144
GRAND BK NORTH EAST	DALLAS	174	104
AMERICAN NB SOUTH	CORPUS CHRISTI	173	103
PLANO B&TC	PLANO	172	216
FIRST CITY NB	EL PASO	171	419
TEXAS BK	WEATHERFORD	170	148
GRAND BANK RL THORNTON	DALLAS	169	223
PLAINS NB OF LUBBOCK	LUBBOCK	167	176
AMERICAN NB OF TERRELL	TERRELL	166	163

UTAH

Name	City	Rank	Assets
PEOPLES FIRST THRIFT	SALT LAKE CITY	266	218
AMERICAN INVESTMENT BK NA	SALT LAKE CITY	218	115
UNITED S&LA	OGDEN	211	207
CITIBANK (UTAH)	SALT LAKE CITY	204	170
CONTINENTAL B&TC	SALT LAKE CITY	186	345

VERMONT

Name	City	Rank	Assets
MARBLE BK	RUTLAND	222	330
GRANITE SVG B&TC	BARRE	216	111
FRANKLIN - LAMOILLE BK	ST ALBANS	188	209
FACTORY PORT NB OF MAN	MANCHESTER CENTER	177	109
PROCTOR BK	PROCTOR	176	191
FIRST VERMONT B&TC	BRATTLEBORO	175	524
VERMONT NB	BRATTLEBORO	171	612
MERCHANTS BK	BURLINGTON	169	504

VIRGINIA

Name	City	Rank	Assets
BANK OF SOUTHSIDE VIRGINIA	CARSON	249	123
CITIZENS & FARMERS BK	WEST POINT	245	126
CENTRAL FIDELITY BK NA	RICHMOND	241	130
BANK OF TAZEWELL COUNTY	TAZEWELL	236	124
GRUNDY NB	GRUNDY	236	112
FARMERS & MERCHANTS BK	ONLEY	223	105
GEORGE MASON BK	FAIRFAX	219	130
AMERICAN NB&TC	DANVILLE	216	167
FIRST VIRGINIA BK COLONIAL	RICHMOND	214	243
SECOND NB	CULPEPER	213	144
FAUQUIER NB OF WARRENTON	WARRENTON	211	108
FIRST VIRGINIA BK	FAIRFAX CITY	211	1,775
DOMINION BK OF N VA NA	VIENNA	208	553
FIRST VIRGINIA BK OF TIDEWATER	NORFOLK	207	374
RIGGS NB VIRGINIA	MERRIFIELD	205	167
UNION B&TC	BOWLING GREEN	205	142
OLD POINT NB OF PHOEPUS	HAMPTON	203	167
COMMERCE BK	VIRGINIA BEACH	202	177
NB OF FREDERICKSBURG	FREDERICKSBURG	202	161
JEFFERSON NB	CHARLOTTESVILLE	200	1,222
FARMERS & MERCHANTS NB	WINCHESTER	199	359
FEDERICKSBURG S&LA, FA	FREDERICKSBURG	198	333
BURKE & HERBERT B&TC	ALEXANDRIA	193	255
FIRST VIRGINIA BK FRANKLIN	ROCKY MOUNT	193	108
FIRST VIRGINIA BK SHENANDOAH	WOODSTOCK	193	139
DOMINION BK RICHMOND NA	HENRICO COUNTY	190	616
PLANTERS B&TC OF VA	STAUNTON	190	191
FARMERS & MERCHANTS NB	HAMILTON	187	136
FIRST VIRGINIA BK - HIGHLANDS	COVINGTON	187	101
FIRST VIRGINIA BK SOUTHWEST	ROANOKE COUNTY	185	287
NATIONAL BK OF BLACKSBURG	BLACKSBURG	185	118
FIRST FS&LA	ROANOKE	178	498
MERITOR SVG BK, FSB	ARLINGTON	178	849
DOMINION BK GRTR HMPDN NA	NORFOLK	177	833
PIEDMONT TR BK	MARTINSVILLE	176	300
CO-OPERATIVE B&LA INC	LYNCHBURG	176	161
FRANKLIN FS&LA	RICHMOND	175	315
PIEDMONT FEDERAL SVG BK	MANASSAS	175	409
PATRICK HENRY NB	BASSETT	171	129
MCLEAN BK NA	MCLEAN	170	174
NEWPORT NEWS SVG BK	NEWPORT NEWS	169	335
COMMUNITY FS&LA	STAUNTON	168	109
PROVIDENCE S&LA, FA	VIENNA	165	202

WASHINGTON

Name	City	Rank	Assets
FIRST INDEPENDENT BK	VANCOUVER	297	336
HORIZON BK A SVG BK	BELLINGHAM	250	238
NORTHWESTERN COMMERCIAL BANK	BELLINGHAM	227	106
WASHINGTON FS&LA	SEATTLE	227	1,871
CITY BK	LYNNWOOD	199	120
BAKER BOYER NB	WALLA WALLA	198	184
CASHMERE VALLEY BK	CASHMERE	196	124
KITSAP BK	PORT ORCHARD	195	144
NORTHWEST NB	VANCOUVER	195	112
YAKIMA FS&LA	YAKIMA	195	409
EVERETT MUTUAL SAVINGS BANK, SFB	EVERETT	194	189
SKAGIT ST BK	BURLINGTON	193	157
AMERICAN MARINE BK	WINSLOW	189	106
FIRST NB IN SPOKANE	SPOKANE	187	114
PUGET SOUND NB	TACOMA	182	1,747
WESTERN COMMUNITY BK	FIRCREST	182	106
WASHINGTON TR BK	SPOKANE	176	504
FIRST INTERSTATE BK WA NA	SPOKANE	175	3,288
FRONTIER BK	EVERETT	174	137
ABERDEEN FS&LA	ABERDEEN	169	126
BELLINGHAM NB	BELLINGHAM	168	166
FIRST FS&LA	WALLA WALLA	168	311
FIRST FS&LA	RENTON	168	168
OLYMPIA FS&LA	OLYMPIA	167	149
PIONEER FEDERAL SAVINGS BANK	LYNNWOOD	167	540

WEST VIRGINIA

Name	City	Rank	Assets
MCDOWELL COUNTY NB WELCH	WELCH	300	102
BANK OF WEIRTON	WEIRTON	262	151
RALEIGH COUNTY NB	BECKLEY	255	177
SECURITY NB&TC	WHEELING	254	195
NATIONAL BK OF LOGAN	LOGAN	242	151
FIRST NB OF MORGANTOWN	MORGANTOWN	230	298
BOONE NB OF MADISON	MADISON	230	103
FIRST EMPIRE FS&LA	CHARLESTON	215	155
WHEELING DOLLAR BK	WHEELING	212	252
EMPIRE NB OF CLARKSBURG	CLARKSBURG	210	100
BECKLEY NB	BECKLEY	206	214
FIRST NB IN FAIRMONT	FAIRMONT	204	136
UNITED NB-NORTH	WHEELING	202	128
MATEWAN NB	MATEWAN	201	106
GUARANTY NB HUNTINGTON	HUNTINGTON	195	138

UNION BN OF CLARKSBURG	CLARKSBURG	191	263
FIRST NB OF BLUEFIELD	BLUEFIELD	189	145
CHARLESTON NB	CHARLESTON	188	392
BANK OF RALEIGH	BECKLEY	184	214
HUNTINGTON FS&LA	HUNTINGTON	184	242
OLD NB OF MARTINSBURG	MARTINSBURG	177	141
COMMERCIAL B&TC	PARKERSBURG	175	107
FLAT TOP NB OF BLUEFIELD	BLUEFIELD	174	150
CITY NB OF CHARLESTON	CHARLESTON	172	109
KANAWHA VALLEY BK NA	CHARLESTON	171	788
CITIZENS NB OF ELKINS	ELKINS	170	115
UNITED NATIONAL BANK	PARKERSBURG	170	589
ONE VALLEY BK MERCER CTY	PRINCETON	168	135
HANCOCK COUNTY FS&LA	CHESTER	166	139

WISCONSIN

Name	City	Rank	Assets
FIRST NB OF KENOSHA	KENOSHA	227	300
SOUTH MILWAUKEE S&LA	SOUTH MILWAUKEE	227	123
TIME FS&LA	MEDFORD	225	115
MILWAUKEE WESTERN BK	MILWAUKEE	219	100
FIRST NORTHERN S&LA	GREEN BAY	219	256
TWIN CITY S&LA	NEENAH	219	143
M&I FIRST NB	WEST BEND	217	156
SECURITY S & LA	MILWAUKEE	216	1,914
WAUWATOSA ST BK	WAUWATOSA	210	193
NATIONAL EXCH B&TC OF FOND DU LAC	FOND DU LAC	210	194
MARINE BANK APPLETON NA	APPLETON	205	237
WEST ALLIS S&LA	WEST ALLIS	204	111
KINNICKINNIC FS&LA	MILWAUKEE	201	121
NORTH SHORE S&LA	BROOKFIELD	201	564
KENOSHA S&LA	KENOSHA	201	317
MUTUAL S&LA OF WISCONSIN	MILWAUKEE	201	953
OSHKOSH S&LA	OSHKOSH	200	149
MARINE BK OF MT PLEASANT	MT PLEASANT	199	262
M&I BANK OF BELOIT	BELOIT	198	122
M7I WEST SUBURBAN BK	BROOKFIELD	198	302
WAUWATOSA S&LA	WAUWATOSA	197	323
PARK ST BK	MILWAUKEE	196	135
LIBERTY S&LA	WEST ALLIS	196	218
ASSOCIATED MANITOWOC BK NA	MANITOWOC	195	180
BANK OF STURGEON BAY	STURGEON BAY	195	160
CITIZENS MARINE NB	STEVENS POINT	194	105
FIRST INTERSTATE BK OF WI NA	EAU CLAIRE	193	153
WOOD COUNTY NB&TC	WISCONSIN RAPIDS	192	130
WAUKESHA ST BK	WAUKESHA	190	203
FIRST NB&TC BELOIT	BELOIT	188	132

WISCONSIN (cont.)

Name	City	Rank	Assets
MARINE BK DANE COUNTY	MADISON	188	200
FIRST WISCONSIN BK MAYFAIR	WAUWATOSA	186	108
EQUITABLE S&LA	HALES CORNERS	186	214
REPUBLIC S&LA	MILWAUKEE	186	465
GREAT MIDWEST S&LA	BROOKFIELD	185	288
M&I FIRST NB	STEVENS POINT	184	135
M&I BK OF HILLDALE	MADISON	183	275
VALLEY BK GREEN BAY	GREEN BAY	183	216
BANK OF BURLINGTON	BURLINGTON	182	119
FIRST INTERSTATE BK WI	NEW BERLIN	180	471
KELLOGG CITIZENS NB	GREEN BAY	179	483
UNITED S&LA	SHEBOYGAN	178	309
ASSOCIATED BK NA	NEENAH	176	210
F&M BK	MENOMONEE FALLS	174	244
FIRST WISCONSIN NB	EAU CLAIRE	173	229
NATIONAL BK OF CMRC IN SUP	SUPERIOR	173	126
VALLEY BK	JANESVILLE	172	174
FIRST NB OF WI RAPIDS	WISCONSIN RAPIDS	171	130
FIRST WISCONSIN NB	MADISON	171	506
PEOPLES MARINE BK	GREEN BAY	170	276
MARINE FIRST NB	JANESVILLE	168	145
ASSOCIATED COMMERCE BK	MILWAUKEE	166	131
FIRST AMERICAN NB	WAUSAU	166	261
FIRST INTERSTATE BK WI	SHEBOYGAN	166	484
M&I MARSHALL & ILSLEY BK	MILWAUKEE	165	2,243

WYOMING

Name	City	Rank	Assets
ROCK SPRINGS NB	ROCK SPRINGS	220	156
JACKSON ST BK	JACKSON	181	108

CREDIT UNIONS

Name	City		Rank	Assets
ALABAMA STATE EMPLOYEES	MONTGOMERY	AL	224	23
ACIPCO	BIRMINGHAM	AL	206	25
SCOTT CREDIT UNION	MOBILE	AL	187	30
ALABAMA TELCO	HOOVER	AL	179	102
SLOSS	BIRMINGHAM	AL	178	24
FAIRFIELD	PINE BLUFF	AR	236	21
TELCOE	LITTLE ROCK	AR	185	29
L.A. SOUTHWEST JAPANESE	LOS ANGELES	CA	248	27
AMERICAN FIRST	BREA	CA	244	107
ESPEE	LOS ANGELES	CA	232	46

ORANGE COUNTY TEACHERS	SANTA ANA	CA	227	506
UNIVERSITY	LOS ANGELES	CA	209	75
LAIRE	LOS ANGELES	CA	205	34
UNIVERSAL CITY STUDIOS	UNIVERSAL CITY	CA	199	27
H.P.	PALO ALTO	CA	197	180
SAN DIEGO TEACHERS	SAN DIEGO	CA	193	130
OAKLAND MUNICIPAL	OAKLAND	CA	190	51
KAIPERM	OAKLAND	CA	189	28
SEA AIR	SEAL BEACH	CA	186	61
PROVIDENT CENTRAL	BURLINGAME	CA	184	355
SOUTHERN CALIF EDISON COM EMPLOYEES	EL MONTE	CA	182	112
L.A. COUNTY CIVIC CENTER	DOWNEY	CA	180	56
CERTIFIED	COMMERCE	CA	179	23
VISTA	BURBANK	CA	176	52
BURBANK CITY EMPLOYEES	BURBANK	CA	173	33
MIRAMAR	SAN DIEGO	CA	173	58
MCCLELLAN	NORTH HIGHLAND	CA	172	83
RICHMOND	RICHMOND	CA	170	20
ORANGE COUNTY POSTAL FEDERAL EMP.	GARDEN GROVE	CA	170	84
SEARS WESTERN	LA HABRA	CA	167	49
AEROJET CENTER	ORANGEVALE	CA	167	30
SAN JOAQUIN POWER EMPLOYEES	FRESNO	CA	167	28
A M FEDERAL CREDIT UNION	COMPTON	CA	166	26
AFTRA-SAG	HOLLYWOOD	CA	166	22
JEFFERSON COUNTY SCHOOL EMPLOYEES	LAKEWOOD	CO	236	29
GATES	DENVER	CO	233	53
COLORADO CENTRAL	ARVADA	CO	216	38
U S CONSOLIDATED	DENVER	CO	184	26
PUEBLO TEACHERS	PUEBLO	CO	177	31
NORLARCO	FORT COLLINS	CO	172	31
MUNICIPAL CREDIT UNION OF DENVER	DENVER	CO	171	37
WATERBURY CONNECTICUT TEACHER	WATERBURY	CT	176	31
BRISTOL TEACHERS	BRISTOL	CT	173	28
NYLON CAPITOL	SEAFORD	DE	171	48
TRANSIT EMPLOYEES	WASHINGTON	DC	227	30
POLICE	WASHINGTON	DC	198	25
DISTRICT GOVERNMENT EMPLOYEES	WASHINGTON	DC	195	26
TRANSPORTATION	WASHINGTON	DC	171	44
TAMPA POSTAL DISTRICT	TAMPA	FL	197	39
OMNI	JACKSONVILLE	FL	186	59
TAMPA BAY	TAMPA	FL	182	51
FIRST FLORIDA PUBLIC EMPLOYEES	JACKSONVILLE	FL	179	49
FPL EMPLOYEES	MIAMI	FL	178	97
TYNDALL	PANAMA CITY	FL	172	144
BUCKEYE EMPLOYEES	PERRY	FL	170	26
TROPICAL TELCO	MIAMI	FL	168	178
NCSC	PANAMA CITY	FL	168	22

CREDIT UNIONS (cont.)

Name	City		Rank	Assets
EASTERN AIRLINES	MIAMI	FL	167	711
ST. PETERSBURG MUNICIPAL EMPLOYEES	ST PETERSBURG	FL	167	21
PINNACLE	ATLANTA	GA	191	28
UNION CAMP SAVANNAH	SAVANNAH	GA	187	37
ROBINS	WARNER ROBINS	GA	177	249
STATE EMPLOYEES	ATLANTA	GA	168	25
1ST RAILROAD COMMUNITY	WAYCROSS	GA	165	74
HC&S	KAHULUI	HI	179	28
CHICAGO PATROLMENS	CHICAGO	IL	210	34
KEMBA INDIANAPOLIS	INDIANAPOLIS	IN	200	23
JET	INDIANAPOLIS	IN	187	21
PERFECT CIRCLE	HAGERSTOWN	IN	182	20
ELKHART COUNTY FARM BUR CO-OP ASSOC	GOSHEN	IN	176	73
MARION INDIANA PUBLIC SCH EMP	MARION	IN	165	26
DEERE EMPLOYEES	OTTUMWA	IA	242	21
DU TRAC COMMUNITY	DUBUQUE	IA	201	88
EDCO	DES MOINES	IA	192	24
SUPER CHIEF	TOPEKA	KS	180	25
WICHITA MUNICIPAL	WICHITA	KS	169	22
ASHLAND ARMCO EMPLOYEES	ASHLAND	KY	243	29
B&W	LOUISVILLE	KY	188	28
GREATER NEW ORLEANS	NEW ORLEANS	LA	204	40
EXXON	BATON ROUGE	LA	176	40
LA DOTD	BATON ROUGE	LA	174	25
KRAFTMAN	BASTROP	LA	171	35
THE NEW ORLEANS FIREMENS	NEW ORLEANS	LA	168	20
OTIS DIVISION	JAY	ME	213	29
FRASER EMPLOYEES	MADAWASKA	ME	169	25
ST. JOHN'S (BRUNSWICK)	BRUNSWICK	ME	165	36
FIRST FINANCIAL OF MARYLAND	LUTHERVILLE	MD	259	104
GIANT FOOD	GREENBELT	MD	223	35
MUNICIPAL EMPLOYEES CU OF BALTIMORE	BALTIMORE	MD	172	214
BOSTON GAS EMPLOYEES	BOSTON	MA	192	21
FRAMINGHAM MUNICIPAL	FRAMINGHAM	MA	180	20
BOSTON POST OFFICE EMPLOYEES	BOSTON	MA	175	47
SOUTHBRIDGE	SOUTHBRIDGE	MA	165	69
MARQUETTE CATHOLIC	MARQUETTE	MI	222	21
DORT	FLINT	MI	216	89
TELEDYNE CONTINENTAL EMPLOYEES	MUSKEGON	MI	206	22
LANSING COMMUNITY	LANSING	MI	204	25
CAPITAL AREA SCHOOL EMPLOYEES	LANSING	MI	202	45
MOTOR CITY CO-OP	DETROIT	MI	191	39
CHIEF PONTIAC	PONTIAC	MI	185	46

WEST SIDE AUTO EMPLOYEES	FLINT	MI	184	92
SOC	MADISON HEIGHTS	MI	183	62
DETROIT POSTAL EMPLOYEES	DETROIT	MI	182	53
DOWNRIVER COMMUNITY	ECORSE	MI	181	42
PARKSIDE	LIVONIA	MI	179	26
COMMUNICATIONS FAMILY	SAGINAW	MI	178	118
CRAFTSMAN	DETROIT	MI	178	34
DOW CHEMICAL EMPLOYEES	MIDLAND	MI	177	236
OMNI FAMILY	BATTLE CREEK	MI	173	42
FIRST FINANCIAL	DETROIT	MI	173	21
JACKSON CONSUMERS POWER EMP	JACKSON	MI	172	67
UNITED	BUCHANAN	MI	172	50
IRON MOUNTAIN KINGSFORD COMM	KINGSFORD	MI	171	32
NORTHEAST CATHOLIC	DETROIT	MI	171	26
FLINT AREA SCHOOL EMPLOYEES	FLINT	MI	170	76
POST EMPLOYEES	BATTLE CREEK	MI	165	30
HURON RIVER AREA	ANN ARBOR	MI	165	34
ST. MARY'S PARISH	SLEEPY EYE	MN	240	34
HONEYWELL EMPLOYEES	MINNEAPOLIS	MN	193	63
HIWAY	ST. PAUL	MN	189	106
MAYO CLINIC EMPLOYEES	ROCHESTER	MN	180	21
RICHFIELD SCHOOLS	RICHFIELD	MN	176	29
INGALLS EMPLOYEES	PASCAGOULA	MS	184	47
AMERICAN ENTERPRISE	LIBERTY	MO	199	21
GATEWAY TELCO	ST LOUIS	MO	177	29
JEFFERSON CITY HIGHWAY	JEFFERSON CITY	MO	166	26
LINCOLN GOODYEAR EMPLOYEES	LINCOLN	NE	172	21
UNITED BROTHERHOOD	BERLIN	NH	253	34
SERVICE	PORTSMOUTH	NH	182	153
GRANITE STATE	MANCHESTER	NH	179	42
DEEPWATER INDUSTRIES	DEEPWATER	NJ	211	27
LUSITANIA	NEWARK	NJ	171	21
MELROSE	FLUSHING	NY	298	205
MIDDLE VILLAGE	MIDDLE VILLAGE	NY	272	23
PROGRESSIVE	FOREST HILLS	NY	265	68
NEW YORK METRO AREA POSTAL	NEW YORK	NY	247	39
LEDERLE EMPLOYEES	PEARL RIVER	NY	211	33
GRAPHIC ARTS	NEW YORK	NY	211	32
JENAPO	BROOKLYN	NY	209	29
POLISH & SLAVIC	BROOKLYN	NY	208	115
SUMA YONKERS	YONKERS	NY	201	28
TURBINE	SCHENECTADY	NY	197	35
SELF RELIANCE NY	NEW YORK	NY	177	127
NCPD	MINEOLA	NY	174	45
UNITED NATIONS	NEW YORK	NY	174	191
AMALGAMATED TAXI	JAMAICA	NY	172	56
GENERAL FOODS	WHITE PLAINS	NY	172	75
SIDNEY	SIDNEY	NY	170	56
BUFFALO TELEPHONE EMPLOYEES	BUFFALO	NY	170	28
ROCHESTER UKRAINIAN	ROCHESTER	NY	169	29

CREDIT UNIONS (cont.)

Name	City		Rank	Assets
LEAGUE OF MUTUAL TAXI OWNERS	NEW YORK	NY	166	76
SEYMOUR JOHNSON	GOLDSBORO	NC	235	24
CONE	GREENSBORO	NC	215	58
PIEDMONT AVIATION	WINSTON-SALEM	NC	190	49
CAROLINAS TELCO	CHARLOTTE	NC	185	135
INTERNATIONAL HARVESTER EMPLOYEES	SPRINGFIELD	OH	257	49
DAY-MET	DAYTON	OH	213	30
COLUMBUS OHIO TEACHERS	COLUMBUS	OH	204	29
MEAD EMPLOYEES	CHILLICOTHE	OH	199	63
TELHIO	COLUMBUS	OH	195	115
801	DAYTON	OH	184	21
TOLEDO TELEPHONE EMPLOYEES	TOLEDO	OH	170	25
GOLDEN CIRCLE	CANTON	OH	167	34
COMMUNICATION	OKLAHOMA CITY	OK	207	94
PORTLAND POSTAL EMPLOYEES	PORTLAND	OR	205	41
TRI BORO	HOMESTEAD	PA	195	39
WHEELING-PITTSBURGH STEEL COMM.	MONESSEN	PA	176	20
UTILITIES EMPLOYEES	READING	PA	175	99
CITADEL	THORNDALE	PA	173	99
READING WORKS	READING	PA	168	32
P R TELCO EMPLOYEES	SAN JUAN	PR	198	28
VAPR	SAN JUAN	PR	197	27
CREDIT UNION CENTRAL FALLS	CENTRAL FALLS	RI	254	169
DEXTER	CENTRAL FALLS	RI	218	37
THE PEOPLES	MIDDLETOWN	RI	188	80
WARWICK	WARWICK	RI	166	29
S. C. TELCO	GREENVILLE	SC	185	37
MEMPHIS KIMBERLY-CLARK EMPLOY	MEMPHIS	TN	178	32
CHATTANOOGA AREA SCHOOLS	CHATTANOOGA	TN	170	37
CITY OF MEMPHIS	MEMPHIS	TN	168	46
L G & W	MEMPHIS	TN	167	32
CONSUMER	GREENEVILLE	TN	167	21
EL PASO EMPLOYEES	EL PASO	TX	243	22
SAN ANTONIO CITY EMPLOYEES	SAN ANTONIO	TX	206	62
EMPLOYEES	DALLAS	TX	203	22
HOUSTON POSTAL	HOUSTON	TX	184	42
RANDOLPH BROOKS	UNIVERSAL CITY	TX	171	290
DALLAS MOBIL	DALLAS	TX	171	31
SOUTHLAND CORPORATION EMP	DALLAS	TX	170	22
ALPINE	OREM	UT	179	22
FAIRFAX COUNTY EMP CREDIT UNION INC	FAIRFAX	VA	238	26
THE RICHMOND POSTAL CREDIT UNION INC	RICHMOND	VA	231	23

MARTINSVILLE DUPONT EMP CREDIT UNION	MARTINSVILLE	VA	204	57
CELCO	NARROWS	VA	194	44
N A E	CHESAPEAKE	VA	186	22
DUPONT FIBERS EMP CU INC.	RICHMOND	VA	165	58
WHATCOM EDUCATIONAL CREDIT UNION	BELLINGHAM	WA	205	42
AGE	SEATTLE	WA	191	41
SEATTLE POSTAL EMPLOYEES	SEATTLE	WA	165	28
STEEL WORKS COMMUNITY	WEIRTON	WV	182	81
ANTIGO CO-OP	ANTIGO	WI	237	52
MILWAUKEE MUNICIPAL	MILWAUKEE	WI	200	33
CO-OP	BLACK RIVER FALLS	WI	184	37
A M COMMUNITY	KENOSHA	WI	179	39
MERC MARINE	FOND DU LAC	WI	175	30
TELCO COMMUNITY	MADISON	WI	172	22
LAKEVIEW	NEENAH	WI	168	22
WARREN	CHEYENNE	WY	218	36

ACKNOWLEDGMENTS

LIKE MY PREVIOUS WORK, *The Great Depression of 1990*, this one is inspired by writings of my mentor, Prabhat Ranjan Sarkar. The ideas flowing through my pen are essentially derived from his thought. I am grateful to John Rickmeier for providing me a comprehensive list of sound financial institutions, including banks, savings associations, and credit unions. I have also benefited greatly from discussions with Glen Linden, Thor Thorgeirsson, Arthur Patton, Rosy Chaudhary, Dan Slottje, and financial planner Jerry Patel. Sanjay Unni, Matiur Rahman, Jamal Abu Rashed, and Sandeep Nanda provided timely research assistance. As with my earlier work, Fred Hills and his associate Burton Beals, at Simon and Schuster, supplied wonderful editorial assistance, and my literary agent, Jan Miller, helped cement my ties with my publisher. Finally, I am grateful to my dear wife, Sunita, for her unfailing support and understanding.

INDEX

Special Offer
Buy a Dell Book
For only 50¢.

Now you can have Dell's Home
Library Catalog filled with hundreds
of titles. Plus, take advantage of our
unique and exciting bonus book offer
which gives you the opportunity to
purchase a Dell book for *only 50¢*.
Here's how!

Just order any five books from the
catalog at the regular price. Then
choose any other single book listed
(up to $5.95 value) for just 50¢. Use
the coupon below to send for Dell's
Home Library Catalog today!

DELL HOME LIBRARY CATALOG
P.O. Box 1045, South Holland, IL. 60473

Ms./Mrs./Mr. _____

Address _____

City/State _____ Zip _____